D0036624

CHICKEN SOUP FOR THE MOTHER AND SON SOUL

is
out
ed.
a
ty.
an
re

CHICKEN SOUP FOR THE MOTHER AND SON SOUL

Stories to Celebrate the Lifelong Bond

Jack Canfield
Mark Victor Hansen
LeAnn Thieman
Barbara LoMonaco

Health Communications, Inc.
Deerfield Beach, Florida

www.hcibooks.com
www.chickensoup.com

We would like to acknowledge the following publishers and individuals for permission to reprint the following material. (Note: The stories that were written by Jack Canfield, Mark Victor Hansen, LeAnn Thieman or Barbara LoMonaco are not included in this listing.)

Adolescence. Reprinted by permission of Lois Wencil. ©2004 Lois Wencil.

Sunshine in the Sand. Reprinted by permission of Duane Bradley Shaw. ©2005 Duane Bradley Shaw.

My Sinking Heart. Reprinted by permission of Cynthia Briggs. ©2003 Cynthia Briggs.

Mother Love. Reprinted by permission of Polly W. Swafford. ©2004 Polly W. Swafford.

A Part of the Team. Reprinted by permission of Cheryl A. Paden. ©2001 Cheryl A. Paden.

Ricochet. Reprinted by permission of Linda Watskin. ©2004 Linda Watskin.

7:07 Prayers. Reprinted by permission of Louise Tucker Jones. ©2005 Louise Tucker Jones.

(Continued on page 339)

Library of Congress Cataloging-in-Publication Data is available from the Library of Congress.

©2006 Jack Canfield and Mark Victor Hansen
ISBN 0-7573-0403-6

All rights reserved. Printed in the United States of America. No part of this publication may be reproduced, stored in a retrieval system or transmitted in any form or by any means, electronic, mechanical, photocopying, recording or otherwise without the written permission of the publisher.

HCI, its Logos and Marks are trademarks of Health Communications, Inc.

Publisher: Health Communications, Inc.
3201 S.W. 15th Street
Deerfield Beach, FL 33442-8190

Cover design by Kevin Stawieray
Inside book formatting by Lawna Patterson Oldfield

OFF THE MARK, *Mark Parisi*, ©*1995. Reprinted by permission of Mark Parisi.*

To our sons,
Mitch, John, Mike, Rob,
Christopher, Oran, Kyle and Travis,
for all the gray hairs and great love!
Your love blesses our hearts
and lives forever.

Contents

3. A MOTHER'S LOVE

4. A SON'S LOVE

5. OVERCOMING OBSTACLES

6. LIFE LESSONS

Acknowledgments

We wish to express our heartfelt gratitude to the following people who helped make this book possible:

Our families, who have been chicken soup for our souls!

Jack's family: Inga, Travis, Riley, Christopher, Oran and Kyle, for all their love and support.

Mark's family: Patty, Elisabeth and Melanie, for once again sharing and lovingly supporting us in creating yet another book.

LeAnn's devoted, loving, supportive family: Mark, Angela, Brian, Dante, Lia, Christie, Dave and Mitch.

Barbara's family: Frank, John, Michael, Robert, Crescent, Christine and Frances, for their unconditional love, enthusiastic support and good humor and for always being there.

Our publisher, Peter Vegso, for his vision and commitment to bringing *Chicken Soup for the Soul* to the world.

Patty Aubery and Russ Kalmaski, for being there on every step of the journey, with support, wisdom and endless creativity.

D'ette Corona, Coauthor Liaison extraordinaire, whose total support on this book went above and beyond the call of duty. Where would we be without your dedication, hard work and knowledge? You are absolutely amazing, and we are lucky to consider you not only a colleague, but also a true friend. Thank you.

Patty Hansen, for her thorough and competent handling of the legal and licensing aspects of the *Chicken Soup for the Soul* books. You are magnificent at the challenge!

Laurie Hartman, for being a precious guardian of the *Chicken Soup* brand.

Veronica Romero, Teresa Esparza, Robin Yerian, Jesse Ianniello, Laren Edelstein, Patti Clement, Maegan Romanello, Cassidy Guyer, Noelle Champagne, Jody Emme, Debbie Lefever, Michelle Adams, Dee Dee Romanello, Shanna Vieyra, Lisa Williams, Gina Romanello, and Dena Jacobson who support Jack's and Mark's businesses with skill and love.

Elisabeth Rinaldi, Allison Janse and Kathy Grant, our editors at Health Communications, Inc., for their devotion to excellence.

Terry Burke, Lori Golden, Kelly Maragni, Tom Galvin, Sean Geary, Patricia McConnell, Ariana Daner, Kim Weiss and Paola Fernandez-Rana—the sales, marketing and PR departments at Health Communications, Inc.—for doing such an incredible job supporting our books.

Tom Sand, Claude Choquette and Luc Jutras, who manage year after year to get our books translated into thirty-six languages around the world.

The art department at Health Communications, Inc., for their talent, creativity and unrelenting patience in producing book covers and inside designs that capture the essence of *Chicken Soup*: Larissa Hise Henoch, Lawna Patterson Oldfield, Andrea Perrine Brower, Anthony Clausi, Kevin Stawieray and Dawn Von Strolley Grove.

All the *Chicken Soup for the Soul* coauthors, who make it such a joy to be part of this *Chicken Soup* family.

Our glorious panel of readers who helped us make the final selections: Michelle Blank, Helen Colella, Christine Del Giorgio, Berniece Duello, Deborah Duello, Richard Duello,

Kerrie Flanagan, Susan Goldberg, Laurie Hartman, Greg Hubach, Ellen Javernick, Karen Kishpaugh, Crescent LoMonaco, John LoMonaco, Mike LoMonaco, Rob LoMonaco, Dahlynn McKowen, Mary McMahon, Linda Osmundson, Nancy Osterhaus, Mary Panosh, Carol McAdoo Rehme, Tracie Ritchie, Christie Rogers, Mary Streit, Terry Tuck and Suzanne Vaughan.

And, most of all, thanks to everyone who submitted their heartfelt stories, poems, quotes and cartoons for possible inclusion in this book. While we were not able to use everything you sent in, we know it all came from your hearts.

Because of the size of this project, we may have left out the names of some people who contributed along the way. If so, we are sorry; please know we appreciate you very much.

A special thanks to Amy Williams, who keeps LeAnn's speaking business booming while she writes . . . and writes . . . and writes.

To Barbara's husband, Frank, and to LeAnn's husband, Mark. Thanks for creating our best jobs of all . . . your wives and mothers of your children.

And to Barbara's mother, Frances, and to LeAnn's mother, Berniece, who taught us the true unconditional love of a mother.

And to God, for his divine guidance.

Introduction

From the moment she hears, "It's a boy!" a special love blossoms in the heart of a mother, and a bond, unlike any other, begins. When he refuses to let her out of his sight, and later refuses to be seen with her in public, her love only grows. In him she sees that she is not only raising this generation, but future ones as well.

Yet, after reading literally thousands of stories submitted for this book, we still had difficulty articulating this unique unconditional love . . . until we discovered these words from the great American writer Washington Irving: *A father may turn his back on his child; brothers and sisters may become inveterate enemies; husbands may desert their wives, and wives their husbands. But a mother's love endures through all; in good repute, in bad repute, in the face of the world's condemnation, a mother still loves on and still hopes that her child may turn from his evil ways and repent; still she remembers the infant smiles that once filled her bosom with rapture, the merry laugh, the joyful shout of his childhood, the opening promise of his youth; and she can never be brought to think him unworthy.*

Indeed, a mother's love is limitless, abundant in joy, support and forgiveness. Though she may loose him from her apron strings, he is forever entwined in her heart.

Savor *Chicken Soup for the Mother and Son Soul*. Celebrate the blessings and bruises, tears and triumphs, happiness and hopes of this unparalleled loving relationship.

1

SPECIAL
MOMENTS

God gave us memories that we might have roses in December.

James M. Barrie

My Son

No language can express the power and beauty and heroism and majesty of a mother's love.

Edwin Hubbell Chapin

The war was far from Saigon when I agreed to escort six babies from Vietnam to their adoptive homes in the U.S. Still, the decision to leave my husband and two little girls had not been easy. When the war escalated, I had begged God for a sign that I could back out of my commitment, but he only filled me with a courage and confidence I could explain to no one. Somehow I knew this was all a part of his plan. By the time I landed in Saigon, bombs were falling outside the city limits, Vietnam was falling to the communists, and President Ford had okayed Operation Babylift. Scores of the estimated 50,000 Amerasian babies and toddlers were herded into our headquarters of Friends of Children of Vietnam in preparation for the airlift.

On my third day there, over breakfast of bread and bottled Coke, Cherie, the director, said, "LeAnn, you've probably figured this out . . ."

I hadn't.

"You and Mark applied for adoption of a son through us, and we told you to expect him in two years." She spoke above the din of dozens of bawling babies. "Obviously, everything has changed. You'll be assigned one of the babies gathered here—or," she paused to touch my hand, "or you can go into the nursery and choose a son."

I was stunned, speechless.

I felt myself flush with excitement—then with fear.

"Really?" I finally croaked. Surely, I had heard her wrong.

Cherie's tired eyes danced. "Really."

"So I can just go in there and pick out a son?"

Cherie nodded again.

Dazed, I turned to my friend and traveling companion, Carol. "Come with me." She jumped up immediately, and we approached the door to the nursery together.

I paused and took a deep breath. "This is like a fantasy. A dream come true."

I opened the door, and we entered a room filled with babies. Babies on blankets and mats. Babies in boxes and baskets and bassinets and cribs.

"Carol, how will I ever choose? There are 110 babies here now."

One baby in a white T-shirt and diaper looked at me with bright eyes. I sat cross-legged on the floor with him on my lap. He seemed to be about nine months old and responded to my words with cute facial expressions and animation. He giggled and clapped his hands.

"We should name you Personality," I said. Then I noticed he was wearing a name bracelet on his ankle. He had already been assigned to a family in Denver. *Well*, I thought, feeling disappointment rising in my throat, *that family is mighty lucky.*

Another child caught my eye as he pulled himself to his feet beside a wooden crib. We watched with amusement as he tugged the toes of the baby sleeping inside. Then he dropped to his hands and knees and began crawling to me. I met him halfway across the room and picked him up. He wore only a diaper, and his soft, round tummy bulged over its rim. He looked at me and smiled brightly, revealing chubby cheeks and deep dimples. As I hugged him, he nestled his head into my shoulder.

"Maybe you'll be our son," I whispered. He pulled back, staring into my eyes, still smiling. For the next hour, I carried him around the room, looking at each infant, touching them, talking to them. All the while, the baby in my arms babbled, smiled and continued to cuddle. I couldn't bring myself to put him down as we went upstairs where the floor was carpeted with even more babies. The hallway was like a megaphone, blasting the sounds of chattering workers and crying babies.

"Let me hold him," Carol coaxed, "while you look at the others." The couch against the wall held a half-dozen fussy infants side by side. I picked up each of them. Most seemed stiff and unresponsive. How sad that cuddling could be unfamiliar to them. I weaved my way to the blanket of babies at the end of the room and sat caressing each of them. As I cradled one in my arms, I could feel the bones of his spine press against my skin. Another's eyes looked glazed and motionless. Sorrow gripped me.

I felt the little boy Carol was carrying for me pat my arm. As I turned to look, he reached out his chubby arms for me. Taking him from her, I snuggled him close, and he snuggled back. Someone had loved him very much.

Downstairs, we meandered from mat to crib, looking at all the infants again. I wished I could adopt them all. But I knew there were long waiting lists at the Denver headquarters of hundreds of families who had completed the tedious, time-consuming application process. Each of these precious orphans would have immediate homes carefully selected for them.

"How do I choose?" I asked myself as much as Carol.

The baby boy in my arms answered by patting my face. I had never missed my husband more. "I wish Mark was here."

I turned my full attention to the child I held, waving my hands in front of his face to check his eyes. He blinked and flashed his dimples.

I snapped my fingers by his ears in a foolish attempt to test his hearing. He turned his head, giggled and grabbed at my hands.

Then I sat on the floor, slowly rocking him back and forth in my arms. I whispered a prayer for the decision I was about to make, a decision that would affect many lives forever. The baby nestled into the hollow of my neck, reassuring me that the choice I was about to make was the right one. I could feel his shallow breath and tender skin as he embraced me.

I recalled all the data we had collected for adoption; all the letters of references from friends, bankers, employers; all the interviews with the social workers.

It had all been worth it for this moment.

We rocked in silence and cuddled. Then, with immense joy, I walked back through the nursery door to the office.

"Meet our son, Mitchell Thieman!" I announced, hardly believing my own words. Everyone gathered around and embraced us. I looked at Mitchell's puzzled face and held him closer. Cherie brought a nametag, and I eagerly scrawled on it, "Reserve for Mark Thieman," and placed it on his ankle.

Joyful tears streamed down my cheeks. For a moment, all my fears were gone. I no longer wondered why I had been driven to make this journey. "This is why God sent me to Vietnam," I whispered.

I had been sent to choose a son.

Or had he chosen me?

LeAnn Thieman

Adolescence

Adolescence is often described as a time of strife and rebellion and a dash toward independence. It seemed, at times, that our eldest offspring was attempting to bend, stretch or break each rule or bond that had developed in his twelve years.

A parenting course and numerous books from the library reaffirmed that we were not the only father and mother forced to endure these difficulties. That information did not help. My mounting certainty that I was a failure as a parent grew higher than the clothes piled on his bedroom floor. The techniques acquired within my parenting group crumbled faster than the blocks we stacked when he was two.

Summer arrived, and Boy Scout Camp loomed ahead. Maybe that would help. Unfortunately, Steve wouldn't be home for my birthday. "Oh, well," I consoled myself, "he's pulling away, letting me go. This is only the first of the many holidays we won't spend together."

One day as he thumbed through his Boy Scout catalog, he said, "Mom, what are you doing this Friday?"

I was prepared for this, the usual pre-camp shopping spree. His list would include new hiking boots, knife, flashlights, batteries and an air pillow. He would try for a new sleeping bag and/or a tent. If I was very lucky and very smart, we might even buy a few things for him to wear upon his return. I had never won the battle against camping dirt.

My husband Bill unexpectedly stayed home. That meant I wouldn't need to bring our daughter through stores in the mall that didn't interest her. Quality time would be ours.

My hopes began to drain away as Steve closeted himself in his room with the phone. However, I heard him tell his best friend that he couldn't go swimming. He took two showers and, ten minutes later, reappeared dressed in pants, not jeans, a dress shirt and tie.

Since he rarely dressed this way, even on Sundays, I thought perhaps I should take him to our pediatrician. He checked the mirror to smooth his hair. "Ready, Mom? Oh, don't bring your purse."

Purse in hand, I followed him out the door and crossed the lawn. John, our neighborhood pre-teen gossip, came toward us on his ten-speed.

Steve gasped. "Keep walking! I'll catch up. He can't see me like this," and dove behind a tree. John turned onto another path.

For the next two blocks, Steve chattered happily about the many merit badges he was planning on earning at camp. They would make it possible for him to move up in rank. We strolled on through downtown, past a few of his favorite shops. He barely even paused to look in the windows. He kept checking his watch. Suddenly, he turned into the most expensive restaurant in town. What on Earth was this about? A waitress approached us. Standing at his full height, which was then the same as mine, his voice lowered as he charmed her with his smile. "I made a reservation for two for lunch."

He took me by the elbow to guide me to my chair (and keep me from falling over in shock!). He held the chair while I sat, then in his most grown-up voice, made suggestions from the menu.

He dove into the whole Cornish hen, stuffed with rice, though I was sure he fervently wished for Kentucky Fried. He hated gravy and stuffing. As he valiantly dove in with knife and fork, Steve commented on the paintings on the walls and the view from the window. He asked about my plans for the following week.

After dessert, he asked for the check and paid for it with his newspaper route pay and allowance, monies usually spent on his model train layout.

As we left the restaurant, Steve said softly, "Mom, I won't be here on your birthday, so we celebrated it early."

He may be letting me go—but not yet.

Adolescence is a transition, a difficult time. My son was becoming a caring, considerate man.

His thoughtfulness was an act of love. There could've been no better birthday celebration—a very special gift.

Lois Wencil

Sunshine in the Sand

A mother's love is indeed the golden link that binds youth to age; and he is still but a child, however time may have furrowed his cheek or silvered his brow, who can recall with a softened heart, the fond devotion or the gentle chidings of the best friend that God ever gives us.

Christian Nestell Bovee

California wildflowers, sea breezes and warm sandy beaches seemed to nourish Mother's spirit. Yet, recent times also dealt health problems. She suffered from blindness, osteoporosis and unsteadiness after a stroke. Nonetheless, even after my dad died, she continued plugging along, living alone and clinging to her independence.

After Father passed, Mom and I spent more time together. It was an amazing journey, and a new variety of unconditional love emerged. We started having dates every Tuesday, rain or shine. After a few trips, it was obvious she liked the suspense of not knowing our destination, so I stopped telling her my plan. The "Tuesday Surprise" always had an aura of anticipation about it from then on.

On one clandestine trip, we set out to explore a stretch of coastline near Bodega Bay, eventually stopping at Salmon Creek State Park. Mom often reminisced about her early years, recalling when, as a small child, her parents frequently took her there. From her many humorous and eventful stories, I gathered the park was just about her favorite place on Earth.

The day began in an extraordinary way, as I drove on a country road near a pasture filled with a herd of Holstein cows. Mom commented, "Look at those cows. They're like spots of black paint on a white stucco wall."

Her statement shocked me! Mom was legally blind and only able to see blotches and blurs.

Then she said, "How beautiful the yellow mustard grass is."

I thought, *Am I imagining this, or can Mom really see today?* Immediately, I knew this moment was special. I wondered, *What are God's intentions?*

About five miles from the entrance to the park, Mother stunned me again when she recognized the surrounding countryside. "Are you taking me to Salmon Creek?"

I confessed, "Yes, and we're going to take a walk on the beach."

I knew the "walk" was probably not feasible. But an hour earlier she could see the cows and the mustard, so I thought, *Why not let God do God's work?* And I hoped for the best.

As I turned into the entrance, I wondered how this could be Mother's favorite place, yet it was my first time here. That thought quickly vanished when I entered Salmon Creek's postage-size parking lot, and we found ourselves surrounded by twenty-foot sand dunes and no beach in sight. Obviously, Mom and I knew she could not walk or even crawl over those mounds to the beach. Nevertheless, neither of us said it.

I was nearly frantic, yet mostly disappointed, by this

dilemma. My heart beat faster than normal. My mind reeled, searching for a quick fix. I thought, *What can I do so Mom will feel and smell the sea breeze, together with the warmth of the sun-dried sand?*

A split second passed, then I eased the car along the parking lot's edge. "Let's spread out a blanket on one of the sand dunes."

Mom agreed. However, my sense of comfort was short-lived. After I opened Mother's car door, she was too weak to get out.

I said, "Mom, I have another idea."

Then, while she was still in her seat, we rotated her entire body clockwise into a comfortable position and slid her legs outside the car door. Elated, I sat down in the sand in front of her.

After a few minutes of conversation, I gently lifted her tired feet, untied her shoelaces and removed her shoes. A moment later, I tenderly slid off her white cotton socks, while massaging her fragile feet. As I set them on the warm sandy granules, I could feel her body calm. I began scooping small handfuls of the hot golden sand into the palms of my hands. Then I let a few drop, like the sand in an hourglass, and watched as they landed on Mom's toes. Repeatedly, I poured them slowly, until a mound formed covering her feet to the top of her ankles. She was as close to emotional pleasure as I had ever seen her. And so was I. Her face showed no frowns, no flaws, no wrinkles or pain—just bliss, pure bliss.

I was thankful to God for doing his work. He manifested all the elements we needed. Mom's sight, the sun, the sea breeze, the warm sand and my most treasured time with her.

Duane Shaw

My Sinking Heart

When thou makest presents, let them be of such things as will last long, to the end that they may be in some sort immortal, and may frequently refresh the memory of the receiver.

Thomas Fuller

Goosebumps rose on my arms. "Hi, Mom. Happy fiftieth birthday!" I heard my son, Brian, say as clearly as if he were sitting next to me. But he wasn't.

Brian was on the USS *Kitty Hawk* on maneuvers somewhere between our U.S. shore and the Persian Gulf.

My party-loving friend, Denise, had invited me out for a quiet fiftieth birthday celebration dinner. It was unlike Denise to let such a special occasion go by without throwing a big birthday bash, so I suspected a surprise party was commencing. When we arrived at the restaurant, I suspiciously scanned the sea of faces in the reception area. I didn't recognize a soul.

As Denise checked on the status of our reservation, I sipped a glass of chardonnay, when once again I heard Brian in my head. "Hi, Mom. Happy fiftieth birthday."

My mother's intuition kicked in. A single, powerful throb stormed through my body, followed by an eerie chill. "I hope he's okay," I said softly.

A wave of melancholy washed over me, and tears welled in my eyes thinking about my twenty-year-old son, who was now married and a terrific father to his own little ones. Was it possible that so much time had passed since he was jumping his bike over jury-rigged ramps in the cow pasture, gobbling down apple dumplings faster than I could bake them and bathing our new kitten in his kiddie pool?

Knowing the intuitive connection between mother and son can be amazingly keen, I wondered if I was psychically drawing Brian to my side to celebrate this hallmark occasion. My eyes spilled over. My heart sank. I was searching my purse for a tissue when Denise returned.

"What's wrong?" she asked when she saw me dabbing at my eyes.

"I think I've had enough wine. I keep hearing Brian wish me a happy birthday," I said, setting my empty wineglass aside.

She gave me an understanding smile. "Our table is ready," she said, ushering me toward the stairs.

"Surprise! Happy birthday to you!"

With beaming faces and rousing voices, friends, family, co-workers, shirttail relatives and perhaps a few people I'd only met casually in the grocery store belted out birthday greetings.

Combining my emotional reaction to Brian's telepathic birthday greeting and the surprise birthday party, I nearly collapsed.

I'd no sooner sat down in the chair of honor when a fireman entered the room, dressed from head to toe in firefighting bunker gear, carrying a sheet cake that looked like it'd been set afire. My heart sank. I'd seen firefighters at other soirées and they . . . well, let's just say they entered the room dressed to put out a raging fire, but exited the room decked out only in their birthday suit. Didn't Denise know this was not only in poor taste, but also downright embarrassing? How could she have let anyone do this to me?

The firefighter set the cake on the table in front of me so I could blow out the fifty blazing candles. "It's time to cut the cake," he said.

It seemed a bit early to be cutting cake, but I was thankful his clothes were still on his body and that he hadn't yet started any dancing gyrations.

I felt a tug on my heart when I saw the cake was a decadent death-by-chocolate flavor, a favorite Brian and I shared. An odd hollowness filled my chest. *He's so far away and so much can happen.*

Once again I heard Brian speak, "Mom, be sure to save me a piece of cake." This time he sounded very far away. *Was he okay?*

I froze in my chair. Was I losing my mind? Was hearing voices another menopausal side effect? My emotional state was fanned by the fear that the fireman might be removing most of his clothing at any moment.

"I'll have some cake as soon as I get this helmet off," the firefighter said. Every drop of blood in my veins flowed to my feet. He was stripping! With one fell swoop, the man grabbed the bottom of the helmet and swiftly pulled it from his head.

"Brian!"

"Hi, Mom. Happy fiftieth birthday!"

Cynthia Briggs

Mother Love

*If you want your children to keep their feet on the
ground, put some responsibility on their shoulders.*

Abigail Van Buren

"Mom, where do you suppose they are?" my slender
ten-year-old son Danny asked for the twentieth time as he
stared out the window toward the pasture.

"They" were our pony mare, Ginger, and her three-year-
old offspring, Charcoal, missing for four or five days—
maybe more.

Our fifty acres of pasture and woods in Miami County,
Kansas, offered plenty of grazing for six horses. However,
spring thunderstorms during the past ten days had
swollen creeks and forced the nearby river out of its
banks. The other horses had come to the barn during the
downpour, but not Ginger or Charcoal.

Danny had learned to ride on Ginger, or maybe she
taught him. At first he had to climb on cement blocks to
reach the stirrups. Charcoal, so-named for his beautiful
black coat, was now Danny's horse, being trained to take
a saddle and rider.

Yesterday when the downpour had subsided, I took Spot, our foxhound, to do some firsthand searching. We sloshed through trees and brush in swamped lowlands near the river. I could smell the fetid water.

All my calling and whistling and Spot's sniffing were in vain.

"I'm sorry, Danny, we didn't find them."

I dialed every sale barn in a radius of one hundred miles hoping someone had found them as strays.

"No, ma'am, we haven't seen either a dappled sandy mare or a black colt."

Without another apparent course of action, I could only worry to myself. I wanted to spare Danny this sorrow.

The next morning, the sun struggled to shine through gray clouds, but dampness hung in the dismal air.

Suddenly, Danny burst in the door. "Mom, come quick! There's Ginger!"

The mare stood at the pasture gate, whickering impatiently and trotting back and forth as if to say, "Follow me."

"Hurry, Danny," I said, "get the bucket with some oats. I'll bring a halter and rope."

Ginger trotted ahead, stopping frequently to look over her shoulder to be sure we were following. She led us down the same path where Spot and I had hiked previously. Overhead, three vultures circled—an ominous sight. When we reached the bottomland, the mare left the path, picking her way through soggy brush toward an inlet creek.

"I see him! I see him!" Danny shouted.

Charcoal was lying on his side, not moving. His right back leg was badly injured, bones protruding and skin blistered. His left leg was seared. Only lightning could have stripped away the hair on his legs, leaving long, ugly, open sores. Flies swarmed about his legs, and maggots crawled over his oozing wounds.

"Oh, Mom, how long do you think he's been lying here with no food and nobody to take care of him?" Tears formed in Danny's blue eyes.

"Probably several days, but we'll never know. Ginger took care of him, though, warding off hungry coyotes." *Or maybe that wild cat the neighbors saw*, I thought.

"What can we do now?" Danny worried aloud. "There's no way to drive the pickup down here in all this mud."

"We'll just have to get him up and lead him out," I said, keeping my voice confident.

So with our cajoling and the lure of oats, Charcoal struggled valiantly, finally managing to stand unsteadily on three legs. I slipped the halter on him. His eyes were dull with pain, yet he was spunky enough to respond to our efforts. This was surely the force of life over death!

What a sight we must have been—Ginger, her beautiful flaxen mane and tail mud-soaked and tangled; Danny with the bucket, marching up the rocky, slippery path through the woods; and I, steadying the injured colt, encouraging him to follow. The hike, ordinarily about thirty minutes in duration, took over two hours. Charcoal could only hop on three feet for a few yards and then rest, while we coaxed him to continue.

"We mustn't let him stop," I cautioned. "If he goes down again, he'll never make it."

A few more hops. The colt stumbled. "Danny, help me steady him. Don't let him stop!"

Up the path in the woods, across a small stream—*Help us, God, to save this horse.*

We crossed the lake's grass-covered dam—water lapping only a foot below. "Keep him going."

"Okay, Mom. The horses know they're almost home."

Through the pasture—at last we straggled back to the barn. Relieved, I gave my son a big hug.

Although our bodies demanded rest, Danny started clearing a corner of the barn to create a stall for Charcoal and Ginger. I hurried to telephone the vet to come as soon as possible.

After cleaning and medicating Charcoal's wounds, the vet told us, "He should heal, but you'll need to treat those legs every day for several weeks, maybe longer." He showed Danny exactly how to apply the medication and cover the wounds.

Then he shook his head and said, "Mares usually detach themselves from their offspring once they're weaned. It's a miracle that this mare, Ginger, who had Charcoal almost three years ago—and even recently weaned her second foal—stayed with him through all the recent storms."

Danny grinned, "Haven't you heard the old proverb, 'God couldn't be everywhere and therefore he made mothers'?"

Polly W. Swafford

A Part of the Team

All things, whatsoever ye shall ask in prayer, believing, ye shall receive.

Matthew 21:22

I couldn't remember a time when it hadn't been his dream to play football. He had watched the Nebraska Cornhuskers since he was a baby. "Some day," he told me, "I want to play with the Cornhuskers."

All through grade school he played flag football at the YMCA. Every spare minute he studied plays, practiced throwing, running, kicking. He never missed a practice or a game. He was going to play at Memorial Stadium in Lincoln some day.

Finally, in eighth grade, he got to go out for football at his junior-high school. The roster came out, and sure enough there was his name and his weight, seventy-five pounds, nearly the smallest on the team. But his father and I had always told him, "You can do anything you set your mind to," and he was going to play football.

The next year he made the team again. This time, though, at eighty-five pounds, he was the smallest on the team. He showed up for every practice and never missed a game. The team was short a second-string quarterback, and he volunteered for the position. The time he had spent studying plays didn't go to waste. He took some snaps, did some handoffs, and the freshman Tiger team went undefeated that year.

His sophomore year in high school was his first year to try out for the reserve team. In the heat of the summer, he sweated the workouts, lifted weights and attended football camps. He made the team, again the smallest member at ninety-five pounds. But he never missed a practice or a game . . . or watching the Cornhuskers on TV. I watched his dedication and prayed, "Lord, I know this sounds impossible, but if you could just find some way to answer this child's desire and let him play on the Nebraska Cornhusker field."

In his junior year of high school, still undaunted by his size, he continued to play on his high school team, which ended the season 2–9. But a losing season did not dampen his enthusiasm. Each time he played, he played to his fullest, and while on the bench, he cheered on the team . . . because if you play at Nebraska, you can't give up.

His senior year came, and he was still nearly the smallest. The linemen weighed over two hundred pounds. My son would be a receiver at one-forty-five. "Lord, it looks impossible that this child can play college football with the Nebraska Cornhuskers, but if you could just find some way to get him onto that field." That year he broke two bones in his hand and had to sit out the middle of the season, but he continued to be at every game, every practice, memorized every play and cheered the team from the bench.

Finally, the orthopedic surgeon gave the go-ahead, and he could get back into the game. The Tigers had a winning season and would be in the playoffs, making it to the semifinals. They would go up against a team from Lincoln High School. But torrential rains and sleet ruined the high-school ballfields, so a substitute field had to be found.

On a bitter cold November night, floodlights filled the stadium like daylight when over the loudspeaker boomed the announcement. "Here come the Tigers!" I watched as my son ran out onto the Cornhuskers' Memorial Field in Lincoln, and I remembered my prayer—and so did God.

Cheryl A. Paden

Ricochet

"Don't worry, Mom. If you're at net and someone hits the ball at you, just hold up your racquet."

"Are you sure about this?"

David had started playing tennis when we moved to a new state and Neil, the only other eleven-year-old boy on our block, played tennis. When you're entering a new middle school in the fall, don't know a soul, love sports and want a friend, learning to play the same game seems incredibly important.

"I need," David had said, "to at least know how to hold the racquet and serve."

My tennis career began and ended in my sophomore year in college. The only instruction I recalled was something about shaking hands with your racquet and love—as a score, or lack of.

The town tennis courts and Little League field were only five minutes away. Since neither of us owned tennis racquets and I didn't want to invest a lot of money, I responded quickly to a two-for-one sale ad. It became apparent, after a morning at the court, that David's great athletic skills allowed him to volley the ball over the net several times before missing a shot. My own shots lacked finesse, positioning or anything approaching power.

David and Neil became fast friends, and within a week I took David to Marshall's department store, bought him two white polo shirts, a pair of tennis sneakers and several cans of vacuum-packed yellow tennis balls.

One day David announced that Neil's mother had signed him up for tennis lessons. So David signed up, too. Every morning for two weeks, David and Neil used a bungee cord to secure a racquet, a can of balls and a thermos to their bike holders, and they rode off for lessons.

About that time, I noticed a local newspaper ad: *Wanted: someone who is a beginner to play tennis—Barbara and a phone number.* Because I also didn't know anyone in my new town and my appetite for tennis blossomed after playing with David, I called Barbara, and we met to play.

Over the next five years, David's love of tennis increased, and he took more lessons, played on the high-school team, entered the town tennis tournament, won in his division and had grown to over six feet tall. My own tennis improved with lessons, but not being athletically inclined, I never really acquired a decent backhand shot. My lob-like serves stayed within the appropriate box, at best.

David's friend Matt played on the high-school team, and his mother belonged to a tennis club, hit a wicked serve, played four or five times a week, and towered over me. One day David came home and announced that Mrs. Armsley's tennis club was sponsoring a mother-son doubles tournament.

"Mom," said David, who excelled in tennis *and* the art of debating, "how can we go wrong? The money goes to a charity that helps kids." Since I taught in a school for children with disabilities, David knew what tack to take.

"Suppose I make a donation?" I offered.

"But," countered David, "how often do we get an opportunity like this? You were the one who first showed me how to shake hands with a racquet and keep score.

"Besides," he added, "it's just for fun, not really competitive." He convinced me I could handle the net and fast approaching balls. We went to the town court and practiced against Barbara and another friend. David gave me some pointers and a lot of one-liners. "Don't worry. Hold up your racquet like this, and the ball will simply ricochet back across the net. Remember, it's for charity. No one is going to play for blood when you're at the net."

The day of the tournament, we both wore whites. By that time David owned a metal racquet with taut strings, and I owned one with a large head. The tournament director divided the boys into age-appropriate groups.

"There are eight teams in my age bracket. If we survive three matches, we'll be in the finals."

"You don't really expect to win, do you?"

David had been right: No one went after the mothers when they played net. The boys quickly assessed if the mother played well. If so, they went all out. If not, they saved the spin and velocity for her son.

We survived three matches. David knew how to move the ball from side-to-side, and I enjoyed the fun of playing with him. The championship game in our age group came down to a match between us and Mrs. Armsley and Matt.

"David, do you realize that the top of my head is even with the second button on her polo shirt?"

All the rules evaporated when we played them. When I stood at the net, it felt like target practice.

"Mom," said David, "I can take the net the entire time. You just pull back, and I'll go to the net."

We did just that. Moving back and forth like a well-oiled machine. The score was tied.

Then a yellow ball, like an errant rocket, came whizzing at me. There wasn't time for David to get to the net, and I remembered, "Hold up your racquet like this, and the ball will simply ricochet back across the net." More for protection than game, I held up my racquet; the ball hit the strings with a resounding ping and rebounded across the net like an unexpected intruder.

I walked away with the prize wristbands, balls and a small trophy—and my son's amazed admiration.

Linda Watskin

7:07 Prayers

Remembrances last longer than present realities.

Jean Paul Richter

I sit with phone in hand, watching the minutes click by on the clock. 7:05. 7:06. 7:07. I hit the button and hear the beginning of a ring. My son answers before it is finished. "Hello, Mom!"

"Happy birthday to you. Happy birthday to you . . ." I finish with my slightly revised version. ". . . Happy birthday, your mom loves you."

"Thanks, Mom," Aaron says, a smile in his voice. We talk. He has been watching the clock too, waiting for the expected call. I tell him how much I love him. "I love you, too, Mom." We hang up. I say a special prayer for a blessed birthday for him and begin my morning activities. But my thoughts remain with him, my oldest son.

Thirty-six years old! How long have I been doing 7:07 birthday songs and prayers? I guess most of his life. I didn't plan it that way. It just happened. Aaron was born at 7:07 A.M. one cold, winter morning. St. Patrick's Day, in fact.

When he was just a toddler, I would wake him at 7:07 and sing "Happy Birthday" and tell him about the day of his birth. It became a tradition. Even when he was away at college, I would hear a groggy "Hello, Mom" as soon as I called. The only time I missed calling was the first year after his marriage when Aaron and his wife, Amy, took a spring-break vacation. Certainly, I wouldn't interfere with this. Later that day, Aaron called.

"Why didn't you call at 7:07?" I could hear the disappointment in his voice.

"Honey, I didn't think it was appropriate, and I had no idea where you were."

He quickly responded, "I told Dad the name of the motel where we would be staying."

Something in my heart began to sing. Our tradition would continue.

But it has become more than a tradition and birthday ritual. Though my prayers are always with Aaron, whenever I look at the digital clock and see 7:07, I know it is a special time to pray for him. No matter the day of the year, whether it be morning or night, I stop everything and say a prayer. Sometimes I awake at exactly 7:07 and immediately begin prayers for him, knowing God has called me to pray at this specific time. Through the years I found that Aaron was in great need of prayer at that particular time. Other times, it remained a mystery. But that's okay. I count it a privilege to pray blessings on my son—any day or night at 7:07.

Louise Tucker Jones

Happy Feet

Those move easiest who have learned to dance.

Alexander Pope

My son Myles was dancing even before he was born. I used to lie in bed and watch as he shook his booty, creating amniotic tsunamis in my belly. On the night he made his first appearance, the nurse laid him on my stomach, and my suspicions were confirmed—he was a boogying baby from the get-go.

When Myles was in second grade, his fabulous teacher asked every student to finish this sentence: "I'm terrific because . . ." and then draw a self-portrait to illustrate whatever sterling feature of their character they chose to highlight. Myles drew a picture of a smiling boy with yellow hair, clad in a tuxedo, dancing on stage in front of a row of footlights, with the caption: "I'm terrific because I can tap dance like Fred Astaire!"

How many little kids know who Fred Astaire is anymore? Myles did, and he also idolized Donald O'Connor, Gene Kelly and Savion Glover, back in his early *Sesame Street* days. We began looking in earnest for a place to get tap lessons, something he had been begging for once he realized that your feet could make noise with the right shoes on. Myles had already choreographed his own dance to a number from "You're a Good Man, Charlie Brown" and brought down the house at the school talent show—a pint-sized Snoopy, dressed in black and white, with a red bow tie, high tops and a black derby. Gotta dance!

As a former tap dancer myself, I began our search for the right place to learn the waltz clog, the time step and the shuffle off to Buffalo. There was no shortage of dance studios where we live. But the search was difficult just the same. Time after time, we would show up during a lesson and survey the teacher, the class and the studio. No boys. Lots of sequins. Pictures sometimes lined the walls: rows of pretty girls in high-heeled tap shoes with high-cut leotards, more sequins and still no boys. We moved on to the next place.

We finally found a home at a studio in Berkeley. Myles visited the class, which had several boys—some his age and some older—and danced across the wooden floor in his Converse hightops. The teacher was a big-hearted woman with a big smile and a loud voice, a head full of ringlets and mismatched earrings. The kids danced to brassy show-biz tunes that got their feet moving. The pictures on the walls were of tap legends: Sandman Simms, Gregory Hines, the Nicholas Brothers and others. Not a sequin in sight. When the class ended and the kids tumbled out the door, I noticed that my son had a new look on his face: His eyes were shining, and his smile was one of joy mixed with gratitude—a wish fulfilled. We signed him up for the class and hurried off to buy his first pair of shiny black tap shoes.

When Myles was around ten, we attended a Jazz Tap Summit in San Francisco, where the living legends of tap performed and spoke to a sold-out crowd of tappers and wannabes. The audience was encouraged to "bring your shoes" and join in at the end for a big jam session. Naturally, Myles laced up and ran onstage with all the others. It was a huge thrill to see him on the stage doing the "Shim Sham Shimmy" with all the big-time tappers. When he returned to our seats, he beamed, "Sandman Simms talked to me!"

"What did he say?" we asked. Proud parents that we were, we waited for some comment on his innate ability, his sense of rhythm or his poise as a performer.

"He said, 'Go this way.' And then he said, 'Now go that way.'"

Myles went on to tap his way through high school and college, including a jam session with the amazing Gregory Hines.

Several years ago, as a terrible fire swept through the hills where we live, I ran through the house grabbing picture albums, jewelry, the pet bird—and Myles's tap shoes. I didn't think to take his second-grade "I'm terrific" picture, but I will always remember the happy boy with the black bow tie, dancing with his feet off the ground.

Risa Nye

"I think I see why you're progressing slowly in music."

©1977 Martha Campbell. Reprinted by permission of Martha Campbell.

Listen to What I Hear

I learned it all from mothers.

Dr. Benjamin Spock

The phone call always came last minute.

"So when are we taking the boys Christmas caroling?" asked my neighbor Mary, cheerful beyond measure with only five days left before Christmas.

Christmas caroling? Was she crazy? The December twenty-fifth deadline for shopping, wrapping, baking and cleaning loomed with Scrooge-like orneriness.

Who had time to sing?

Yet passing up the opportunity to take my three young sons and her little guy out into the crisp night air to belt out Christmas carols for our neighbors would haunt me like the ghost of Christmas past.

"How does the twenty-third look?" I asked, mustering as much enthusiasm as I could.

"Perfect!" said Mary, who doubles as a highly organized art teacher. "I'll send out flyers for our neighbors to leave on their porch lights if they'd like us to stop. You bring the hot chocolate."

With that, she hung up. There was no backing out now. The event was rolling along like the final verses of the Hallelujah Chorus.

"When are we going Christmas caroling?" asked an eager son hovering nearby.

"The day after tomorrow," I answered.

"I get the sleigh bells this year!" all three yelled together.

Two days later, the mystery of a winter night bloomed dark, frosty and beckoning. The three boys and I stuffed ourselves in as much warm clothing as allowed us to move, filled the thermos with hot chocolate, grabbed a bag of cups and marshmallows, and snatched the sleigh bells from the mantle.

Just about the time we started to sweat, Mary called to say they were on their way.

"Meet you at the end of the driveway," she said.

"Let's go!" the boys yelled, dashing out the door into the welcome blast of cold night air.

Across the street and down the hill came Mary and Brad.

As we gathered in the road, the boys let out whoops of joy at the sight that greeted us.

"Wow! Look at that!" Brad said.

Mary's flyer had done the trick. Beacons of porch lights, like a string of constellations, twinkled around our horseshoe-shaped lane, directing us to a waiting audience.

"We better do a warm-up before we go," Mary suggested.

Like a rowdy Midwestern version of an English boys' choir, our four guys launched into a rousing rendition of "Jingle Bells," our caroling opener, ringing their bells with enough gusto to spook even Marley's ghost.

As they hit the last note, they were off and running to the nearest house to see who could push the doorbell first. Mary and I lagged behind, struggling to keep up with their energy.

As soon as a neighbor swung open the storm door, the boys broke into song. One by one, more friendly faces began to pop up behind the first one until we had a small ensemble bobbing with our beat. Ending our short medley with "We Wish You a Merry Christmas," the boys were rewarded with candy canes and Christmas cookies.

Of course, Mary and I had to have some, too.

Then it was onto the next welcoming porch light as more shivering neighbors shouted to family members, "Come quickly, come quickly, it's the Christmas carolers!"

After five or six houses, our throats were ready for a short intermission. Sipping the soothing hot cocoa, we looked skyward through the sculptured arms of a huge, old oak tree, studied the stars and embraced the sudden stillness of the night.

In that simple moment, I found the peace of Christmas.

Soon the rustle of jingling bells indicated it was time to move on. One of our favorite stops was at Bill and Paula's. Although Bill's speech was impaired from a stroke, he opened the door like a king welcoming his favorite minstrels to his court. Paula appeared right behind him with an array of cookies made just for us.

The boys' repertoire for Bill differed slightly from the rest. They knew his favorite song was "Silent Night," and they sang it with all the sweet, awkward tenderness that their innocent, young voices could muster.

Like the crystalline beauty of a snowflake drifting through a moonlit night, a moment of magic hung in the air as the boys ended their song. With misted eyes, Bill broke into enthusiastic applause, and with great effort he called each boy by name.

"J-John, B-Bob, T-Tom and B-Brad, that was wonderful!" he joyfully proclaimed.

The boys beamed with the happy awareness that somehow they had given a gift.

As our guys grew older, musical instruments began to replace the bells. Two trombones, a trumpet and a drummer made up a caroling band, with Mary and me as backup singers.

Some years we sang in soft snowfall, and some years the nights were so cold the boys' instruments stuck to their lips. Sometimes visiting grandmothers trudged along beside us, and occasionally the new voices of other children who had moved into the neighborhood joined the swell. Once we even sang "Away in a Manager" to a neighbor's stabled horse.

Always there were porch lights beckoning and sweet songs answering.

Sometime during the teenage years, the caroling phone call stopped coming. Band concerts, dates and sports took over the boys' busy schedules, and we all moved on to other Christmas activities.

Like the imperceptible beat of angel wings, time flew by. Our boys became young men, Bill passed on, and after twenty-six years as my neighbor, Mary moved away.

Yet even now, when the hectic holidays threaten to turn me into a humbug, I'll step out into the night and look up through the gnarled arms of an old oak to the sparkling stars. The cold quiet warms my soul. And if I listen closely, I can hear the peace of Christmas in the whisper of young boys' voices serenading back to me, "All is calm, all is bright."

The echo, forever, will be a hymn in my heart.

Marnie O. Mamminga

2

BOYS WILL BE BOYS!

The greatest happiness in life is the conviction that we are loved, loved for ourselves, or rather in spite of ourselves.

Victor Hugo

Getting Even!

*My mother had a great deal of trouble with me,
but I think she enjoyed it.*

Mark Twain

Several years ago, my son was attending a college out of
state. He called one evening and asked if he could come
home for spring break. I reassured him that he was welcome. There was a pause and he asked, "Can I bring my
sweetheart, Deanna, with me?"

"Sure, Jeff," I said. "We'd love to meet her."

As I hung up the phone, I started remembering all the
times this particular son had totally embarrassed me. Like
the time I asked him to pick out a box of cereal at the store,
then turned around to see him doing his stammering
Elmer Fudd imitation to the delight of fellow shoppers. Or
the time I was speaking from the pulpit at church and saw
him sitting in the pew wearing glasses with bloodshot
eyeballs springing from the lenses, swaying back and
forth. His pranks were never-ending.

"So," I said to myself, "this is my chance!" I decided to
show up at the airport to meet him and his sweetheart in

less than my conservative manner of dress. I donned a black leather miniskirt, patterned hose and six-inch patent leather heels. I wore a gold sweater that sparkled and glowed in the dark, accented by earrings swaying from my ear lobes to my shoulders. I spiked my hair and moussed it orange.

When my husband came home that evening, he took one look at me and said, "What is this? The bachelor party I never had? You aren't going to go through with this, are you?"

I nodded. He drove me to the upper level of the airport and let me out of the car, refusing to walk with me to the gate.

It was a long walk through the airport. I found myself looking down a lot. I found out what men think of women dressed like I was. I found out what women think of women dressed like that. But when Jeffrey got off the airplane, *ohhhhhhhhh,* it was all worth it! I ran, arms outstretched toward him.

I squealed, stretching out his name as if he was a long-lost relative. "Jeffrey!" He looked away as soon as he saw me, the color quickly fading from his face. Deanna stood behind him, grinning—or was it grimacing?

"Aren't you going to introduce me?" I asked.

"No," he said abruptly. I looked at Deanna, smiled and reached forth my hand.

"Oh hi, Deanna, I'm Jeffrey's mom."

She seemed not to know whether to laugh or cry. A snort of disbelief came from her as she covered her face to disguise her reaction. I looked back at Jeffrey, whose horrified expression looked as if he'd experienced his worst nightmare.

I smiled.

About now, his father showed up, and as they walked together to baggage claim, Jeff asked, "What in the world has gotten into Mom since I left for college?"

His dad whispered, "A severe midlife crisis."

I chatted nonchalantly all the way home. Jeffrey and Deanna clung to each other and barely spoke. When we got home, I jumped in the shower and washed the orange out of my hair. I entered the living room in slacks and a sweater, looking like the mom Jeff knew and remembered. A look of relief flooded his face, and he burst out laughing. "You got me, Mom!"

We hugged and laughed and spent the next several hours giggling and reminiscing about the tricks Jeff had pulled on all of us.

The next trip home for Jeffrey and Deanna was in December after they were married. I went to the airport to pick them up. I arrived at the gate just as the doors opened and cheerful seasonal travelers filed off the plane. I noticed two large reindeer coming toward me in full fur and antlers, one with a blinking red nose.

I hugged Rudolph.

"You feel a little silly this time, Mom?"

"No," I laughed. "Don't you?"

Somehow we were even for all those times he had totally mortified me.

Or were we?

Suzanne Vaughan

The Mother's Day Note

As a single mom, my treasures consist of things my sons, Luc and Sam, have said or written. My most recent treasure came from Luc on Mother's Day.

I felt doubly blessed sandwiched between both teenagers in church that morning, listening to our pastor speak about families rather than just mothers. His message was encouraging and uplifting, with instruction directed to both parents and kids about showing your love for each other.

During the sermon, Luc scribbled on a piece of paper and handed it to me. My heart swelled as I began unfolding his written declaration of love. I hoped I wouldn't cry in public, as I anticipated his declaration that I was the best mom in the world. I bit my lip to contain my emotion as I read, "Watch the Lakers game today for me while I'm at work."

Jeri Chrysong

Chalk It Up

There are only two things a child will share willingly—communicable diseases and his mother's age.

Dr. Benjamin Spock

Decal. Ptck. Appten. Septwo.

Would you believe that the above message when deciphered means: "Dentist called. Patrick has an appointment at 10:00 A.M. September 2"?

This is one of the easier messages to translate since we have an eleven-year-old scrawling messages on the new blackboard next to the telephone. We don't miss any more phone messages in this house, but unfortunately, something is often missing in the translation.

This has led to some very embarrassing situations.

Take, for example, the call I got from the president of the Women's Club, Mrs. Burton. I was out shopping when she called to ask me to sell tickets for the upcoming dinner-dance.

My dutiful son Steve wrote down the message, "Mrs. Burton called." This was very commendable on his part.

Unfortunately, not one to overlook the opportunity of having chalk in his hand, he also wrote a tribute to his eight-year-old brother: "Patrick is a turkey."

When Patrick spotted this, he erased it, but in his haste he erased only "called" and "Patrick." The message now read, "Mrs. Burton is a turkey" in letters bold enough for all to see. Guess who came over to deliver the tickets just as I was arriving home and saw the blackboard? The only consolation is that at least now I don't have to sell tickets.

Then there was the time I was a religion teacher, and the education coordinator called me. She told Patrick, "This is Sister Loyola. Tell your mother there is no class at the church tonight. Please tell her I called."

When I came home I saw the message scribbled on the board in childish script. Patrick had enlisted the help of eleven-year-old Steve to write: "Your sister called from her Toyota. There's no glass in the church, and she's cold."

I knew there was something wrong. I don't even have a sister.

Barbara Adams

It Is What It Is

When I grow up, I want to be a little boy.

Joseph Heller

Jesse was playing inside a big cardboard box and, as is typical of a four-year-old, found a good afternoon's worth of an active imagination to sustain his interest. The box was large enough that he could get inside and pull the flaps closed. He carefully selected which of his toys would accompany him inside it. When I checked on him after a good length of time, he was clearly having a ton of fun. So I asked him, "What is that, Jesse? Is it your house?"

"No, it's not a house," he said.

"Is it a castle?" I queried.

"No," he answered.

I pressed on. "A cave?"

"No."

"A tent?"

"No."

"Your secret hiding place?"

"No."

"Okay, I give up. Jesse, what is it?"

Jesse poked his head up through the flaps, looked me straight in the eye and said, "It's a box."

Gertrude Stein wrote, "A rose is a rose is a rose." I will forever smile in remembrance that one so young could promote thinking "outside the box" from inside the box.

Karen Brown

Making the Grade

One of the virtues of being very young is that you don't let the facts get in the way of your imagination.

Sam Levenson

Being the youngest of our four children, my son Shawn tried so hard to keep up with the three older ones, two of whom were brothers, and the competition was fierce.

We strived hard for our children to do well in school and rewarded them for excellent grades. Shawn had to work hard for even average grades in first grade, but he never gave up.

The going rate was one dollar for each "excellent" that they received on their grade cards. Being in first grade, excellent grades appeared as the symbol "O" for outstanding.

I anxiously waited on the front porch the day that he was due home with his first grade card, knowing he would be so proud of whatever grades he had. He stepped off the bus, and his little feet never hit the ground. He was so excited, he screamed, "Mom! I got two Os!"

He jumped onto the porch and ripped open his school bag and said, "Look, two Os, Mom. I did it!"

I hugged him and was so proud, but then I looked at his grade card. The two Os were zeros for days missed and days tardy.

Nothing would burst his bubble that day. I told him how proud I was of him and gave him the two dollars anyway.

Susan Pasztor

"Hard day at school. Every time I raised my hand,
Ms. Dirk called my bluff."

©1990 Martha Campbell. Reprinted by permission of Martha Campbell.

A Place in the Sun

It's been years since my sons were in Little League baseball. I get a bit nostalgic as I see the neighborhood children going off to their games, looking sharp and proud in their uniforms with a number on their backs they will never forget.

In 1963, Colin, my eldest son, played centerfield for the Tigers, a Little League team in Hampton, Virginia. In his first year, his father told him that keeping a ball firmly gripped in his baseball glove would help form a good pocket in his new glove. We'd often find him sleeping with the glove still on his hand, baseball gripped tightly.

I made sure I was at all of our sons' games, even when I was pregnant with number-four child (another future Little Leaguer) and pushing my youngest daughter around in a stroller. The older daughter was already old enough to help whenever I had concession-stand duty. It was our family entertainment every night of the week during baseball season.

The most unforgettable game came at the conclusion of the '63 season and Colin's last year of Little League baseball. He was on the all-star team, and this game would determine who went on to compete in the regional playoffs. Our all-stars needed to clinch this one. It meant traveling out of town to an unfamiliar field, but we went in hopes of watching our boys beat the socks off the opposing team.

Tied, the game went into extra innings. It was a hard-fought game and a toss-up right to the final hit deep into midfield. In some ballfields, it might have been considered a homerun, but standing tall and ready to save the day far out in center field stood my son with his eye on that fly ball all the way. He seemed to hesitate as he stood there, anticipating the trajectory, and then he began his dash for the landing zone. I sat in the stands praying this wasn't going to be one of those days that Colin got ahead of his size-thirteen feet as he watched the ball heading into no-man's land, a weedy patch of knee-high grass and low trailing vines. It arched high, stalled and became lost to us in the lowering five o'clock sun. From the stands, the players were silhouetted against the glare, their mouths gaping open as they followed the ball into the raw afternoon light. Collectively, we held our breath, frantically squinting against the sun for a glimpse of Colin and the ball as it dropped toward the outfield where maintenance had long since been abandoned.

Parents sat mute, resisting their usual sideline coaching. It was the quiet of a golf tournament. Colin took off, feet following his steady concentration on the baseball; first attempting to run, then leaping through the thick and tangled weeds and vines until he appeared to be right under the descending ball. He had his glove stuck out before him. It looked as though he was attempting to correct his position, but then he stumbled backward, vanishing from view.

The crowd in our bleachers groaned as one.

The other team jumped up and down in their dugout, and their parents cheered and whistled.

We fixed smiles on our faces for the sake of our team's spirit, which would soon be congratulating the other team as victors and league champs. At the same time, we strained our eyes to see if Colin was going to get up to chase the ball.

Then above the weeds, we saw an arm with a mitt raised high. Someone yelled, "He caught it!" The umpire nodded.

The crowd went wild. I thought our bleachers would fall apart with the pounding of feet.

Such a game fulfills the dreams of heroics for little boys and their parents there to witness it. It may be the best day they remember, when they had their place in the sun . . . and a pocket in their glove!

Rosalie Griffin

The Gotcha Game

Laughter is the shortest distance between two people.

Victor Borge

It all started one autumn afternoon when the children came home from school carrying paper sacks filled with all the goodies they'd collected from their Halloween parties.

"Look what I've got, Mom!" said my young son. Austin put his hand in his sack and rustled his fingers around in the candy wrappers and papers. With a huge grin on his face, he pulled out his prize. A rubber mouse!

"Eek!" I said, pretending to be scared. It really was ugly with its gray skin and painted red eyes. The long rubber tail wiggled like the real thing. Somebody's mother had probably bought a bag full of toy mice for her child to pass around at the classroom party.

"Gotcha, Mom!" he giggled. What better fun was there for a boy than to surprise his mom with a lifelike rodent?

"Take it to your room," I said in mock reprimand. He laughed as he ran up the stairs. *Little boys,* I sighed to myself. *Hopefully in a few days he'll tire of this new toy, and it'll slowly sift to the bottom of his toy box where I won't have to look at it.*

That night before turning in, I washed my face and reached into my makeup drawer for my moisturizer. I felt something soft and rubbery, and jerked my hand back! There, amid the eyeliner and foundation, lay the gray mouse, its bright red eyes staring up at me.

"Austin!" I yelled down the hallway. Muffled laughter came from his darkened room. He had probably been lying awake in bed, waiting for his mother to discover the surprise hidden in the drawer. *All right,* I thought with a smile, *two can play this game.*

The next morning, Austin came down the stairs and climbed up onto the barstool at the kitchen counter. He rubbed his eyes sleepily. Suddenly, they opened wide with surprise. Peeking around the edge of his cereal bowl was a little gray nose with black whiskers.

"Hey, my mouse!" he chuckled. "You got *me* that time!" He picked up the toy and stuffed it into his jean pocket. He grinned widely at me, no doubt anticipating his next move in this new game.

I didn't have to wait long. As soon as I slipped into the driver's seat of my pickup, I was once again victim of the Gotcha Game. Perched on the steering wheel was the mouse, looking right back at me.

The next few weeks were filled with moments of surprise for both of us. Sometimes I set the mouse on Austin's pillow just before bedtime or sent it to school in his lunch bag. A couple of times I hid the critter in his boots or shoes. Then I'd find those painted red eyes peering at me from my crochet basket or deep within my purse. Once I noticed it sitting on top of the telephone like it was waiting for an important call.

One day I realized it had been a while since I'd seen our little gray friend. Somehow it had become misplaced or simply lost in the hectic flow of our daily lives. I found myself looking for it anyway, expecting—almost hoping— to see it in the oddest places.

While I was picking up a few things at the store one day, I spotted a sale table full of leftover Halloween items. I looked through the boxes of decorations and found a bag of gray rubber mice with bright red eyes. Memories came flooding back, full of laughter, giggles and calls of "Gotcha, Mom!"

I bought two bags.

Pamela Jenkins

The Asparagus Costume

Maternal love! Thou word that sums all bliss.

Channing Pollock

I am not what you would call an artsy-craftsy mom. I can follow directions that are given to me, but I don't have a lot of creativity when it comes to doing art projects.

Halloween was rapidly approaching, and my three-and-a-half-year-old son, John, was old enough to really get into the spirit of the whole thing. Even though he had gone trick-or-treating before, he had really not participated in the selection of his costume. He had been too young to care and was happy with whatever I bought for him.

This year was different. He had very definite opinions, and he knew just what he wanted to be: an asparagus! An asparagus? Where in the world did that idea come from? We had never even seen a costume like that in the stores, and with my sewing abilities I certainly wouldn't—or rather, I couldn't—sew one for him. What was a mother to do?

I had the perfect solution. I would convince him he wanted to be a monster for Halloween. Monsters I could do. I would dress him all in black, slick down his hair and make up his face. Oh, would I make up his face! There would be no sewing involved, and that's a good thing.

Being the thoughtful person that he is, and since we couldn't find any asparagus costumes, he agreed to be a monster. But he wanted to be "the scariest monster in the whole wide world." I told him not to worry and that I would take care of everything.

A few hours before dark on Halloween, the transformation from boy to monster began. I sat on a small chair in the bathroom so we were at the same level, looking eye to eye. I got all of the makeup out of my drawer, lots and lots of half-used cosmetics that for some reason I'd never thrown out. When they were all mixed together, the concoction became wonderful monster makeup. And so I got to work.

John had his back to the mirror while the transformation took place. He practiced making appropriate monster noises so he would be ready when we hit the streets to trick-or-treat. I slathered his beautiful, little face with all kinds of goo. When I was finished, it was bluish purple with scars, gashes, gouges and blood from his forehead to his chin. There was not a speck of skin showing. The scariest of all were his eyes. They were really hideous. I must say I was really pleased with the results. I had thoughts right then and there of giving up being a stay-at-home mom and becoming a professional makeup artist.

It was now time to show John the results of my artistic abilities. I knew he would be delighted and impressed to see his goal of being "the scariest monster in the whole wide world" achieved. I turned him around slowly, telling him to keep his eyes closed until he was facing the mirror. Then I told him to open his eyes. He did. He *screeeeeeamed!* So loud he could be heard all over the neighborhood! I had done such a fabulous job that he was scared of himself!

Not knowing who that monster was in the mirror, he couldn't stand to look at himself and he started to cry. Loud.

Being the sensitive mother that I am, I started to laugh. I tried to explain to him that there was no need to be afraid. The face in the mirror was John, and beneath all that glop was still a sweet, loving, little boy. Well, he would have none of that explanation. So I turned him around, hugged him and spent the next ten minutes wiping his face clean of all traces of that monster and drying his tears.

When he was back to being John, I turned him around again. He kept his eyes closed, but I finally convinced him to open them. His smile said it all. He was back. The monster was gone. He was happy.

We did go out for Halloween that night. I slicked back his hair and put just enough dots of blue eye shadow on his face to satisfy him, but not enough to cover up his face and make him unrecognizable. We were not exactly sure what he was supposed to be—maybe the blue-dot monster— but at least he didn't scare himself.

Where was that asparagus costume when I needed it?

Barbara LoMonaco

The Cowboy Suit

Of all animals, the boy is the most unmanageable.

Plato

Christmas was a wonderful time for me in 1962 when we had just moved from Alabama to Texas. The tree didn't have a lot of gifts under it, but there was one big one with my name on it.

Finally, Christmas morning rolled around, and we gathered around the little tree to open gifts. I grabbed mine with eager hands and ripped it open to find a genuine cowboy suit, just like they wore in Texas. It had a big, ten-gallon hat, chaps, a leather vest, a badge, a pair of cowboy boots and a two-pistol holster. I was blessed. All my sisters got were silly old dolls. I could think of nothing better for Christmas, except maybe a Superman suit with cape and all. The thoughts of a super hero leaping tall buildings would have to wait another year, but in the meantime, I was going to be a cowboy sheriff. I pinned on the silver badge with pride.

Dad seemed to enjoy my gift more than his new shirts and blue jeans. Being an adult was tough, and all he could do now is play with the toys his son got for Christmas. My dad was a big western fan, and we watched those cowboy movies together. I loved the Lone Ranger and Will Rogers. I shot up a whole roll of caps in no time working on my quick draw, with Dad's coaching, of course.

I went to bed that night thinking of me slinging those two six-shooters and twirling those pistols in grand fashion, just like Roy Rogers. I could smell the gunpowder.

The next morning arrived bright and early. I was out of bed, loading my two six-shooters and donning the whole cowboy suit to include the boots. You know the kind—no matter which way you put them on, they always look like they are on the wrong feet. I was ready for a shootout, and I knew right where it was going to happen. I got my imaginary friend, Will Rogers, and we started for the old barn. I knew Mom was there milking the cow. She'd be surprised when I stepped into the barn and started my shootout. I just knew Mom would beam with pride.

Stepping in, I noticed the cow busy eating hay and Mom sitting on a stool squeezing squirts of milk into a bucket on the dirt floor. She was so busy with her chore, she didn't notice my arrival.

I stood there, fully dressed, cowboy hat and all. The only thing missing was a good set of spurs on my boots, but not to worry. I stood bowlegged as if I had been riding a horse for about a week anyway. I looked into the barn, imagining that at the other end stood five mean, old cowboys with black hats and dirty-looking, as though they needed a shave and a good scrubbing with Mom's scrub brush.

I raised my hands ready above each pistol to await their move. I said, "Mean Joe Whiskey, I'm here to run you out of town. Either get on your horses right now or make your move." I waited about a minute, and then I caught a movement that told me the bad guys were going for their guns.

It happened so quickly. I whipped my two six-shooters out and started shooting. *Bam! Bam! Bam!* Maybe the cow didn't like cowboys. Maybe it didn't like cap pistols either. Anyway, it spun around, knocking my mother to the floor. The mad cow tossed the stool and milk bucket against the wall, then turned on me and my shiny six-shooters. It lowered its head, and for the first time I saw those sharp, dangerous horns. The cow plowed toward me in a rage of steam and snorts. I stood there, frozen, helpless, watching death charge right at me.

Maybe I closed my eyes or perhaps I just blinked, but how my mother passed that cow still amazes me. Was she really that fast, or could she fly? All I knew was I was looking at a set of mean-looking horns on an even meaner-looking cow, and out of nowhere came those hands that lifted me into the air—not only into the air, but rising up to clear the gate to the field and land on the other side. Immediately, I heard the raging cow collide with the gate.

It left a dent that would remain there as a reminder that a super hero was leaping that Christmas after all.

G. E. Dabbs

My Hero

I watched out the kitchen window of our old house for my eight-year-old to come up the path. He knew not to dawdle when he got off the school bus, but like most little boys, he could be easily distracted, even in the rain. I had a dry towel ready, knowing he'd be soaked from the downpour.

Charlie came in the door, immediately sat his backpack down, and pulled out a wriggling creature. A cat!

"Isn't he neat, Mom? Can we keep him?" he asked, batting his big brown eyes. I looked askance at the feline, a mangy little thing, soaking wet, shaking water from his dripping fur—not a kitten, but not quite a cat either.

"I think someone abandoned him," Charlie explained, tears forming in his eyes. "I picked him up out of the ditch because he was all wet and scared. I promise I'll take good care of him, and he won't be any trouble at all. Can we keep him, pleeeease?" he entreated me.

My son had always had a tender heart and was especially compassionate when it came to animals, but the last thing I needed was a *cat*. Cats were a lot of trouble, and it was quite likely that after a few days, Charlie would forget all about it and the care of his pet would fall to me. Besides, I had asthma and was sometimes allergic to animals.

"Well," I fudged, "why don't you feed him some milk and line a box with an old blanket for him to sleep in, and we'll see how it goes, okay? We'll check with the Humane Society in the morning. You can at least keep him overnight."

"Not him . . . Horatio," Charlie said shyly. "I already named him Horatio."

Later on that night, I was washing dishes when I heard a strange rustling sound. I dried my hands and headed for the living room, but what I saw stopped me cold and turned my spine to jelly. It looked like a snake poking its snout out from under the bathroom door, easing slowly into the hallway!

Charlie came up behind me. "What's the matter, Mom?"

I heard myself take in a tight breath, and then, as if in a dream, I put my hands behind me, dropped the dishtowel and made fluttering motions with my palms to signal Charlie to back away. He was a smart kid, and I sensed him departing slowly and quietly. Moments later, I heard his tremulous voice on the phone, "911? We need help!"

The snake turned its ugly head and slithered toward me. The rescued cat, Horatio, sat nearby, very still, like a sentry. Then I heard a hiss! I thought it was the snake striking at me, and I was terrified. Then I saw something streak by me so fast I couldn't tell what it was.

The next thing I knew, a nice paramedic was holding my head and waving a bottle of some kind of ammonia under my nose. Wrapped in a blanket, I felt warm and cozy—then suddenly panicked, and I jerked my head, looking around, but the paramedic must have read my mind.

"Whoa, it's okay; your son is out there in the police car staying warm," he said, pointing to a black-and-white car in the driveway.

About then another police officer approached. I thought I was going to pass out again—he held a long stick with something scaly wrapped around it. He glanced at it almost proudly and said, "Hope you're planning on being real good to that cat; he killed an eight-foot-long diamond-backed rattlesnake!"

Charlie ran to my arms, holding the cat. He looked up at me and said, "Horatio is a hero, right, Mom? Aren't you glad we kept him now?"

I held my son close and nodded my assent. Horatio was his hero. And *he* was mine!

Anita Biase

A Heart of Compassion

Children are God's apostles, sent forth day by day to preach of love and hope and peace.

James Russell Lowell

"Mom, he's picking on me again!"

I cringed at the shrill sound of seven-year-old Austin's voice rising above the rap music on the radio. Between the radio, the rumble of the truck's diesel engine, the whirl of the air conditioning and the snickering coming from the back seat, my nerves were stretched taut.

"Devin! Didn't I tell you to stop it?" I glanced into the rearview mirror, making eye contact with my middle son, freezing him in some act of mischief.

"He started it!" came the disgruntled reply.

"How many times do I have to tell you? If you don't want him to do to you what you're doing to him, then don't do it in the first place!"

Under the brim of the red baseball cap, a strange, confused look crossed Devin's face. I cringed at what I had just said. No wonder he was confused. I backtracked and rephrased it before his attention wandered onto ideas of more turmoil he could put his younger brother through.

"If you don't want him to tease you, then don't tease him. I mean it! Leave him alone!"

When I looked back into the mirror, clear understanding showed on his nine-year-old face.

"Let's see if we can make it to the baseball field without any more fighting, okay?" My two younger sons pretended to listen while my sixteen-year-old ignored us all.

Austin's game was scheduled to start in fifteen minutes, and I was, as usual, running late. Dealing with work, kids in school and now baseball games caused my husband and me to rearrange and adjust our schedules to fit the kids'.

I sign up my three sons to play baseball every year to give them a chance to learn an athletic skill and, hopefully, good sportsmanship. I wonder at times if the morals I am trying to instill in them are filtering through. There are usually no outward signs that they have absorbed these things. This worry weighs on me at times, like that day.

Steering the extended-cab pickup into an empty spot near the field, I cut the engine then issued instructions to the boys. My sixteen-year-old, John, nodded, his CD headphone wires swaying, and jumped out. He sauntered off in the direction of the Majors field without a word, while Austin and Devin tripped and shoved each other on the way out the truck door.

"Mom, can I get something to drink?" Devin was the first to ask.

"I want something, too!"

"All right. Austin, go on and meet your coach. Devin and I will bring you something."

I heard Austin's coach call out to him. "Hey, buddy, you gonna hit us some home runs tonight?"

"Yep!" came Austin's excited answer. With two older brothers honing his skills, Austin was one of the best players on the team. They expected him to hit home runs, and he did, two to three a game.

Smiling, I crossed over to the concession stand and waited at the end of the line. A friend of Devin's ran to him, and they were off to play ball. "Stay where I can see you." The words were barely out of my mouth when he ran to a grassy triangle section between two of the fenced-in fields.

Alone, I walked the rest of the way to the dugout and gave Austin his bottle of water and sunflower seeds. Standing there watching the kids, I listened to seven-year-old co-eds tease the other players on their team, as long as the coach didn't hear them. My son, of course, was exempted from this teasing because he played a little better than the other kids.

"Hey, guys, maybe you should try helping each other instead of cutting each other down." I spoke to no one of the kids in particular, hoping that at least one would pay attention. They all froze and looked up at me with wide, innocent eyes. Guilt, I have found with my sons, is a taught emotion. I was satisfied they would stop for the time being, and I took a seat at the top of the bleachers.

The game started and excitement built. Family members cheered and hollered advice to the little ones as they played. Midway through, I felt a tap on my arm. Kevin, my husband, had arrived.

"How's the game?"

"Good, it's running about even," I told him, my eyes riveted on a little boy named Justin coming up to bat. I felt empathy for the dark-haired child. He tried so hard, but didn't seem to catch on. Standing as rigid as a soldier, he reared back and swung, completely missing the ball. The third swing produced a short, low ball, easily caught by the pitcher and thrown to first base. Justin made his first out for the night.

"Aw, poor baby!" I spoke softly to Kevin as I watched

the boy half-walk, half-run off the field. "Justin tries so hard. I think he's the only one who hasn't made a base hit all season. The kids were giving him a hard time earlier. He has the heart, but he hasn't developed the skills yet."

"He'll get there," Kevin muttered. His voice grew louder when Austin stepped up to the batter's box. "Hey, Austin, keep your eye on the ball. You can do it, buddy."

Sure enough, our son made his first home run for the night. His fellow players cheered him and clapped him on the back when he jogged into the dugout. This scenario continued throughout the game—Justin got put out, and Austin had home runs. Kudos were handed to Austin, and Justin got nothing from his fellow players except groans when he came up to bat.

In the last inning, Justin's hit was repeated. As he stumbled, defeated, into the dugout, head down, shoulders slumped, I noticed Austin standing by the gate watching him. When Justin stepped inside the dugout, Austin wrapped his arm around his shoulders and patted him as he walked him back to the bench. His head lowered to the boy's ear. They sat side-by-side, Austin talking and Justin nodding every now and then.

My heart swelled. I silently thanked God for showing me our son had a heart of compassion. I don't know what Austin said to Justin, I didn't ask him, but the fact was, he saw a person in need and reached out to him.

On the way home, in the dark, the interior of the truck was quiet and still for about five minutes. During this peaceful time, I basked in the knowledge of my son's kindness, feeling we had succeeded as parents. Soon, whispers and commotion started from the back seat. Before I could ask what was going on back there, Devin's voice piped up.

"Mom, Austin said I was adopted!"

Judy L. Leger

Big Hair

We imitate only what we believe and admire.

Robert Aris Willmott

It was the '90s, the time of big hair. Being a young mom and not wanting to be out of style, I had big hair. Curly, big hair.

Of my three sons, my middle son, Mike, looked the most like me. He had my face, my blue eyes, my crooked teeth before braces, and my silliness and sense of humor. He also had curly hair.

One summer he and his high-school friends decided to have a contest to see who could hold out the longest before getting a haircut. The contest began the last day of school in June and would go until there was only one boy left standing—the boy with the longest hair. The weeks went by, and Mike's hair got bigger, curlier and longer. So did his friends' hair.

By the middle of the summer, all of the boys were looking pretty scruffy, unkempt and hot under all that hair. But they all thought that this was great fun—that is, until just before school was to start again in September.

All of the kids had a party to celebrate—or mourn—the fact that summer was almost over and school would be starting soon. I had arranged to pick them up later, but in the meantime at the pool party, the big-hair guys were swimming and having a great time. Mike got out of the pool and went into the house to get something to eat. When he came back outside, his hair was just about dry and had ballooned out to incredible proportions. As he was walking back to his friends, he heard them yell, "It's Barbara!"

Mike thought I had arrived earlier than expected, but, much to his amazement, all of his friends were laughing and pointing at . . . him!

He went the very next day and had his curls cut off.

No contest is worth looking like your mother.

Barbara LoMonaco

Wassup?

What a spendthrift he is of his tongue.

William Shakespeare

One of the challenges I encountered with my son during his teen years was meaningful communication. At the age of sixteen, he no longer spoke in traditional sentences. Rather, he spoke in one or two words that conveyed the main idea. For instance, upon meeting a friend in the mall, an exchange would go something like this:

"Wassup?"

"Chillin'."

"Cool."

"Later."

"Later, man."

After finally comprehending this new means of "teen-speak," it became clear to me why he always got this glazed look when I tried to talk to him. Too many words, I suppose, for his hormone-soaked adolescent mind to process. So instead of fighting it, I decided to try it. One morning I walked into his room, pointed in the general vicinity of the floor, which hadn't seen daylight in weeks, and said, "Room, rank, clean, today." Worked like a charm!

Even though I'd cracked the code, I still longed to connect with him in the traditional, full-sentence way, but how? The answer came quite by accident. Late one night, I decided to pop some corn and watch a chick-flick. The buttery, aroma drifted into his room and enticed him to investigate the source.

Without warning, he plopped beside me on the couch and put his huge paw in my bowl. The mantle clock chimed midnight. Something about the bell tolling twelve and the warm, fluffy kernels really loosened his lips. The kid talked about everything. He told me things I wanted to know and some things I'd rather not have known.

He said his girl dumped him. I didn't know he had one. Oh well, she didn't deserve him anyway.

He talked about his career choice—a video-game tester. Hmm, maybe this wouldn't be a good time to talk about medical school.

Last week, his best friend threw a cool party while his parents were gone. No parents? Mental note to self—never leave town.

Conversation flowed for at least two hours. I was exhilarated. In heaven. On cloud nine. Finally, we were communicating in full sentences. We connected. I crossed the barrier with popcorn at midnight.

The next morning my heart still sang of the progress made just a few short hours earlier. I couldn't contain my excitement when I called him to breakfast. What would we discuss? The possibilities were endless.

However, I realized moments like the night before were small gifts to tide me over until my son achieved manhood, when he walked in the kitchen and said, "Wassup?"

Linda Apple

Raising Eyebrows

Laugh if you are wise.

Latin Proverb

It was the most fragile summer of my life to that point—the summer before my first year of junior high. Of course, I wanted all the girls to swoon when I graced the hallowed halls on my first day. But, just as my last days of elementary school came to a close, my sister Tami informed me, "You're not going to have any girlfriends when you get into seventh grade."

"Why not?" I asked in pure disbelief.

"Because your eyebrows connect. They're all one thing. Joe P.'s eyebrows connect. He has no girlfriends, and you won't either," she admonished in that nasty tone only older junior-high sisters can take with their little brothers.

Terror struck my heart. Every day, I looked at my unibrow, ruing the fact that it would be the demise of my junior-high career.

One day early that summer, I watched Tami in front of the bathroom mirror, primping and preening. She gooped foreign things on her face that transformed her into the teen idol she thought she was. She put some foam stuff on her eyebrows, and a few seconds later wiped it off to reveal the picture-perfect browline.

A week later, my parents went out for the evening, and Tami was babysitting over at the Kings'. As I was putting dinner dishes into the dishwasher, a great idea hit me with an enormous wallop. I went to the bathroom medicine cabinet, took out Tami's eyebrow stuff and slathered it on mine. I really wanted it to work, so I left it on longer than Tami did. I went back and finished my dish chores. When it began to itch, I guessed that was a signal my eyebrows were ready for their debut.

I entered the bathroom thinking, *Girlfriends, here I come!* With tissue, I wiped the foam away from my right eyebrow. My stomach did a somersault. To confirm that the mirror wasn't playing a nasty trick on me, I looked into the tissue, and sure enough, there were my eyebrow hairs—all of them. In panic, I wiped the foam from the other eyebrow—and stood gazing at the eyebrow-less wonder staring back at me from the mirror. With shaky, cold, wet hands, I picked up the phone and called over to the Kings'. When my sister picked up, I screamed in rapid-fire, incoherent cadence, laced with utter terror, "Tami! You told me I had one eyebrow! No girlfriends! Now I don't have any eyebrows! It's your fault!"

"Put on mom's eyebrow liner and get over here," she gruffly instructed and hung up.

Mom's color didn't match, and my shaky hand did nothing to make it look anything close to normal. So I put on a baseball cap as low as I could pull it over my brow and tore down the street to the Kings'. Tami was waiting at the door. The kids had been put to bed extra early for reasons they could only wonder about. When she looked at me, a strange mix of horror and humor crossed her face. Her creative, almost-eighth-grade brain went into overdrive.

In Mrs. King's medicine cabinet we found false eyelashes. Tami quickly cut them up to create eyebrow prostheses, but there was no more sticky stuff to put them on. We scrapped that plan.

Then Tami had another brilliant idea. She ordered me to sit down at the kitchen table and, "Shut up!"

She tugged and cut at the back of my hair, and then, with deft precision, took tweezers and dipped the hairs one-by-one into strawberry jelly and applied them where my eyebrows used to be. Flies buzzed around my head, landed on my face and stuck to the jelly mess. We were out of answers.

I put the baseball hat back on, went home and had an epiphany before I hit the door. *I'll put Band-Aids on my eyebrows!* "Yep, that's it! I fell down and broke my eyebrows!" So wearing Band-Aids and a baseball cap, I went to bed.

The next day my older brother, Kirk, jumped on top of me in bed, saw the baseball cap and paused. I could see the "You weirdo" look in his eyes as he ripped the cap from my head and began slapping me to wake up. He looked at the Band-Aids and stopped mid-slap—then took the ends and pulled them both off at the same time.

I thought he was going to pass out. He thought he'd ripped my eyebrows right out of my head and went screaming for my mom and dad and all the rest of my six siblings. They all came down to my bedroom where I sat looking madly for the Band-Aids and crying. They just stared. My father grunted and looked at my mom. Everyone took their cue from him and looked over at her as well. My mom, bless her heart, said in her most pitiful and "oh-Lord-please-keep-me-from-laughing" voice, "This is going to remain a secret in the family."

Everyone took that as orders to leave before any laughter could commence.

All summer long, I was taunted as I wore a baseball cap

pulled down over my injured eyebrows. Kirk pulled it off in public when he was feeling especially nasty. I cried every time. Uncle Tom came to visit, I assumed to counsel me on my eyebrows. He said if I watered them, they would grow back more quickly. So I did. All day long. I carried a small canteen around with me, and when no one was looking, I patted water on the site.

Magically, they grew back just before I set foot in Grant Junior High School on the first day.

For years my herd of a family brought up "the eyebrow story" at the most inopportune times. I got mad every single time. Sometimes, when no one was looking, I cried from embarrassment. I seemed to be everyone's favorite idiot.

Finally, following yet-another rehashing of the stupid story, I could no longer hold back. I blew with an out-of-place anger that surprised everyone. I was going into high school, after all, and it was time to let it all go.

Mom took me aside and calmly and empathetically said, "Honey, it'll probably take you a long time before you see that the eyebrow story is actually very hilarious. The moment you learn to laugh at the story and laugh at yourself, you'll have just as much fun with it as everyone else."

I actually reflected on her advice, putting it through the acid test of a young mind. "Did she laugh at herself when we reminisced about the goofy things she did?" The answer was a resounding yes. My mom still laughed at her follies as if they were someone else's. She knew that laughter is medicine, and that laughing at yourself is the most potent elixir of all.

So today, when I do something goofy, which hasn't changed a lot from junior high, I just raise an eyebrow and laugh.

Scott Halford

Sounding Bored

He'd been so disrespectful lately. Of me, his teachers, his sisters. Of girls in general. I recognized that my rough-and-tumble son was thick in the throes of a seven-year-old's revolt against the female race. His play was rough, his actions rowdy. He even spoke a foreign language consisting solely of sound effects: guttural growls, deafening detonations and rumbling motors. It was obvious he'd O.D.'d on police shows: too much of the wrong thing.

In an attempt to override those influences, I engaged him in more conversations. I encouraged calmer activities like reading and origami and board games. I urged him to spend less time in front of the television and more time playing with his sisters.

And it seemed to work. He acted out less and was more conversant overall.

One day, I watched and listened as the kids played "wedding." My daughters, of course, organized it all and played the important roles of both bride *and* groom. They assigned my son the part of preacher. Rolling his eyes at me when I nodded approval, he obliged—yet was obviously bored with the ceremony, even though he allowed his sisters to boss . . . er, *instruct* . . . him through it. I was pleased to hear only words, nothing disruptive. And then it was time to exchange vows.

He stiffened. He narrowed his eyes. He cocked his head toward the "groom" and —with no hesitation at all—spit out the words he knew best, the ones he knew by heart.

"You have the right to remain silent," he said with authority. "Anything you say can and will be held against you. You have the right to have an attorney present."

"Now," he smirked in satisfaction, "you may kiss the bride."

Carol McAdoo Rehme

READER/CUSTOMER CARE SURVEY

CF5G

We care about your opinions! Please take a moment to fill out our online Reader Survey at **http://survey.hcibooks.com**.
As a **"THANK YOU"** you will receive a **VALUABLE INSTANT COUPON** towards future book purchases as well as a **SPECIAL GIFT** available only online! Or, you may mail this card back to us and we will send you a copy of our exciting catalog with your valuable coupon inside.

First Name		MI.	Last Name	
Address				
State	Zip		Email	City

1. Gender
- ❏ Female
- ❏ Male

2. Age
- ❏ 8 or younger
- ❏ 9-12
- ❏ 17-20
- ❏ 31+
- ❏ 13-16
- ❏ 21-30

3. Did you receive this book as a gift?
- ❏ Yes
- ❏ No

4. Annual Household Income
- ❏ under $25,000
- ❏ $25,000 - $34,999
- ❏ $35,000 - $49,999
- ❏ $50,000 - $74,999
- ❏ over $75,000

5. What are the ages of the children living in your house?
- ❏ 0 - 14
- ❏ 15+

6. Marital Status
- ❏ Single
- ❏ Divorced
- ❏ Married
- ❏ Widowed

7. How did you find out about the book?
(please choose one)
- ❏ Recommendation
- ❏ Store Display
- ❏ Online
- ❏ Catalog/Mailing
- ❏ Interview/Review

8. Where do you usually buy books?
(please choose one)
- ❏ Bookstore
- ❏ Online
- ❏ Book Club/Mail Order
- ❏ Price Club (Sam's Club, Costco's, etc.)
- ❏ Retail Store (Target, Wal-Mart, etc.)

9. What subject do you enjoy reading about the most?
(please choose one)
- ❏ Parenting/Family
- ❏ Relationships
- ❏ Recovery/Addictions
- ❏ Health/Nutrition
- ❏ Christianity
- ❏ Spirituality/Inspiration
- ❏ Business Self-help
- ❏ Women's Issues
- ❏ Sports

10. What attracts you most to a book?
(please choose one)
- ❏ Title
- ❏ Cover Design
- ❏ Author
- ❏ Content

TAPE IN MIDDLE; DO NOT STAPLE

NO POSTAGE
NECESSARY
IF MAILED
IN THE
UNITED STATES

BUSINESS REPLY MAIL
FIRST-CLASS MAIL PERMIT NO 45 DEERFIELD BEACH, FL

POSTAGE WILL BE PAID BY ADDRESSEE

Chicken Soup for the Mother and Son Soul
3201 SW 15th Street
Deerfield Beach, FL 33442-9875

FOLD HERE

Comments

Do you have your own Chicken Soup story
that you would like to send us?
Please submit at: www.chickensoup.com

3

A MOTHER'S LOVE

Before becoming a mother I had a hundred
  theories on how to bring up children.
  Now I have seven children and only one
  theory: love them, especially when they
  least deserve to be loved.

Kate Samperi

Ready or Not

I think I'd be a good mother—maybe a little over-protective. Like I would never let the kid out—of my body.

Wendy Liebman

"I'm not ready for this," I told my husband as he drove me to the hospital for the birth of our second child.

"Not ready for what?"

"This." I pointed to my belly. "I can't do it. Not yet."

He laughed—actually laughed—at me. "You don't get much choice in the matter at this point." Despite my protests, he proceeded to shepherd me out of the car, through the hospital doors and into the delivery room.

The nurse helped me change into a gown, the doctor administered medication, and still I asked for a recount on the delivery date. "I'm not ready."

"The baby is, dear," the nurse said, patting my tummy.

I'd already had a baby, so I knew what this one would involve. Although I'd been scared the first time, I was nearly paralyzed with fear this second go-round. At least with the first child, I was expected to be an idiot, asking about formula temperatures and diaper rash. Forgetting the pacifiers melting in a boiling pot of water was funny, not moronic.

But with the second child, the pressure was greater. Now I had to perform, like a circus elephant that knows the routine. I'm a mom, a member of the elite nursery club. If I've forgotten the secret handshake and the password, then I deserve to be booted from the roster.

I'd had more time to prepare for my first child. I quit working in the sixth month of pregnancy and had twelve leisurely weeks to decorate the room, stock up on baby food and practice diapering on a stuffed bear. I read all the books, went to Lamaze class, cooked and froze dinners in advance. I was ready.

When my daughter came home from the hospital, I didn't go back to work. We spent lazy afternoons napping together on the couch, took daily morning walks. It was a quiet, peaceful time with few demands on me besides her needs.

By the time I got pregnant with my second child, my daughter was nearly five. There was school and parent meetings, church and Sunday school, field trips and lunch money. I worked full-time at home as a writer, often staying up until the wee hours to make a deadline. Throughout the pregnancy, I felt unprepared. Hit the rewind button. Start over. I need more time.

When labor got underway, I didn't have a single meal cooked, had forgotten to sign up for the refresher Lamaze class and hadn't assembled the crib. I was five days away from a writing deadline, my house was a mess, and my daughter still had a week of school left.

Try as I might to delay the inevitable, our son arrived right on time. I was in a panic for the first three days after Derek was born, convinced I couldn't handle a second child. I begged my husband not to return to work, but he left me all the same.

I gazed at the laundry pile, now a mountain. The breakfast dishes mingled with the lunch plates. Dust bunnies had taken up permanent residence. By one o'clock, my son and I both needed a nap.

I snuggled his little body against my chest and lay down with him on the couch. Within seconds, he was lulled to sleep by the steady rise and fall of my chest. A sense of peace stole over me, the kind that seems to come wrapped with the soft scent of a new baby.

"I'm ready," I whispered to him.

Shirley Kawa-Jump

A Girl

I did the nursery in dusty blue, peach and mint green, figuring it would be fine for either a boy or a girl, but with my "mother's intuition" I was sure our first child was a girl. In 1989, sonograms were not yet a routine part of doctor visits and pregnancy, so because there were no signs of trouble, I didn't have one. I did all the silly tests expectant mothers do to predict the sex of the baby, like swinging a threaded needle in front of my protruding belly. If it swung sideways it was a girl, up and down was a boy. Mine went side-to-side. The doctor even told me on one of my visits that the heartbeat sounded "like a girl."

I picked out a girl's name right away—Sara Kathleen. (Kathleen is my mother's name.) I loved the name and used to talk to "her," like all mothers do when they're alone. I imagined her as a darling little blonde, blue-eyed angel, taking after both her daddy and me.

I was the third and last child in my family of three girls. I looked at pictures of myself as a little girl, with thick curly hair, dressed in velvet dresses my mom had sewn, with matching patent leather shoes, polished to a high shine. When I told my mother I was expecting, she sewed a beautiful white bassinet cover, matching blanket and pillow to match the nursery colors. Mom said, "Sara will like it."

My mother-in-law had had three boys, so she was excited at the prospect of a granddaughter. I said I didn't care whether the baby was male or female, as long as it was healthy, but secretly I really wanted a little girl. Boys just weren't as much fun to dress, and first-time moms certainly do have a lot of fun doing that.

I probably wouldn't have even picked out a name for a boy if I hadn't watched a movie with a character named Connor McLeod. We decided that if we had a baby boy, his name would be Connor Byron. (Byron is my dad's name.) I felt certain I was having a girl. I even worried to myself that I wouldn't love a boy as much.

Time passed and the big day arrived, starting at two A.M. We drove to the hospital and things progressed quickly, but got stuck, literally. After trying everything he knew, my doctor said he'd have to do a Cesarean section. After three hours of pushing, I told him, "Get on with it, man!" As I was rushed into the operating room, I remember thinking what a story I would tell my daughter when she was older.

Then I heard a loud, strong, beautiful cry of a new life coming into the world. My husband, who had been sitting at my head throughout the surgery, stood up and yelled, "It's a boy!"

All I heard was the sound of my child crying as they cleaned him up in what seemed like five seconds. Then the pediatrician introduced me to my swaddled and now quiet son. I will never forget the rush of love and joy I felt when the doctor held up Connor for me to see. I looked at my son with his little rosebud mouth and cleft chin, just like his daddy's, and knew he had to be the most beautiful baby ever born in the history of the world. My son! My little boy! The one I'd been waiting so long for was here at last.

He opened his eyes at that moment and looked at me. I know they say newborns can't see, but he was looking at me, I know it. With tears running from my eyes, all I kept saying was, "Thank you . . . thank you . . . thank you" to the doctor, who with tears in his eyes held Connor closer so I could kiss his forehead. Never in my life has a day equaled that one.

As for Sara, we finally got one seven years later when Connor wanted a pet rat for his birthday. He picked out the one he liked best at the local pet store. She was a sweet little girl, with white blonde hair and dark brown eyes. He loved her.

Me, I liked her, too, but she was a girl. . . . I just couldn't imagine having a girl.

Laurie Hartman

The Threads That Bind

*Blessed be the hand that prepares a pleasure
for a child, for there is no saying when and
where it may bloom forth.*

Douglas Jerrold

After enduring a few stitches and a couple of minor surgeries, it was a relief when the most recent operation was
successful. My seven-year-old son, Drew, was thrilled.
These were always rough times for him, but the older he
got, the easier they became. With this last attempt, a few
more months, maybe even a year, was added to the life of
his favorite blanket.

With a look of sadness and concern in his blue eyes, he
had approached me one morning holding his blanket like
it was a wounded animal. His blond hair stood in all
directions, obviously the result of a rough night's sleep.

"Mom," his voice cracked. "There are more holes. Can
you fix them?" I looked at the wounded piece of fabric
in his hands. I gently picked it up by the corners to
assess the damage. Big holes and frayed edges. Careful
not to pull on any of the life-bearing threads, I said to

him, "I'll see what I can do, honey."

Like a skilled surgeon, I carefully examined the patient. This was not going to be easy, but I came up with a plan. I called Drew over for my prognosis. "Your blanket isn't looking so good. If it is okay with you, I will sew it to some other fabric and patch up the holes. Okay?" He agreed and then reluctantly put his priceless possession into my hands before we left for school. I felt I should have had him sign a medical release form before he left, freeing me from all responsibility should something go wrong. (I am not the best at sewing; truth is, I am not very good at all.)

After an hour of skillful work (luck, actually), the surgery was a success. My reward—a big smile showing both of his adorable dimples, a hug and a "Thank you, Mommy," that oozed with sincerity.

Some people may say Drew is getting too old for a blanket and I should just throw it away. Part of me agrees with that, but then another part remembers wrapping him up in that same blanket and rocking him to sleep. This blanket has been more than just a source of comfort at night; it has been a super-hero cape, a bandage for wounded stuffed animals, a spread for a picnic and a memory keeper for me. I miss holding him in my lap, his head resting on my chest, the powdery fragrance of a freshly cleaned baby.

I could tell him he is too old for a blanket and that it is time for him to grow up, but why? If you think about it, adults have favorite "blankets," too: an old nightshirt full of holes or a car stranded in the garage we swear we are going to fix some day. We would never admit we have favorite "blankets," things in our lives that provide us comfort and that we'd have a hard time doing without.

So what will I do when Drew needs me to fix his blanket again? I'm not sure. For now, I kiss him goodnight, tuck his blanket snugly to his chin and tell him to have happy dreams. I slip into my favorite holey nightshirt, grab my favorite quilt and a family photo album, and nestle into my favorite chair. With a big sigh, I open the album and begin reliving moments of the past seven years—many with a little boy and his favorite blanket.

Kerrie Flanagan

The Bedtime Story

Making the decision to have a child is momentous. It is to decide forever to have your heart go walking around outside your body.

Elizabeth Stone

"Once upon a time there was a lady who had blonde hair and a man who was tall and balding . . . ," I began, as I looked down at the three-year-old toddler dressed, ready for bed, in footed orange-fleece pajamas.

He was lying on the bed with his left leg drawn up and his right foot resting at an angle on top of the other knee, waiting for the next word. I finished picking up toys and crawled up on the bed beside him. He had asked for his favorite bedtime story, a story I had been telling him since he was two. I continued, ". . . who were very lonely because they didn't have any children—no boys, no girls, not even a little baby. They very much wanted a child to come to live at their house so they would be a family. They went everywhere trying to find a baby. They talked to people. They called people. But no one had a baby they could take home. The lady and man were very sad because there were no children to play at their house."

My voice was low and soft as I stroked his soft red hair. *It really needs to be cut again*, I thought. *It grows like crazy and looks like a mop.* He was gazing expectantly at me, so I went on.

"But finally, after many months of waiting, they got a telephone call. A lady on the phone said there was a little red-haired baby boy the lady and man could come see. If they liked him, they might be able to bring him home."

My voice rose, and I spoke faster with the excitement of suspense. My listener was hanging on every word.

"The lady and man were so excited. Maybe this would be the baby to make them a family. Then the lady could be a mommy and the man could be a daddy.

"Before they went to see the baby, they thought they had better get some baby things. So they went out to the store and bought blankets and diapers and sleepers. They bought bottles and T-shirts and bibs. Then they went on a long trip to see the baby. They thought they would never get there; they were so excited. When they finally saw the baby, they could hardly believe their eyes. He was the most beautiful baby in the whole world, and he had the most beautiful red hair!" I exclaimed. "The lady was really pleased because her hair was a little bit red, too.

"The lady and the man said they would really like to be mommy and daddy for this beautiful baby," I continued, emotion stealing into my voice. "They were sure they would love him forever.

"So they put him in the clothes they had brought and wrapped him in the new blanket and took him home. After that, they had to sign some papers so they could keep him forever. This is called adoption. They were so happy to have the little red-haired baby at their house. He turned out to be the best baby in the whole world, and they lived happily together.

"And do you know who that little red-haired baby was?" I asked. At this point, he pointed to himself and smiled with delight. The story always ended this way. Then I hugged him and tucked him into bed, as usual.

The very first time I told him the story—when I told him that *he* was that beautiful baby with the red hair—his eyes grew big and serious and bright as he fit the pieces together.

Now my son is twenty-something, and his hair has gone to strawberry blond. I don't know whether he remembers hearing this oft-told childhood story, but I know I'll never forget . . . it is still *my* favorite.

Sylvia Gist

Coach for a Day

*L*et *France have good mothers, and she will have good sons.*

Napoleon Bonaparte

On the first day my six-year-old son began to play organized sports, I became his biggest fan and most enthusiastic cheerleader. At every Little League baseball game, undaunted by cold or drizzle, I could be counted on to be sitting proudly in the bleachers, rooting for my son and all of his teammates. Season after season, while my husband continued to coach every team—teaching the boys new skills and encouraging their competitive spirit— my position remained consistent: cheering the teams to victory and comforting them in defeat. Between innings, I was on call with Band-Aids, icepacks, Gatorade and chips—the eternal "Team Mom." With our roles clearly defined, Little League remained a shared family activity.

When our son Craig was ten, thanks to the talent of a determined and hardworking team, the leadership of their coach and the spirit of their team cheerleader, we made it to the finals. The week before the championship game was filled with practices, pep talks and optimistic plans for a victory celebration at the local ice-cream parlor. Nothing could stop the Mighty Magicians!

That was, until the phone call, the night before the big game. A business catastrophe left my husband no choice but to leave the next morning to deal with the emergency—leaving his championship team without a coach. Several last-minute phone calls brought disappointing responses. One dad had just started a new job, another was on jury duty, a third away on vacation. As I saw the panic growing on my son's face, I knew we had run out of options.

"I'll do it," I volunteered, more confidently than I felt.

"What?" Both my husband and son looked at me in disbelief.

"Well, why not?" My defiance was bringing with it a new strength. "I know every kid on the team, and after all these years, I know all of your strategies and all of the rules of Little League. And the rest . . . I'll wing it." I took a deep breath. "After all, how hard could it be?"

Silently, shaking their heads in unison, they knew they had no choice but to agree.

After a sleepless night, I kissed my exasperated husband good-bye, wished him a safe and successful trip, packed up the pretzels and thermos of Gatorade, and grabbed the clipboard with the team roster and starting positions my husband had left for me. By the time we arrived at the field, the news of my husband's absence had spread, and my presence as coach was met with nervous looks from my son's teammates. I pretended not to notice the snickers from our opposing coaches. I ignored the expressions of doubt facing me from the parents of our team as I announced the starting lineup. One brave mother offered to coach third base. I gratefully accepted her charitable gesture and called our team into a pre-game huddle. I refused to acknowledge the look on my son's face—a mix of embarrassment and fear—and gave him a smile that I hoped would be more reassuring than I felt.

"Batter up!" I heard the umpire call. I took my position near the dugout and said a silent prayer.

"Come on, Bobby Bear!" I shouted to our pitcher. When out of the corner of my eye I saw my son cringe, I realized that our ten-year-old pitcher left that nickname behind in kindergarten. When Bobby struck out the first two batters, it was all I could do not to run to the mound and hug him. But when Russell, our catcher, caught a high pop-up to make the third out, my resistance melted. I grabbed him, spun him around and threw my arms around him. And when Bobby came off the pitcher's mound, he too got an unsolicited hug from the coach.

The next few innings didn't go as well. Our opposing team scored seven runs. As their jeers grew louder and their cockiness more blatant, our team was beginning to deflate. I couldn't bear to look at the defeated expression on my son's face. I was beginning to agree with him— maybe it was a mistake to let me coach.

But there was no time for introspection. There were three innings remaining in the championship game, and for the Mighty Magicians, I was the only coach they had.

Before our first dejected batter headed for the plate, I quickly assembled our team for my last shot at a pep talk. Digging into my resource pool of ideas swimming frantically inside my head, I offered them a sixty-second mix of strategy changes—mostly to restore their confidence that I actually knew what I was doing: Positive reinforcement— "You are the best! We are the champs!" Revenge—"Let's kick the butts of those cocky Sharks!" Bribery—"Double sundaes for everyone if we win!"

They half-heartedly high-fived and returned to finish the game.

Bobby Bear's grand slam homerun put us ahead and rekindled our team spirit. Though I'd like to take credit, it was likely that hit and luck that secured our ultimate victory that afternoon. The look on the faces of our opposing team when *my son* drove in the winning run in the bottom of the final inning was my triumph.

The team whooped and hollered and jumped up and down, then crowded around me for a group hug. The image of my son's face when his beaming teammate said, "Craig, you have the coolest mom!" is my ultimate trophy.

Linda Saslow

"Let me give Mom a kiss so she doesn't
trade me from my home team."

©2005 Jonny Hawkins. Reprinted by permission of Jonny Hawkins.

Spencer's Mom

Nature's loving proxy, the watchful mother.

Edward George Bulwer-Lytton

Sooner or later a mother is confronted with the reality that her son no longer needs her. I just didn't expect it to be at the tender age of six.

On a whim, and with no prior acting experience, Spencer attended a local audition and was selected to be one of the orphans in the film version of John Irving's *The Cider House Rules.* One of the first major signs of his blossoming independence came when he went off to audition with the director he had never met, in an apple orchard where he had never been, and came skipping back twenty minutes later with an apple in his hand, saying, "This is my lucky apple. I got the part. I'm Curly."

From that moment, and for the next six weeks of filming, my relationship with my son was transformed. He was the actor. I was the guardian required by his contract to accompany him to the set each day. The actor has his hair done and sunscreen and moisturizer applied in the makeup trailer, while the guardian stands out of the way, gawking.

The actor is given a warm down jacket, long johns and toe-warmers by the wardrobe people. The guardian hops up and down in the snow, hoping to avoid frostbite. From the time he arrived at the set each day, Spencer had dozens of people hovering over him, all concerned with his well-being. I reluctantly blended in with the backdrop.

Spencer was provided a tutor who worked with him when he wasn't rehearsing or filming. "Sorry, no room for the guardian in the school tent," I was told. He had an acting coach who played improv games with him between schooling and filming. "It's best if guardians wait outside so the kids don't feel inhibited." He was very well fed by a talented group of chefs who provided an endless array of kid-friendly food and sugary between-meal snacks on the "craft services" table—a definite improvement over the boring, nutritious fare he was accustomed to at home.

I always tried to be physically near Spencer while he was working. Depending on the actual location of the shoot and how the cameras were arranged and the number of people involved, I was only marginally successful. Sometimes I could find a small, unobtrusive niche in close proximity, but more often I was kept a good distance from the action. I didn't like this feeling of separation, but I was too intimidated to speak up. I wanted to shout, "Hey, I'm his mother. I'll tie his shoes and rehearse his lines." But, of course, I didn't.

Then one very late night toward the end of all the filming, on the set of the interior of the orphanage in the old state hospital, I was paged. "We need Spencer's mom; has anyone seen Spencer's mom?" I leapt to my feet. I wasn't exactly dozing, but my job as "guardian" didn't require much alertness either.

"That's me. I'm Spencer's mom." Of course, after six weeks, they knew that already, but it was the only name they knew me by.

"Spencer needs you. He says his left lung hurts."

That's all I needed to hear. I flew into the dormitory where my son was sitting on the edge of the bed, surrounded by the assistant director, medic, wardrobe and technical friends. He was crying. They cleared a path for Spencer's mom. The crew was uncharacteristically quiet.

"What is it, honey?" I asked. "What's wrong?"

"My left lung hurts," he said, pointing vaguely to his chest.

"Oh, I'm sorry, sweetie. Do you think it might feel better if I get you a hot chocolate?"

He nodded and clenched my hand.

The assistant director said, "Okay, everyone, let's break for twenty minutes. Everything is all right. Spencer's mom is here."

I smiled to myself.

Sometimes even independent young actors who have directors, tutors, coaches, chefs and many doting assistants need more than a guardian—they need their mother.

Robin Geller Diamond

The Rustic Rink

A mother understands what a child does not say.

Jewish Proverb

To this day I can't tell you why that Cub Scout roller-skating party was so all-fired important to me. But for some reason, I was obsessed with going to the Rustic Rink with my fellow Cubs and lacing on a pair of heavy black rollerskates.

But there was a problem. It was a Cubs-and-parents affair, which meant I had to invite Mom and Dad. Now, don't get me wrong. I loved my parents. But I had long since figured out that they were a little different from most of my friends' folks. For one thing, they were older—Dad was fifty-three at the time; Mom was forty-seven—and physically less active than other parents in the neighborhood. My friends would go skiing and camping with their parents. Mine let me sit and watch "The Mickey Mouse Club" nearly every day.

Which is why it surprised me a little when Mom responded so enthusiastically to the skating party when I finally brought it up.

"But I never learned how to rollerskate," Dad protested. "Then it's time you learned," Mom replied. "Besides, you used to ice skate."

"Wanda, that was forty years ago."

"Oh, you know how it is with those kinds of things," Mom assured him. "Once you learn them, you never forget them." She placed her hands lovingly on my shoulders. "It means so much to him, Bud. Don't you think we should at least give it a try?"

Dad looked at me with mock frustration.

"All right," he said with a shrug and a chuckle. Then he pointed a finger directly at me. "But you better plan on following right behind me so I can land on you when I fall."

The way it worked out, that job fell to Mom. Since she had actually skated when she was a little girl, she was designated as The Skating Expert. It was her task to support Dad as he made his herky-jerky, clackety-clacking way around the rink and to go down with him whenever he fell, which was about once every twenty feet or so. They would sit on the floor for a few seconds after each fall, giggling like teenagers, and then struggle to their feet and begin again.

Clackety-clack. Thud. Ha-ha-ha.

Only I wasn't laughing. Most of the other parents skated pretty well. Ron and Don's dad could skate backward, for Pete's sake. But there was my roly-poly Mom trying to support my nearly white-haired father, who just couldn't grasp the concept of gliding on skates. They went down—again and again—in an embarrassing gale of laughter, making enough noise that you could barely hear the Beach Boys tunes blaring from the rink's loudspeakers.

I didn't even tell my parents "thank you" as we drove home from the party that night. I vaguely remember hearing my mom joke that her back was a little sore, but mostly I sat solemnly, up to my earlobes in humiliation and self-pity.

My mortification turned to shame of another sort when

Mom awakened in the middle of the night in agony. Dad gave her aspirin. He alternated putting a heating pad on her back and then massaging it. Mom tried to be brave, but she couldn't keep from moaning in pain—low and guttural—and tears rolled down her cheeks until her pillow glistened with moisture.

I tried to sleep through it, but it was impossible with the remorse that enveloped me. As the first light of day peeked over the mountains, Dad prepared to take Mom to the emergency room. I heard him sadly tell my sister that it was his fault for being so darn clumsy.

But I knew whose fault it really was. When I finally saw her in the hospital, I was almost overwhelmed with guilt. She had slipped a disc in her back and was in traction, which looked to me like something straight out of a torture chamber. Her head was held in place by an ugly assortment of cables and harnesses that kept her looking straight ahead. A stack of weights pulled her feet, like a painful game of tug-of-war.

And I had put her there. For all I knew, she was dying. Because of me. For the first time I understood how selfless her love for me had been. And how selfish I had been.

"Mom . . ." I could barely speak.

"Joey? Is that you, son? I'm sorry, I can't see you." Again she was apologizing for something that wasn't her fault. I figured it was my turn to ask forgiveness.

"Mom . . . last night . . . the rollerskating . . ." I couldn't even form the words.

"Oh, yes—the rollerskating," she said. Then she beamed a smile as best she could in that contraption. "We did have a wonderful time, didn't we?"

Thankfully, Mom didn't die from the injuries she suffered at the Rustic Rink. But her back was never the same.

And neither, I hope, was I.

Joseph Walker

The Yellow Boat

Like so many things one did for children, it was absurd but pleasing, and the pleasure came from the anticipation of their pleasure.

Mary Gordon

I bought my first boat when I was sixty-nine years old. I did not fish. I was not a sailor. I did not swim. I was afraid of the ocean. I'd never been on a boat sailing anywhere. But nonetheless, I bought a boat.

I was in debt and lived frugally, but I spent $2,000 for a boat. It was in good shape. I knew because someone experienced checked it out for me. After all, when you fall in love, someone has to have some good sense and check things out. And I fell in love with the yellow boat. Though no one else understood, the first moment we met, I knew I had to buy it. "Be brave," it said. "You can do this. I can see it in your eyes. The excitement. You know where I belong."

My grown son Steve was a fisherman. When his father was alive, they dreamed together of the day they would take their own boat into the ocean. My husband passed on before their someday dream could come true. And now it had become my son's dream.

It was Steve's fortieth birthday. I wanted to give him something special. Something to fill up the space left by his father. I could not take the pain away, but I wanted to help heal it. Steve and his father had been best friends. They had shared so many father-and-son moments I could not replace, but perhaps I could add moments of our own. And so I gifted my son with a boat for his fortieth birthday.

I knew it would sit in my long driveway. The ocean, the river and bay were nearby. It was easy enough to attach the boat to the station wagon and journey to water. This way, I got to see the yellow boat. Every day. Each time I looked at it, I smiled. It is not easy to smile sometimes. Being a widow isn't fun. Nor is being a cancer survivor. Nor is struggling to make a living. None of it brings me instant joy. But the boat did. Part of the reason it brought me such joy was that it brought me my son as a bonus.

Busy with a young family and his job, he had made the one-and-a-half-hour trip to my home as often as he could.

But now there was the boat in the driveway. Beckoning. Tempting. It drew him like a magnet to my shore house. "Mom, I'm coming down to go fishing," became a familiar telephone message. Sometimes he brought his two young sons and his wife. Other times he came with a friend. And once in awhile he'd come alone. And we would have our best moments together. In the driveway. On the boat. While he puttered around, wiping things down and repairing what needed to be fixed, he told me of his work as a teacher. We found it easy to talk sitting on the boat. About life. About his father whom we both missed. Sometimes I brought a cup of tea. Sometimes we ate lunch.

I did not need the sea to set me sailing.

These moments with my son did that.

Harriet May Savitz

Homecoming

When you are a mother, you are never really alone in your thoughts. A mother always has to think twice, once for herself and once for her child.

Sophia Loren

As a teenager during World War II, my mother had the unpleasant experience of watching her young friends go off to war, with some never coming home. Twenty-five years later when the U.S. Army sent me to fight in the Vietnam War, her memories of those days returned with added anxiety, because this time it was her son who was being sent into the unknown. Since I was in the infantry, Mom knew that combat duty would often be dangerous, but her frequent letters never once hinted that she was not coping with my absence. In fact, Mom's ability to keep up my spirits while I was so far from home made it easier for me to deal with the uncertainty of the war.

As my yearlong tour was coming to an end, the Army gave me an eleven-day early release. I decided not to tell my parents I was leaving Vietnam ahead of schedule because I thought it would be more memorable to surprise them by me unexpectedly walking through the front door. As it turned out, we all got a surprise.

My cousin Donald secretly picked me up from the airport, and on the way home we fantasized about how I would make my entrance. When we arrived at the house, we were amazed to find it locked up tight and no one at home. My family had taken a trip out of state and was not expected back until late that evening!

Unsure of what to do next, I decided to get out of my uniform and change into civilian clothes. I did not have a key, so the only way I could get into the house was by crawling through an unlocked window. Once inside, a warm and inviting feeling rushed over me; I was really home! I fondly inspected the familiar surroundings and was happy to see that nothing had changed; even the clothes in my closet were just as I had left them. The only thing different was a map of South Vietnam hanging on the kitchen wall identifying all the places I had written home about. I still wanted to keep my arrival secret, so I decided to spend the night at Donald's. I was careful not to disturb anything or leave any evidence that someone had been in the house.

Shortly after midnight, my tired parents shuffled into the house, and my mother suddenly proclaimed, "Artie is here! He's home!"

Whether or not there is such a thing as mothers' intuition, Mom had somehow detected my presence. Knowing that I was not due home for at least a week, my father laughed at the notion, claiming that Mom was simply tired from the road trip. Yet she insisted that I was hiding in the house and called for me to come out. When there was no response, she began searching. After checking the closets, under the beds and in the attic, Mom finally gave up but could not shake the sensation that I was near.

Her antics put the family on edge, and although no one said anything, they shared the eerie feeling that perhaps I had come home but not in the flesh. They worried that I might have been killed in the war and that my spirit returned to say good-bye. Needless to say, they had a restless night.

Early the next morning, Donald called my parents to make sure everyone was awake because he wanted "to drop something off." When I triumphantly walked through the door, my father, sister and brother gawked at me without speaking a word.

"Hi, everyone," I cheerfully sang out, only to be confused by their silence and darting glances as they suddenly recalled Mom's announcement that I was home.

"What's the matter with you guys?" I asked, noticing that my mother was not in the room. "Hey, where's Mom?"

"Still sleeping," my father sputtered, choking on the words as his eyes followed me down the hall.

The moment I stepped into my mother's room, her eyes opened, and she tilted her head back as if she was expecting me. When I said, "I'm home," Mom gently replied, "I know, you were here last night." Before I could ask how she knew, Mom leaped from the bed and crushed me with a giant hug to make sure I was real. Tears rolled down our faces as she cried, "I knew you were safe. I knew it all along."

For my mother, the war and the waiting were over.

Arthur Wiknik, Jr.
Previously appeared in Nam Sense

Welcome Home

*Let there be peace on Earth, and let it begin
with me.*

Seymour Miller and Jill Jackson

My nightmare was over. My son, Lance Corporal
Robert Bautzmann, was finally returning from war in Iraq.
I drove with my other children, Demi, Kaila and Drew, to
the town of Twenty-Nine Palms to await the arrival of our
hero.

There, we joined others in decorating the gym to welcome them home. After three hours of nonstop work, we
wandered to the PX, where several people stood looking
up at the sky. The security personnel had just warned that
a tornado was headed for Yucca Valley. There was no way
the boys were going to make it back to the base today.
Even if the tornado dissipated, the roads would still be
flooded. We were instructed to stay on the base where it
was safe until the tornado threat passed.

I glanced over at Jeri, another Marine mom I had
become close to during the last worrisome nine months.
Our eyes shared the same feelings. We had come so far,

been through too much, for them not to come home today. Speechless, with the wind blowing strong, we watched a whirl of clouds to the west of us.

The National Weather Service announced the tornado had touched down. Highway 62, the road the Marines were coming in from March Air Force Base, was closed.

We headed to the hotel to wait. Sections of road flooded so high that water lapped the floorboard of my truck. I gasped to see a car floating down a side street. Chunks of the road broke free.

Finally, we reached the hotel. I pried my fingers from the steering wheel and breathed a sigh of relief. Okay, so I was not going to welcome Bob home today. I guess I could deal with that. As long as he was out of Iraq, I could deal with just about anything.

As the sun pushed away the dark clouds, crews were working hard to clear the roads from all the mud, debris and water. Just as we had all started to relax from the harrowing drive, the phone rang. The Marines were still coming home today! We should head for the base within the next hour. Joy filled the air until I realized that meant driving back through the flooded roads again. At this point, I was willing to do just about anything to see my son again. No flood was going to stop me from being there when the buses arrived.

The roads were better—still a challenge to maneuver, but better. The families were told to wait at the gym. My heart filled with excitement and joy. I waited—and waited—and waited some more—for over three hours.

A local radio station was monitoring their progress. Finally I heard the words we had waited so long to hear. "They are on the edge of Twenty-Nine Palms!"

Cheers, smiles and tears broke out among the anxiously waiting families. Now everyone was standing, hoping to catch a glimpse of the seven white buses bringing our loved ones home. I glanced at Jeri again. Our eyes shared the same feelings. The radio DJ announced they had entered the main gate of the base. Families stood in anxious anticipation. We all knew they had to turn their weapons in before they would be driven to our area. Once again, we waited—and waited—and waited some more—for two hours.

I'll never adequately describe the emotions flowing through my body at the moment. All the heartache, all the worry, all the sleepless nights were over. My son was almost home. I grasped my youngest son Drew's hand as our family wove through the mass of people. The buses arrived, and we jumped and waved, hoping beyond hope that Bob would see us.

We stood at the last bus, watching the smiling Marines exit. Family members shouted welcome home to each Marine and then asked if their particular Marine was on the bus. We joined in. "Has anyone seen Bob?" The bus was emptying. I became a mom on a mission: Operation Find My Son.

Bus after bus, no sign of Bob. Now fear was rising. Where is my son? Did he miss the plane? Tears rolled down my face, down Demi's face. Kaila's stomach ached. We turned and once again walked up to each bus, crying out, "Bob! Bob Bautzmann!" We must have looked pitiful because not one but two officers joined us in calling, "Bautzmann!" All around us, families hugged with tears of joy. Little children got their long-awaited hugs from their daddies. New dads met babies born while they were gone. Wives and moms cried, holding tight to their Marines. Two Marines went down on their knees to propose to their girlfriends.

But where was my son?

With compassion overflowing from his eyes, one officer looked at me and said, "Don't worry, we will find him."

Suddenly, out of the crowd I heard the voice that caused my heart to skip, "Mom! Mom!"

There was Bob, a huge grin on his face as he called out, "Mom!" In my mind I had imagined this moment and how it would be. Everyone would want to hug Bob; I would wait and let them go first. Now that moment was here. I made one beeline for my son and his waiting arms. The tears I had held back on many of the rough days now flowed nonstop. "You're home, you're safe. I missed you so much . . ."

"Mom, it's okay. I'm okay."

Drew looked up at his older brother in awe. Bob seemed taller, older, standing there in his desert camies. His eyes twinkled, just as they had when he was a little boy. He swept up Drew and gave him a hug. Then he put him down to embrace his sisters. I couldn't stop touching him. Neither could Drew, Demi and Kaila, so we all wrapped our arms around each other in a major group hug.

Bob introduced us to many of the Marines close by. In all the confusion, I had lost track of Jeri. Now as I looked up, I saw my friend with a smile on her face, holding tight to her son Chris's arm. Our boys were back. God Bless America! God bless our heroes!

Debi Callies

A Mother's Bond

Even he that died for us upon the cross, in the last hour, in the unutterable agony of death, was mindful of his mother, as if to teach us that his holy love should be our last worldly thought—the last point of Earth from which the soul should take flight for heaven.

Henry Wadsworth Longfellow

I'm eighty-eight years old now and am sometimes still asked the impossible question, "As a mother of eight children, which one do you love the most?" My answer is the same now as always: "Love isn't divided; it's multiplied and equal, but the one that is away or sick is thought of the most."

In 1965, as a farm wife and the mother of eight children, I was busy and tired when night came. I'd never been a good sleeper, especially when the Vietnam War was escalating and our second son was in Danang in the midst of it all. My thoughts and prayers were constantly with him.

One night, I was awakened by his voice—I clearly heard him crying for me. "Mama! Mom!" I lay there trembling, devastated, fearful until dawn. I didn't want to upset or scare the family, so I kept my secret from my husband and children.

I did, however, call my best friend and asked her to meet me in a nearby town where we frequently met for lunch and shopping. I told her of my nightmare. "But it wasn't a dream," I insisted. "I heard his voice calling for me." She believed me.

Three days later, about midnight, I was awakened again when a telegram was delivered. Our son was hit in Vietnam—on the same day I'd heard him in the night—multiple injuries to head, chest and arms—serious condition—being moved to a hospital in San Francisco.

My husband left the next day and spent many months with him. He was very instrumental in giving him hope in wanting to live. Later, my son's rescuers from the field in Vietnam visited him. They told him, "When we picked you up, you kept calling out, 'Mama! Mom!'"

Berniece Duello

4

A SON'S LOVE

Love makes its record in deeper colors as we grow out of childhood into manhood; as the emperors signed their names in green ink when under age, but when of age, in purple.

Henry Wadsworth Longfellow

"You followed the recipe but it's missing
the secret ingredient: Mom."

©2000 *Patrick Hardin. Reprinted by permission of Patrick Hardin.*

Voicing My Wish

Presents which our love for the donor has rendered precious are ever the more acceptable.

Ovid

One evening, while writing the first draft of my book, I attended a writer's group for feedback. There were so many people there that discussion was limited to just a few stories. When I arrived home, my thirteen-year-old son shrugged off my disappointment and asked me to read the excerpt to him instead. So I settled into a chair and read a rough draft of my reflections on spending my allowance as a nine-year-old child.

The experience I wrote about was a metaphor for how choice and risk were handled by a child affected by alcoholism. Each week at Woolworth's lunch counter, I dreamed of someday ordering a banana split. Above the counter twirled an umbrella with colorful balloons hanging from each rib. The sign read: *Pop a balloon and pay 1 to 63 cents!*

Imagine paying one cent for a banana split! But I never had more than fifty cents, and I shuddered at the thought of Woolworth's calling my parents for more money if I got the sixty-three-cent balloon, so I kept my wish to myself. I never thought of asking anyone for more money. It seemed way too risky, and risks were dangerous in a world where alcohol made even benign requests subject to rage.

Frankie sat at my feet, listening intently, as I read the final sentences of the chapter:

> Each week as I watched others select a balloon to pop, I fantasized about proudly taking my chance. But it never happened. Pink, blue, orange and yellow balloons called out to me, daring me, taunting me and, eventually, defeating me. Inevitably, when the waitress strolled up to my spot at the counter and smiled, indicating that she was ready to jot down my order, I mumbled, "I'll take a Coke, please," and then turned my back on the umbrella.

Frankie was silent. After thinking for a moment, he said, "So you never got the banana split?" A long discussion ensued, and eventually he seemed to understand that it was my own belief that limited me. I never took the chance of voicing my wish. It was a pattern that took years to break.

The next morning, Frankie casually announced that he was going out for a little while. When I asked where, he smiled and said, "I can't say."

My mother's instinct told me he wasn't up to anything dangerous, so I agreed. Frankie left, and I busied myself upstairs packing for an upcoming camping trip.

In a short time, I heard the back door open and then the sounds of chairs scraping, kitchen cabinets slamming and muffled conversation. Soon my nine-year-old daughter Sarah announced through giggles that I could come downstairs. "Eyes closed—except for stairs," she said.

Once downstairs, Sarah held my hand and helped me stumble my way through camping equipment and into the kitchen.

"Open your eyes!" Frankie and Sarah shouted in chorus.

I couldn't believe what I saw. The kitchen table was covered in a pile of balloons. Frankie walked up to me and handed me two quarters and a fork. His eyes were lit with anticipation. "Pop one!"

Tears welled up in my eyes. I stared at the balloons in disbelief and then jabbed one. When it popped, Frankie and Sarah laughed as I let out a loud whoop. A piece of paper fell out of the balloon. I opened it and recognized Frankie's awkward scrawl.

"What does it say?" he prompted.

"Fifty cents," I whispered, too choked up to speak loudly.

Frankie got business-like and asked, "Well, do you have fifty cents?"

I handed him the two quarters he'd given me moments earlier.

"Okay then!" Frankie walked over to the refrigerator, pulled out a homemade banana split on a Tupperware plate and handed it to me. Mounds of vanilla ice cream were covered in chocolate sauce, Cool Whip and peanuts. Underneath it all was a banana, split in two. I hugged Frankie hard and kissed the top of his head, still sweaty from all the effort. My eyes stung with tears as I held the banana split Frankie lovingly made to right an ancient wrong.

Theresa Goggin-Roberts

The Necklace

*E*very gift, though it be small, is in reality great
if given with affection.

Pindar

My younger son, Kelly, started preschool when he was
four, attending twice a week for two hours each time. I
soon noticed he was always the last one to leave the classroom, so I asked the teacher if he was having problems.
"No, no," she assured me. "He is doing fine—just involved
in a creative project."

Once I asked through the classroom door if he was
ready to leave. He yelled, "Don't come in! It's a surprise."
So I waited patiently each day until he finally emerged,
smiling and mysterious.

"What are you doing in there?" I asked.

"Making something," he said.

My curiosity was getting the best of me. What held his
attention for such a long period of time? He liked building
things by stacking alphabet blocks, then attaching Lincoln
Logs until he made a structure big enough for parking his
Hot Wheel cars.

Eventually the day arrived when he led his class out the door carrying his creative project, with both hands. His eyes rarely left the tissue-wrapped package as he carefully walked to the car, instead of running as usual. He handed it to me. "Here, Mom, it's a surprise. I made it just for you."

Carefully I lifted the tissue off first one side and then the other. Inside nestled a string necklace made of hand-colored macaroni pieces—red, yellow, green, purple and every other color in his Crayon box.

"It's beautiful," I said, holding it carefully and turning it this way and that so the sun shone on it through the car window. "It looks like a rainbow necklace."

He leaned on my arm and stared at it with me. "I made it," he said confidently, "all by myself."

The necklace caused a lot of excitement at home. Kelly's dad, his older brother and both younger sisters admired it. I carefully stowed it in my jewelry box so it would not get broken.

After dinner I left on a short walk to the grocery store for some milk. "Wait, Mom! Wait!" Kelly yelled as he ran down the sidewalk after me. "You forgot your necklace!" I bent down, and he tied it around my neck. "You look pretty," he said.

My new, brightly colored macaroni necklace caused quite a stir at the market. "Nice necklace," a stranger said. Then my neighbor remarked, "One of your kids make it?" I nodded. The grocery checker even commented, "I want one, too."

Nothing I have ever worn created more comment than that necklace, and I wore it often, enjoying every word.

Over time, however, the macaroni pieces broke one-by-one and slipped off the string. Kelly forgot about the necklace, and I stopped wearing it hoping the pieces would last longer. One day the last piece crumbled and joined the other broken bits of macaroni at the bottom of my jewelry box. The necklace was no more. I remembered how hard he had worked and how proud we had been of his efforts. I got a lump in my throat when I thought about wearing it to church, school events or Grandpa's. It was a memorable gift, and I would miss wearing it for our special family occasions.

Over twenty-five years later, on Christmas Eve, Kelly handed me a small box. "I remember when I was four and wanted to give you a present, but had no money, so I used some string and macaroni to make you a surprise. You were such a good sport about wearing that macaroni necklace, and each time you put it on, you made me feel very special. So this gift is to make up for the macaroni one that didn't last."

He plucked a beautiful string of pearls from inside the red velvet box and placed it around my neck.

"Did you make it?" I asked jokingly, barely able to speak.

"No," he chuckled, "but I did pick out each pearl. I hope this necklace makes you feel as special when you wear it as I felt when you wore the other one. Merry Christmas, Mom."

Gloria Givens

Reel Love

*I love these little people; and it is not a slight thing
when they, who are so fresh from God, love us.*

Charles Dickens

"It's just you and me, buddy. What do you want to do
this afternoon?" I asked Jake, our eight-year-old son. My
husband and other two boys already had plans, leaving
me a little one-on-one time with our youngest. I guessed
he might want to see a movie, eat an ice-cream cone or
play tennis. Instead, he surprised me.

"I want to go fishin'."

I did say he could pick whatever he wanted to do . . . "Umm,
well . . . okay. But I don't really know where everything is,
do you?"

"Yeah, it's in the garage in Daddy's fishing bag." My
husband is an avid fly-fisherman with enough gear for a
family of five and their friends.

"I don't even know which fly to use, or how to even tie
one on. Are you sure you want me to take you fishing?
Maybe Daddy could take you tomorrow."

"No, you can do it, Mom. I'll show you how."

Underneath his red, worn baseball hat, his blond curly hair stuck out, and his bright brown eyes lit up with the idea that he could show me something. *How can I possibly say no?* But all I could imagine was untangling the line and hook from the trees and shrubs all afternoon. Then the story about my husband hooking his mom's friend in the cheek when he was young and learning to fish popped into my mind, sending a shiver of fear down my spine and reminding me to stay far away from Jake as he cast.

"All right," I said with hesitation. "Why don't you get together everything you'll need, and I'll take you to the kids' fishing pond on the creek path."

I gathered up a few things, like a couple of water bottles and granola bars, and even my book—wishful thinking. I looked out the kitchen window and saw Jake in the driveway, hard at work. He had put together the fly rod, attached the reel and was putting the fly-line through the eyelets on the rod. He had to lay it on the driveway and carefully pull the line through each section because the rod was more than twice his size. I went down to help him tie on the fly, which he selected from my husband's vast collection.

I really had no idea how to tie it on. I tried to tie my own kind of knot, hoping we wouldn't lose too many flies today. Then Jake said, "Mom, that's not how you do it. You're supposed to loop it through the hole, go around the top of the hook seven times, and then tie it. Here, I'll do it." It was a little too tricky for his tiny fingers, so I did the looping, and then he grabbed the end of the line and tightened the final knot.

We stuck the rod in the back of the truck, jumped in with my husband's fishing bag and drove to the pond. On the road, I thought, *What if he really does catch a fish? I can never get them off those hooks.* "Jake, do you know how to get the fish off the hook and throw it back before it gets hurt?"

"Yes, Mom," he said and rolled his eyes at me.

We unloaded the gear, and Jake started fishing. I sat down far enough away to not get hooked, yet close enough to help. I breathed in the crisp autumn air—it felt like taking a refreshing drink of cold water. The late afternoon sun magnified the beauty of the fallen red, yellow and orange leaves that decorated the pond. I soaked in the beauty around me. Jake stood casting his fly into the water, concentrating intently, as he gently pulled the line toward him through the water, and then casting again. The light behind him caused a glow around his little body; he looked like an angel. Better than Brad Pitt in *A River Runs Through It*.

Within ten minutes he caught his first fish. He reeled it in, quickly took the hook out of its mouth and gently set it back in the water to swim away. Thrilled, he went at it again and caught another . . . and another . . . and another. People stopped along the path to watch him and talk to him. Then out of the blue, he announced, "Mom, the next one I catch you can reel in."

I knew that giving up the thrill of catching the "big one" and offering his mom the chance to experience that thrill was a huge sacrifice for him. But he wanted to give me something, and in that moment, that was the biggest and best thing he could give me.

Sure enough, he caught another one. He hollered, "Come reel it in!"

I quickly put down my book and felt a twinge of excitement as he handed me the rod and instructed me on how to keep the tip up and gingerly pull the fish in. It wasn't a very big one, but in my heart I'd experienced the catch of a lifetime. Jake and I smiled at each other as he wrangled the slippery fish to the ground, removed the hook and placed it back in the pond.

"Good job, Mom!" he beamed up at me, reminding me that the way a boy shows his mom how much he loves her can be simple. In this case, an act of "reel love."

Jean Blackmer

Sharing Flowers

Flowers are love's truest language.

Park Benjamin

His stubby little fingers struggled to remove the shriveled blossom from a petunia.

"I did it," my six-year-old son Clay exclaimed, flashing his sideways grin, his cowlick dancing above his curly brown hair. He loved to help me in my flowerbed.

"Can I pick some pretty ones for Mrs. Rieke?" he asked.

"Sure. A stingy florist gets few flowers," I said.

"What does that mean?" he asked, scrunching his eyebrows.

"We had a neighbor years ago who taught people how to garden. He told me God made flowers to be picked and shared. In return, I'd get more flowers over the season."

"Is that because you were good?"

"That, and it makes the flowers healthier and their roots stronger."

He picked his favorite candy-striped petunias. Off he went to see our neighbor, Mrs. Rieke, his surrogate grandmother. My generous little florist returned with a chocolate face and cookie crumb tracks down his shirt. "She liked 'em a lot," he said.

A week later, I got a call from another neighbor. "Did you know Clay and Lisa are giving away daffodils?"

"No. They're not even supposed to be out of the yard."

"They've got their red wagon loaded with flowers. They told me they're sharing with everybody so Mom can get more flowers," she said.

I checked outside. They'd plucked every daffodil in my front yard.

I followed the trail of yellow petals and green stems. By the time I caught up to them, Clay had his four-year-old sister, Lisa, in the Radio Flyer delivery truck, giving her a ride home. She clutched the only remaining daffodil.

"We saved the last one for you, Mommy," she announced.

"You aren't supposed to be out of the yard without permission," I said, trying to put on my best stern look. "You need to ask before you leave. What were you doing this far down the street without me?"

Clay said, "We're being good florists. God made flowers to share, remember?"

Spring progressed to summer, and baseball and swimming kept Clay's attention away from my flowers until the climbing roses came into full bloom.

In late August, the excitement of starting first grade occupied him for several days, but spending a full day at school affected him more than I realized. One Sunday evening, my husband and I had a retirement dinner to attend. We hired a teenage neighbor to baby-sit.

"Will you be home before I go to bed?" Clay asked as he tugged at the end of my jacket. "Will I get to see you before I go to school tomorrow?"

"You'll be asleep before we get home tonight, but I'll see you in the morning," I reassured him. "You be good for Sheila. Get to bed early. I don't want you too tired for school." He climbed up on the arm of the sofa and gave me a bear hug and a kiss good-bye.

The party ended early, and we arrived home to a sober household. Clay had been sent to his room for tearing up my roses and arguing with Sheila.

"He tore dozens of roses off the bushes. I found them thrown all over the house and garden," Sheila said. "I think he did it because I wouldn't give him the flower clippers. I didn't know if he was allowed to use them. He insists he didn't do anything bad."

That didn't sound like Clay, but I charged upstairs to confront him, angry he had caused a problem. I found him sitting on his bed clutching his well-worn Snoopy dog.

"Why did you tear up my roses?" I asked. "I thought you loved them as much as I do?"

His eyes brimmed with tears, and his jaw quivered. I knelt down beside him. He defiantly folded his arms across the front of his Batman pajamas. He turned away and refused to answer my questions.

"Why did you do it?" I demanded.

"I didn't tear up any flowers. And I didn't throw them all over the house!" he shouted.

I took a minute and studied the upset little boy bending over his Snoopy and wiping his runny nose on his sleeve. When I tried to put my arm around him, he scooted away.

I replayed the problem in my mind. It didn't sound right. Clay wouldn't intentionally destroy my flowers. Then I realized I hadn't asked for his side of the story.

"What were you doing with the roses?" I asked.

"I wanted you to know I loved you and wanted you to remember me tomorrow. I put them every place you'd be so you wouldn't forget you had a little boy at school."

My heart shattered, and I hugged him. "Thank you, sweetheart. I'd never forget you. You're my only little boy, and I love you very much." I tucked him in and kissed him on the cheek. "I'm sorry I misunderstood." He reached out from under the covers and handed me a crumpled red rose he had in his fist.

"I had one left for your pillow when Sheila caught me."

"I'll explain it to her. You get some sleep," I said and turned out the light.

Downstairs, true to his word, I found a rose on the dishes in the sink, on my sewing machine, one each on the washer and dryer, and dozens of others scattered throughout the house and garden. To the unsuspecting eye, it looked like random mischief.

Twenty years later, Clay still brings me roses. Once their beauty dims, I snip off the heads and add them to my rose jar, a reminder of my flower-loving son and the importance of understanding intentions.

Carolyn Hall

Tea Party

He gives not best who gives most but he gives most who gives best. If I cannot give bountifully, yet I will give freely, and what I want in my hand I will supply by my heart.

Arthur Warwick

I believe every little girl deserves a tea party at some point in her life. Most women have memories of backyard tea parties complete with a little table and chairs, plastic pink tea sets and, of course, the tea. Their moms supplied the good stuff like hot cocoa or soda for tea, or they just used pretend tea. Of course, dolls were invited.

Growing up in the projects of St. Paul, Minnesota, a tea party just never happened for me. I lost my mom one month before I turned nine years old. Her death and my dad's chronic gambling left no room for normal kid stuff. I was too busy raising myself to have a tea party. The county provided food stamps, but tea was not a high-ranking staple.

Sitting on other people's doorsteps became a daily routine. I can still feel the roughness of those concrete stairs, but an eight-hour sit was worth it, knowing that on the other side of the door was a family who might ask me in for a meal and let me play house with them. I lived in a world of make-believe tea parties, family vacations and meals around a real table.

When I married my husband, Rick, nine years later, many of those things were fulfilled . . . except a tea party. Ten years into my marriage and living in a beautiful home on Lake Superior, I bought my first miniature porcelain tea set at a local gift shop. Over the years I collected many of them, in part to recapture those girlish things, even if it meant only pressing my nose up against my hutch and dreaming about tea parties that might have been.

One perfect spring day, our eighteen-year-old son Marc walked in the dining room as I stood staring at the tea sets.

"Mom, why do you collect those anyway?" he asked.

"I love thinking about what it would have been like to have a tea party as a little girl."

"Why is that so important now?"

"I never had a tea party as a young girl. I miss that connection between a mother and a daughter at a tea, the heart-to-heart talks, the pretending and the silly laughter." I sighed.

At six-feet-two and 225 pounds, Marcus was captain of his football and wrestling teams. As I told my story, I knew he would quickly bore as I reminisced. I peered back into the hutch.

He quickly responded with, "Oh, that's cool . . . gotta go now," as he got up to leave the house. I understood. After all, this "mom story" had nothing to do with touchdowns or pinning an opponent.

Fifteen minutes later, I noticed Marc's car was still in the driveway. I heard his voice call from the three-season porch, "Mom, can you come in here for a minute?"

As I walked into the sunlight, I couldn't believe my

eyes. Tears immediately filled them. There at the little round glass café table were two chairs and a tea set for two. He pointed to the seat across from him and with a big smile said, "This chair is for you, Mom."

As Marc filled my cup, I noticed foam oozing out of the spout.

"Sorry, Mom, but root beer was the closest match I could find," he said apologetically.

It wouldn't have mattered to me if the pot were filled with air; I never wanted this moment to end.

The kid-like pretense started a silly laughter in both of us, followed by heart-to-heart conversation between mother and son. Watching him go through the motion of sipping tea with his big fingers was such a spontaneous gesture of unselfish love that it will be etched in my heart and mind forever. An unexplainable bond formed that perfect spring day, and when we finished drinking our root-beer tea, Marc reminded me, "See, Mom, it's never too late."

Today—fourteen years later—as I gaze into my hutch at the little china tea set that my son so quietly took out that day, I recall the memory of the best tea party ever. It's the only one I'll ever need because it was fulfilled in the most unexpected way . . . on my *own doorstep*, with my only son.

Gloria Plaisted

Paul's Bike

It is the will, and not the gift, that makes the giver.

Bruno Lessing

Late one June evening, our oldest son, his dad and I discussed a newspaper route with a morning delivery manager. From the dining room I could hear the television where a younger son, Paul, watched his favorite program.

The man described two available routes. "And if you keep a route for at least a year, the bike we loan you becomes yours to keep."

"How old do you have to be to have a paper route?" Paul piped in.

I stared at Paul. How long had he been sitting at the other end of the table?

"How old are you, son?" asked the manager.

Paul stretched himself as tall as possible. "Ten."

"Well," answered the manager, "we like the boys to be at least eleven."

"But you have two routes in our area. I could do one," insisted Paul.

"Okay, if your parents agree that you can do it. Let me know tomorrow."

After the man left, I laid out some rules. "If you take these routes, they are yours, not mine. Don't expect me to drive you when the weather is bad or you get up late. I don't want to remind you to collect each month either."

The manager trained the boys for two days. On Saturday he presented each boy with a paper-route bike.

The bike was one-speed, large, fat, tired and ugly red. A basket rested over each side of the back fender to hold papers, and a large canvas bag hung from the handlebars.

I watched Paul's face. He smiled, rode the bike down the driveway, then parked it in the garage. After the first week of riding the bike to school, he chose to walk.

Each morning Paul got up early on his own to deliver his papers. Even if I offered to drive him in the freezing cold, he refused. He finished his collections on time without my urging. Each month he cashed his checks at the local drugstore, paid his paper bill and hid his profits in a sock in his underwear drawer.

With Christmas a couple of months away, the boys and I made many trips to Target. Each boy went his own way. I'd find Paul in the bicycle department.

"Why are you always looking at bikes?" I asked him. "You have one that you seldom ride."

"Mom, the kids make fun of my clunky paper-route bike. I want one like everyone else has. By Christmas I'll have enough money to buy this one."

Every day after school, Paul counted his money. On each trip to various stores, his brother showed me Christmas gifts he'd purchased. Paul never bought anything. He spent the whole time sitting on new bikes. In December he did his collections early.

On our final Christmas shopping trip, I again discovered Paul at the bicycle department. His shopping cart was empty. "Are you buying the bike?" I asked.

"I have enough money," he boasted.

"Well, hurry up. We'll wait for you at the front." We waited and waited. At last Paul came out carrying one little bag to the car.

Each boy took his turn in my bedroom, secretly wrapping his gifts. Paul didn't take long. He placed a few small packages under the tree.

That night I went to tuck the boys into bed as usual. When I entered Paul's room, he lay on his back, staring at the ceiling. His brown eyes sparkled. "I can hardly wait for Christmas," he said. He put his hands behind his head, and his face filled with a huge smile.

"Why, Paul?" I dreaded his answer. "Will your new bike arrive soon?"

"I didn't buy it, but I spent all my money!" He looked happier than I'd ever seen him. "Everyone's going to love what I got them for Christmas!"

Linda L. Osmundson

The Love of His Life

No joy in nature is so sublimely affecting as the joy of a mother at the good fortune of her child.
Jean Paul Richter

With his sixth birthday just days away, my son, Jake, has outgrown Mickey Mouse, his favorite teddy bear and many other little-boy things in our home. But not me.

Since he started school, Jake has broadened his horizons, meeting tons of new friends. He's become devoted to his principal, art teacher and coach and has found a new expert on all things universal—his kindergarten teacher.

But even though I'm no longer his source for all knowledge . . . even though there are many days he would rather fish with his dad than spend time with me . . . he still loves me with the unconditional love that exists between a six-year-old and his mother.

In the morning, he rolls over in bed and asks, "Where's my dad?" But at night, tucked in for sleep, his teeth brushed, hair fresh with the scent of shampoo, he waits in bed for my final check on him. I poke my head in his doorway, and he looks up with a radiant smile that nearly bursts with his love for me. He's so happy to see me, you would think it had been days instead of just minutes since I saw him last.

Soon enough, I know, the other girls in his life will take center stage, and I will move willingly, but a little sadly, to the side. The days of Jake holding my hand in front of his friends and giving me good-bye kisses are numbered, and I try to remember that when it feels like he wants too much from me. Soon, he'll go his own way, and I won't be needed as much anymore.

I may be sad. I may be devastated. That's when I'll remember the Valentine's Day carnation.

Student council members at his school were selling the flowers as a fundraiser, and I gave Jake money to buy carnations for two lucky girls in his class. He picked his friends, Samantha and Caroline, to buy flowers for.

But before I dropped him off at school, Jake said, "Mom, can I have one more dollar? There's someone else I need to get a carnation for."

I handed him the dollar, and his eyes were shining with excitement. "I can't tell you who it's for; it's a secret." He practically bounced in his seat. "It's a special someone that I love a lot." He chattered all the way to school. By the time I dropped him off, I had more than a clue who the special someone was.

At the end of the school day, Jake sat on the pick-up bench with the rest of the kindergarten kids. His hands moved dramatically behind his back as he saw me approach him. Then he held out his white carnation with a flourish. "Here, this is for you, Mom," said my son, "because I love you."

"I'm so surprised!" I said, hugging him. He grinned and held my hand tightly all the way to the car.

So on the day that Jake is embarrassed to hold my hand or kiss my cheek, I'll remember the sweet, sweet smell of that carnation.

Sue-Ellen Sanders

A Swing of Fate

The manner of the giving shows the character of the giver, more than the gift itself.

John Casper Lavater

The memory was morning fresh.

"Close your eyes, Mom," Kyle had ordered.

"What?"

"Don't ask questions and don't peek. Just close your eyes!"

Grabbing the backs of both my elbows, Kyle pivoted me from the kitchen sink and paraded me through the house and out the back door. "Are they still closed?"

I squinched my eyes even tighter and nodded.

"Okay, you can open them now." He grinned. "Happy twenty-fifth wedding anniversary!"

The entire family had gathered on the patio. My other three children. My husband. All smiles, they huddled in anticipation, eager to catch my first expression.

My gaze jumped from them to our old battered porch swing . . . with a fresh paint job!

Wait! This wasn't the same swing; it was another, even

older swing, still pungent with new paint. It was . . . No, it couldn't be. Could it?

Kyle's moon face broke into a wide smile. "Do you recognize it?"

"Of course, I do." I beamed.

"Here, sit down. Try it on for size."

Escorting me across the patio, Kyle brushed aside a stray pine needle from the plank seat and a lone tear from my cheek.

Squeezing my eyes against more threatening tears, I settled in, my body recognizing the size, the shape, the slope of the old swing. Even the comforting creak hadn't changed.

I had been drawn to the swing the moment I first saw it twenty-three years ago. As seasoned as the vintage house itself, it hovered under the large covered porch. Ancient even then with its layers of chipped paint, the swing summoned me, invited me, awaited me. I had cuddled with my husband there, listening to night harmonies, awed at owning our first home. Sitting with mounded tummy, I had pushed the swing rhythmically with the toe of my shoe, spinning dreams of impending first motherhood and crooning whisper-soft lullabies.

So many times I had regretted not bringing the swing with us when we moved from Kansas to Colorado two decades ago. How often had I mentioned it through the years?

Obviously, Kyle had heard and understood what the swing symbolized.

"I can't believe you managed this, Kyle! But—how? And—when?" I choked.

"Do I have a story to tell *you*, Mom!" In typical Kyle-style, he launched into a hilarious and lengthy tale about an undercover adventure to secretly locate the old Wichita home, an aborted plan to kidnap the coveted swing, and a timely and fortunate rendezvous with the swing's under-standing owner.

"This is wonderful, Kyle! The best gift ever. Honestly, you'll never top this," I said. "So don't even try."

Now, a mere six months later, I bent over his hospital bed in the Trauma Unit at County Hospital where an inert Kyle lay, the victim of a hit-and-run accident. Trying to ignore the tendrils of tubes and cords vining his body, I admired the seeping pink color beginning to replace yesterday's gray cheeks.

"Kyle," I whispered close to his ear, "I was wrong. You've topped the porch swing. I just received an even better gift—the very best gift ever.

"The doctor says you are going to live!"

Carol McAdoo Rehme

Song-and-Dance Man

We pardon as long as we love.

François de La Rochefoucauld

After nineteen years of marriage, I made the most difficult decision of my life. The divorce turned my thirteen-
year-old son Mike's world upside down. He lived with his
dad, and the days strung out between my visitations
every other weekend. During that time we struggled, each
in a private whirlpool of emotion, often unable to commu-
nicate adequately with one another. A typical teen, his
need to be with peers left us little time together. I feared
not living under the same roof would permanently damage the positive relationship we'd once had. I prayed often
that somehow we'd uncover the common ground the past
years of mindful parenting had forged—an irrevocable
bond between us. I could see, hear and feel his anger. How
could he not be? I didn't know what to do. I had to let go.
I had to let God handle it. I asked God to help my son cope
with the upheaval the divorce caused in his young life. I
fervently prayed that somehow, someday, my son and I
would have a healthy relationship.

Eventually technical rock climbing became a mutual pursuit, with Mike and me literally trusting our lives to each other on the ropes. From there we seemed to rebuild our relationship, but I still wondered if he held latent resentment toward me. I worried that he'd soon find other people and activities to fill his time and drift farther away from me.

By his late teens we seemed to overcome the obstacles of separation and busy lives. I relished each time he'd stop by to give me a ride on his newest motorcycle or show off improvements he'd made on his truck. When he began dating, I enjoyed meeting his girlfriends, always offering to have them over for a dinner date. Sure, I wanted to save Mike the expense of a restaurant, but mainly I wanted the pleasure of his company. Not exactly selfless of me, but it worked! I got to see him a bit more often, and he didn't seem to mind.

Then he met "the right one," and they began to plan their life together. Thrilled for them, I couldn't help but wonder what he may have confided to his fiancée, what he might still harbor inside.

Their wedding arrived, highlighted by a ceremony and reception that impressed everyone. It was a joyous celebration of their love—elegant, meaningful and sincere. They paid attention down to the smallest detail; organized and thrifty, this pair thought of delightful touches, large and small, that lent festivity and significance to their event, creating numerous reasons for guests to "ooh and ahh."

He and his bride chose a well-recommended DJ who, by reputation, knew how to get everyone up and having fun. They had decided to skip the customary "special dances" at the beginning of the reception and simply get down to the music right away. The DJ energetically welcomed all present, and I figured he'd soon be cajoling one and all out onto the floor with his rollicking antics. Imagine my surprise when I heard the announcement, "The mother of the groom is immediately requested on the dance floor." I hesitated, but when I saw the DJ gesturing directly to me, I hustled over. The lights dimmed, and my freshly wed son stepped up to me. I could see my new daughter-in-law smiling and nodding at me from behind Mike.

"How's your two-step, Mom?" Grasping my hand, he chuckled, knowing how I tread on toes with my two left feet. The music began. In one tender motion he began to lead me around the dance floor. Since he stands a full head and shoulders above me, I had to tilt back my head to see his face. I stifled my giggle when I saw the earnest look in his eyes . . . I didn't know what to expect. "This is called 'She Was' by Mark Chesnutt," he said, and then began singing to me.

I wasn't familiar with the song or the artist, but Mike knew the words and the melody well. I found listening and dancing at the same time quite a challenge. I tripped and lost the beat. Mike laughed softly and got me back on track, but he never stopped singing, ". . . she started her new life ten dollars in debt . . . never thought twice. . . ." As I caught the bits and pieces of lyrics, I began gradually to comprehend what was happening. He continued to squire me around the room, singing, ". . . she tried to be everything to us . . . those precious moments turned into years in what seemed like the blink of an eye." The room hushed. My vision blurred with tears. It became evident to all the guests who were aware of our history that my son was using the song to say something profound to his mother. Mike squeezed my hand to gain my full attention and looked directly into my eyes. I could see he meant the words he was singing with all his heart, ". . . a woman like her would be hard to give up. . . ." At that moment I got it. He hadn't drifted away from me at all! The healthy relationship I'd feared gone was at this very moment being publicly declared. I was thunderstruck. By the time Mike sang the last line, ". . . If there ever was a picture of love, she was," my shoulders heaved, tears coursed down my face, and my feet would not even move. Gently he glided me off the dance floor, bent down and kissed me on the cheek. I tried but could not speak. Our eyes met. Mutual understanding, forgiveness and respect passed unspoken between us.

Maryjo Faith Morgan

Captain Kirk

It is generally admitted, and very frequently proved, that virtue and genius and all the natural good qualities which men possess are derived from their mothers.

Theodore Edward Hooke

I was seventeen and, at first glance, the strangers crowding around us would have guessed I was with my grandmother and not my mother. A year of chemodialysis had ravaged her once sturdy frame until she tottered at barely half of her normal weight. Her once lustrous black hair was almost completely gray, and deep lines of pain and weariness etched her face.

It was a rare day, unusual enough just for Mom to be out of bed. With no doctor's appointment scheduled that morning, we had gotten a ride across town to a *Star Trek* convention at a local auditorium. It may seem strange to have taken someone as sick as her to a science-fiction event, but her eyes shone as we paid for our tickets, and she seemed to regain a lost spring in her step as we made our way through the mob and toward the stage.

You see, William Shatner, the renowned Captain Kirk of the original *Starship Enterprise* was, himself, the guest speaker at this year's event. My mother had been raised far from the nearest town, on an eastern Oregon cattle ranch. Divorced nearly all of my life, she was an old-fashioned, wholesome soul who blushed at the slightest profanities, or what she called "racy jokes." She had never remarried, or even dated, deferring all of her love and energy to me, her only child, and, of course, to William Shatner.

Many nights, as a child, we sat together to watch the epic adventures of the *Enterprise* and her crew, Mom gazing adoringly at her ideal of masculine perfection. On her dressing table sat a photograph of the actor, obtained by me after joining his fan club. Now, years later, she was about to see her idol in the flesh!

I managed to elbow us a path through a horde of Klingon-clad enthusiasts, until we were seated in the front row. Mom waited with great patience as the obligatory outtakes and unseen episodes flashed across the screen. Finally, the moment came, and Shatner himself strode onto the stage. He was a bit older than I remembered and seemed to have lost some of his Starfleet physique (haven't we all?), but it was obvious from Mom's shining face that she still saw the Captain in all his glory.

Mr. Shatner, a gracious and entertaining speaker, shared witticisms and backstage gossip, keeping his audience enthralled for the better part of an hour. Finally, he began to wrap up and asked if anyone had any questions. A thought struck me. Dare I? I raised my hand. We were in the front row so Mr. Shatner could hardly have missed me, but one by one, he called on other hands around the room until he had time for only one final question. Boldly, I stretched my arm even higher. I think he must have seen the desperation in my face. He hesitated—then pointed to me.

I stood, half facing the audience. I was either about to become a hero or look like a complete fool.

"Mr. Shatner," I said, "my mother thinks that you're about the most wonderful man who's ever lived, and she's been a fan of yours since I can remember. It would mean a lot to her if she could come up on stage and give you a hug."

I heard my mother gasp in the chair beside me, but dared not turn to look. My pleading eyes locked with a man who had probably dealt with more than his share of obsessed admirers. Silence hung over the auditorium for a moment. The Captain nodded. The room erupted into deafening cheers. I held my mother's arm and steadied her as she made her way slowly up the stairs and across the stage. He had turned off his microphone, but I was close enough to hear him ask her name. Then he thanked her and kissed her cheek.

I will remember this day vividly as one of the happiest of my life. My mother fairly floated through the rest of the show. Just a few weeks later, on the night before my mother passed away, she retold this story to her doctor. She still smiled and blushed at the memory of her kiss from Captain Kirk.

I'm so glad I dared to boldly go where no man has gone before.

Perry P. Perkins

Goodnight, Mom

A man loves his sweetheart the most, his wife the best, but his mother the longest.

Irish Proverb

I listened intently from the kitchen to an unremarkable conversation occurring in the bedroom.

"You need to put your slippers there by the edge of the bed."

"Oh, okay . . ."

"If you don't, you'll forget they are in the middle of the floor. If you have to get up in the middle of the night, you might trip and break your neck!"

After a girlish giggle, the second voice answered, "Okay, I'll move them now."

Though the conversation was not unremarkable, there was only one person in the bedroom.

My mother could best be described as the original earth-mother with Victorian sensibilities. In another time, she loved to garden and feel the warm earth in her hands. Her recreation was being driven along some mountain road watching for wildlife—she never learned to drive.

She was always simple in her lifestyle and had spiritual ideas that were a curious blend of the 1960s and a more pious religious era. She saw God in all things natural, and yet was very modest and believed it was important for people to dress modestly. She did not attend church, but tithed, read scripture and subscribed to religious magazines. She believed in "live and let live" and yet was highly offended at the freewheeling, open expression of the '60s.

Her health and her mental function had been deteriorating slowly in the past year, and she increasingly talked to herself. It was not a conversation, but a monologue. But that changed one day. Probably some unknown, unseen bit of plaque on the wall of an artery somewhere had dislodged and then obstructed a small blood vessel that fed some small area of my mother's brain. Suddenly, she became fearful, even paranoid, and the monologues become a dialogue. There was a child-like voice and one that seemed adult, which I called "the protector." That voice alternatively praised, reminded and admonished the girlish voice. But, and I don't say this with impertinence, for several weeks that two-in-one person got by and together made almost a whole person as we took my mother to innumerable doctor visits and medical tests. Unfortunately, the two voices soon became three and then five.

The diagnosis was Alzheimer's, although it is not classic Alzheimer's, as I understand it. Whatever its name, it does not change the fact of what it is.

The realization came to us, her family, but not to her, that her eighty-five years of independent life were gone. We faced the horrible choice that all too many face—how to care for someone who requires more physical and mental care than a family can provide. We made the heart-wrenching decision to place her in a nursing home.

I sat one night in her wheelchair by her as she sat on the edge of her bed. I asked if I could help her undress and put on her nightgown. She answered, "Why, thank you."

She unbuttoned her blouse as she chatted with her unseen companions. The medications made them less intrusive and her less fearful. I helped her take off her blouse.

"Can you unhook this?" she said referring to her bra.

I knew at that instant the mother I had known and loved all my life was in a very real way gone from this world. She would have never disrobed in front of me. Certainly, the body lived on, but my mother's essence was gone.

I got her into her nightgown and tucked her into bed. I touched her cheek with the back of my forefinger, smoothed her hair behind her ear and said, "I love you, Mom," as I kissed her on the cheek. "See you another day."

"Goodnight," she said as I headed for the door.

I turned and smiled, and then turned again and walked out the door.

I heard the protector voice say, "Who was that?"

"I don't know," another voice responded.

The girlish voice said, "He's nice."

Their conversation faded as my footsteps echoed down the polished hallway and walked toward the Alzheimer unit's locked door. A nurse's aide let me out of the unit, and I walked past the nurses' station and out the door.

It was raining lightly as I walked across the parking lot. It was as if there were tears from heaven to match my own.

Daniel James

His Mother

It is the general rule that all superior men inherit the elements of superiority from their mothers.

Jules Michelet

"But what happened to *you?*"

"My mother was thirsty and hadn't eaten for days."

"But what happened to *you?*"

I looked into the dejected eyes of the man from Kosovo, now temporarily relocated in the United States. Mr. B. was middle-aged, a bit shy, but very articulate as he sat humbly across the small table from me.

It was 1999, and I was part of a team of workers documenting testimony about terrible human-rights abuses experienced by him and thousands more. My assignment was to precisely record the testimony of these refugees to help understand their persecutions and, hopefully, eventually hold their perpetrators accountable. Men and women, young and old, visited our makeshift office, pointed at maps, drew pictures and recalled for our team unthinkable tales of being forced from their homes and unmercifully abused. I was overwhelmed with awe and admiration for their courage as survivors and, now, witnesses.

This interview was particularly compelling for me—not because it was more brutal than the others; indeed all of the testimony was shockingly violent and terrifying—but because this man's story revolved not around himself, but his mother. He seemed absolutely incapable of talking about himself. His own experiences seemed entirely swallowed by empathy for his mother. Yet, knowing that first-person accounts were most valuable to separate facts from hearsay, I aimed my gentle questions to encourage him to talk about his experiences.

"What happened to *you*?" I coaxed gently.

"My mother had to flee her home."

"And you, Mr. B. Where were you?"

"My mother was chased far distances—over dangerous territory—to the relocation camps."

"I see. And Mr. B., where were you?"

He paused. "Carrying her." He shook his head, as if still in disbelief. "Mama was very sick."

"Tell me about it, Mr. B.," I said softly.

"Mother needed medical attention . . . she had to get past the soldiers to get help in the camp . . . she was so sick."

Again, he went on and on about his mother, with no mention of himself until I coaxed him for details of *his* involvement. Then he told, as if it were a trivial matter, of taking a life-risking step—approaching a group of soldiers to beg for medical assistance for his mother. For this he was severely beaten, nearly to death. But from his perspective, this was of no importance to the story.

"I survived that," he said, "and lived to take care of Mama."

As I continued documenting details of their journey, he reported it as though his own experience was practically irrelevant and his mother's all-important.

Indeed, thanks to her son's courage and care, his mother

had escaped with him. Although she was still too ill to provide testimony herself, I was honored to meet her one
evening a few days later. As I entered their quarters at the
facility, I contemplated her son's devotion and wondered
where a man could learn such perfect selflessness.

Then I saw the frail woman gaze into her son's eyes and
stroke his cheek, and I realized the answer.

He learned it from his mother.

Angela Thieman Dino

5

OVERCOMING OBSTACLES

*Good timber does not grow with ease.
The stronger the wind, the stronger
the trees.*

J. Willard Marriott

A Constant Presence

*Woman is the salvation or the destruction of
the family. She carries its destiny in the folds of
her mantle.*

Henri Frederic Amiel

Our son Mason came into this world the usual way.
Dave and I married late in life and were very eager to start
our family. When we did get pregnant, we shared every
moment of those nine months, from doctor visits to ready-
ing the nursery to baby showers and even gaining weight!
Mason finally arrived in October 2003 . . . just in time for
his daddy to be deployed to Iraq.

A longtime member of the California Army National
Guard, Dave had received his orders just days before
Mason came into this world. He left us for an eighteen-
month tour in the Middle East when Mason was only
three weeks old.

As a new first-time mom—a new, *single* first-time
mom—I found myself with a baby boy. *A boy*, I cried to
myself. Boys need their dads to help mold them into
men. Through many tears, some from fear of my husband

fighting in a war zone and many from postpartum blues, I made the decision to mother Mason with strength, joy and, most important, Dave's presence. I set my goal to provide a safe and loving environment for our son and to bridge the gap between our home in northern California and the hot, sandy deserts of Iraq.

I was determined to make sure Mason not only knew his father when he finally came home, but that he would be excited to see him. I purchased six-inch wooden letters that read "My Daddy," as well as several picture frames, filling them with large photos of Dave, both in uniform and in civilian clothes. Then I arranged them all on the wall overlooking Mason's crib, screwing everything into place so he couldn't pull them down on himself.

Next, I laminated pictures of Dave and gave them to Mason to play with, put in his mouth, carry around the house, give to the family dog or whatever he wanted to do with them. The goal was for Mason to learn his father's face, his daddy's eyes and smile.

One day, when Mason was just seven months old, we were at our favorite local restaurant when a soldier entered wearing the traditional camouflage. Mason stared at him, obviously recognizing the uniform. My plan was working!

Meanwhile, greeting cards began arriving in the mail from Dave. Before he was deployed, he must have secretly purchased lots of beautiful and funny cards to send as a surprise, along with wonderful letters. This amazing gesture of love by Dave equated to some of my most favorite mother-and-son bonding times. The two of us snuggled in the special rocker in Mason's room, with me reading the letters out loud while he gummed the cards, making a slobbery mess. And even though I sometimes read Dave's letters through my tears, I felt strongly that Mason understood that the letters and cards were from his daddy. I knew he realized that there was more to "us" than just him and me.

As Mason grew and his development progressed, I put the telephone to his ear when Dave called home. His eyes would light up; he squirmed all over my lap with excitement. At eleven months, Mason started bringing me his play telephone, holding out the receiver and saying, "Da-Da, Da-Da."

Time passed quickly, and finally my son and I headed to the base to pick up Dave. The question kept running through my brain: Was I successful in keeping Dave's presence a constant in Mason's heart and in our home? Would his baby boy know him? I fretted that since Mason had experienced very little physical contact with his daddy after his first three weeks of life, he would not know his father.

Then Dave stepped off the bus and raced toward us. Mason immediately reached for him, took his daddy's face in his little hands and exclaimed with a big smile, "Da-Da!"

Kathleen Partak

No Limits

God could not be everywhere, and therefore he made mothers.

Jewish Saying

"I'm not doing it, Mom. She can give me an F!" said my third-grader with conviction.

When my son Billy began talking, it was immediately evident there was a problem. He would choke on his words, as if there was an obstruction in his throat depriving him of air for a few seconds in every word he said.

I took him to a speech therapist, who referred him to a speech pathologist. He ruled out stuttering. Billy's condition, Spasmodic Dysphonia, was caused by the vocal cords overlapping each other. Surgery was ruled out because patients ended up with high-pitched voices.

Since he was so young, we were advised to wait until he was three to begin speech therapy. But it could not wait. A mother knows no limits to what her son can do, so the therapy began.

The therapist had a meeting with the family first, to give us some rules: Except for the therapist's office and the fifteen minutes of daily work at home with the flash cards and breathing exercises, Billy's speech impediment did not exist. We agreed he should be aware of it as little as possible. He also told us that this would not be cured in a couple of weeks—it would take years.

As a mother, I was still very concerned when it came time to start school. Although his speech had improved a little, it was still difficult to understand him if you didn't know him well. I made his teacher aware, but I worried about his classmates. However, as time passed, my concerns proved unfounded. He made new friends and was a well-rounded, happy-go-lucky kid. He played sports and was a member of the school band where kids had to keep up good grades. And he had many little girlfriends always ready to help him after school with his flash cards and breathing exercises, which now, all of a sudden, he didn't hate anymore.

Billy never showed frustration or lack of confidence due to his speech until one day in the third grade. A friend of Billy's told me they had to give a short speech in front of the class the next day, and Billy was getting an F because he refused to do it. No one in the family could persuade him to even try. "I'm not doing it, Mom. She can give me an F!"

All of a sudden around 5:00 P.M., I remembered a book I was reading called *Get Me Ellis Rubin*. It was about the famous Miami-based criminal lawyer and some of his most famous cases. In the book, it mentioned that as a child Mr. Rubin had suffered from a severe speech impediment. I thought, *What if Mr. Rubin could talk to Billy and give him encouragement?* But the chances of that were slimmer than me being the first woman to play and win the Masters. However, the thought kept nagging me, so around 5:30 P.M., I called Miami information, and a few minutes later I was talking to his secretary. I couldn't believe the office was even open. I told her why I was calling. Mr. Rubin wasn't in, of course, but she took my message.

At least I tried. A mother knows no limits to what her son can do, and I still had two and a half hours before Billy's bedtime to work on him. At 8:00 P.M., the phone rang. I answered and a man said, "This is Ellis Rubin." I couldn't believe it. I quickly explained the situation, and he asked to speak to Billy, who knew about him from my book. Boy, was Billy surprised! They talked for twenty-five minutes, and then he asked to speak to me. He wanted Billy to call him, collect, the next day and report to him about the outcome of the speech.

I didn't ask Billy about the conversation. That was between them. All I knew was that Mr. Rubin had convinced my son to give the speech and what to say to the class beforehand. "I have a speech impediment. If at any time you do not understand what I say, raise your hand and I will repeat it."

My son came home the next day with the biggest smile on his face! He called Mr. Rubin immediately (not collect). "Mr. Rubin, this is Billy. I made an A. Thank you, sir. Oh, yes, and I got a standing ovation."

That day was a new beginning for Billy. He continued speech therapy through junior-high school, and today, at the age of thirty-one, he is a fine, tall, confident, handsome young man whose speech is much improved.

There is no limit to what a mother—and her son— can do.

Deisy M. Flood

Hearts in Our Eyes

Childhood shows the man as morning shows the day.

John Milton

Due to Cody's debut in this world as an extreme preemie at one pound, six ounces, he underwent eye surgery to prevent blindness. His nearsightedness meant glasses and close monitoring by an ophthalmologist for the rest of his life.

Cody wore glasses with great pride, making it abundantly clear to his little brothers that Mommy and Daddy also wore glasses, and wasn't it a shame that they didn't have any themselves? This usually prompted a round of begging from his siblings that they get glasses, too.

With bated breath, we watched Cody enter kindergarten.

One day, a couple of boys at recess derailed Cody's bright outlook on having glasses. One said, "Your glasses look stupid, Cody." Another yanked them off his face and bent them.

Cody was a timid, small child. Seeing tears well up in his eyes as he reiterated the event wrung our hearts dry.

Just recently, though, something changed his outlook. Literally.

It was the morning of Valentine's Day. I shut off the alarm and groped around in the dark until I found my glasses. I donned them and, without turning on the light, blindly made my way to the bathroom. I flipped the bathroom switch, and there I discovered why it was extra dark in my bedroom. My husband had stuck two red heart stickers on my glasses, partially blocking my view.

Plastered all over the antique mirrors above the bathroom sinks were the same stickers.

"VALENTINE," my husband had scrawled on one mirror, "I LOVE YOU THIS MUCH!"

In one mirror was drawn a stick arm with a hand pointing west. And in the other mirror was the same thing pointing east. I was chuckling under my breath so as not to wake the rest of the household. I penned my response in the mirror. "Thanks to you, sweetie, I've got hearts in my eyes!"

While dressing Cody for school, he whispered, "Mom?"

"Yes, big boy?"

"You got hearts on your glasses."

"Yep, I sure do."

"You're funny, Mom," he said, his eyes sparkling.

We both climbed into the cab of the pickup truck, where other hearts ambushed us. Stuck to the steering wheel was a heart. Another one was on the rearview mirror, on the stick shift, on my truck key and on my wallet. All compliments of my heart-happy husband.

I peeled the hearts from my glasses and handed them to Cody. He stuck them carefully on his own glasses and smiled the whole way to school.

I parked in front of his school. "Get your bookbag, sweetie."

"Mom, can I wear my hearts to class?"

I debated it for a moment. Pulling a stunt like this could go either way. But the pleading in his eyes sealed it for me. How could I deny him what may turn out to be a fun opportunity?

"I don't see why not, big boy."

I placed two more hearts on my own glasses, and together we entered his school, hand in hand, parting the crowd in the hallway on our way to his classroom.

"Ha! Look at Cody Oliver! He's got hearts on his glasses!" one observer called out.

"Oh, look at Cody! How cute!" shouted another, pointing and giggling.

Cody smiled shyly, gripping my hand for dear life.

When we arrived at the doorway, classmates gathered around my little guy, while I saw him trying to shake the biggest grin from his face.

"That's neat! Hearts on your glasses!"

"Cody, can I try them on?"

"I wish I had glasses."

I knew then without a doubt that Cody's outlook was back on track.

Just by having hearts in his eyes.

Jennifer I. Oliver

Cerebral Chaos

Teach children to think and read and talk without self-repression, and they will write, because they cannot help it.

Anne Sullivan

"No! You can't go outside!" my mother yelled. "You're on restriction for a week!"

My blood boiled upon hearing the horrid word "restriction." You can't ban an eleven-year-old boy from his BMX bike and buddies—especially during the summer!

But I had disobeyed my mother. She told me to be home at two; I didn't come home until seven that evening.

I stomped toward my bedroom, but before reaching the doorway, a hard grip around my elbow curtailed forward progress.

"Don't walk away from me!" My mother pointed at the couch. "Sit down."

I folded my arms across my chest, my forehead furrowed. I turned to the couch and slammed my bottom on the cushion.

"Oh, okay," my mother said, nodding, "since you think

you can ruin the couch *I* paid for, you can't sit there. Get up."

So now we were playing musical chairs. I rolled my eyes and stood up. Mom grabbed my wrist. We walked through the kitchen into the dining-room area. "Sit down."

I pulled out a chair from the dining table, plopped down and fixated on the wall. I pushed my spine against the curved iron back, but I ignored the slight discomfort and leaned back defiantly, folding arms and pouting my lips.

My mother took a pen and pad of paper from a kitchen drawer. "I have an assignment for you."

Assignment? I thought. *School is over!*

She dropped the pad and pen in front of me. "You must be a genius," she said, grinning. "Something in that hard-headed noggin of yours convinced you it was a good idea to come home so late."

I gazed at her, head tilted. She had something up her sleeve.

"So," she continued, "since you have such a creative mind, let's see you prove it. I want you to write a story every night of your punishment . . . starting tonight."

I twisted my face as if a raw odor had stunned me. I stared at the paper, then looked up at her. "Write about what?"

"Anything you want. You have an hour, and I'll read it when you're done." She walked into the kitchen. "I'll warm up your dinner, so get goin'."

Talk about ball and chain. Bad enough I had to stay in the house, but now my mother wanted to torture me. No TV, no Atari, no handheld video games. Just me, the dining-room table, a pen and a blank pad of paper.

I grabbed the pen. With a scowl, I transferred my anger through my thin fingers—and wrote. I didn't care about plot or structure; I wanted my revenge on paper.

My hand didn't stop. I wrote myself as the main character

and hero; my mother became the villain and enemy to kids of the world. Of course, I defeated the evil villain with supersonic weapons.

I ate as I wrote, and I finished an hour later. When my mother read my story, she asked why I wrote about bad things happening to her. I didn't respond, just shrugged. My eyes fixated on the wall again, bottom lip sticking out.

To my surprise, my mother said, "I love the story and can't wait to read another one tomorrow night." I sucked in my bottom lip to keep from smiling. Dang it, I was still mad!

But I felt good inside. I'd written a story—something I'd never done before—and my mother praised my effort.

The next night, I banged out another story. Mom was still a villain, but this time I used my mental powers to make her an ally.

As my mom's eyes scanned the pages, she chuckled once or twice. Again, she praised my art of storytelling. She kissed my forehead, and I felt my hard resolve against her fading.

The third night, I wrote a little earlier than usual. An idea had been bouncing in my head, and I itched to create another "masterpiece." My fingers whipped across the page and, within minutes, I had created a story about a kid taking his own life. I'd seen a TV special on teenage suicide once, and I always wished I had the power to prevent such tragedy.

A look of sadness draped my mother's face. After she read my story, she hugged me and said she loved me. I didn't ask how she felt about the story. Her glassy eyes said it all.

Sleep didn't come easy that night. Characters crystallized and swam in my head, much like in my dreams. I saw their faces, heard their voices, knew their likes and dislikes—everything.

And they wanted out.

Luckily, I had brought the pen and paper to bed with me. With so much tug-of-war in my mind, I had plenty of ideas to create more stories for my mother. I wrote a story for myself this time.

For the next few days, the stories kept coming. I looked forward to Mom's comments, but I didn't have to wait on the hour she had allotted for writing. I had plenty of time to write in my room. And with so much "cerebral chaos," I could create any adventure I wanted. Being stuck in the house couldn't limit my mind.

That same cerebral chaos stayed with me even after my mother lifted the outdoor ban. It carried on through my teenage years—and lives with me today as a man. The people in my head still hold me captive sometimes—until I release them. Only this time, I use a laptop to set them free.

I never told my mother why I was so late that day twenty years ago. In the downtown library, anyone could lose track of time in the wondrous world of Encyclopedia Brown, Charlie Brown and Snoopy, and choose-your-own-adventure books.

I still immerse myself in books, and sometimes my mother still buys me some for special occasions. But I also create my own novel-length manuscripts. Although I haven't published a novel yet, the thrill of seeing my name in print doesn't drive me. Cerebral chaos does—thanks to my mother's "assignments."

James W. Lewis

"I hope you realize you're spoiling the
carefree days of my youth!"

©2000 Dan Rosandich. Reprinted by permission of Dan Rosandich.

The Optimist

They say an optimist reports happily that the jar is half full; the pessimist complains bitterly that it's half empty. Our son, Tom, has always been an optimist. However, there was a time when the merit of this character trait was lost on me.

When he was a freshman in a new high school, Tom struggled with algebra. Since most people in our family seem to possess a genetic deficiency in math, I was sympathetic. I studied his book and relearned the basics of algebra, which I attempted to teach him. At the end of each hour, we came away with nothing more than headaches and a mutual sense of failure. I met with his teacher, who suggested he go back and start with the basics. His father, who finds math fun, took over. Tom still couldn't grasp the concepts. Needless to say, it put a strain on the father-son relationship, and my husband's frustration grew exponentially.

"You're going to pass algebra if it kills all of us," I said, and hired an expensive tutor.

The tutor was a very nice college kid who was majoring in calculus or something. He also thought math was fun. So naturally, I had my doubts. But the quarter test was just weeks away, and math had become a four-letter word in our house, so the tutor was our last resort.

Every Tuesday and Thursday evening he showed up wearing a hopeful grin. Two hours later he left, rubbing the back of his neck as he shuffled out of our front door. Tom would sigh and head to his room before I could question him about how the session had gone.

Finally, the dreaded day came for the big test. *If he doesn't do well on this, he might just give up on school,* I thought. I picked him up from school and watched him saunter toward the car. I tried to read his face. He didn't look upset, but he didn't look especially happy, either. As he slid into the car I asked, "How'd you do?"

"I got a D."

"Oh, Tom," I said, "I don't understand how that happened."

"I don't either." Then he smiled. "I guess the Lord was looking out for me."

Margaret P. Cunningham

Wishing Upon a Son

"I'm trapped in the house with a two-year-old," my friend Tanya tells me. I hear the sound of imminent breakage in her voice, a voice that has shrieked out too many NO's, a voice that has sung along with *Sesame Street* too many times, a voice that has not been able to talk about books, relationships or gardening in too many hours.

When Nicholas was born, a bunch of us gathered to have a coming out party for him. Like benevolent fairy godmothers, we created a circle and bestowed wishes upon the child. I held the infant in my arms while we fantasized about the attributes of the fairy-tale man, a sort of New-Age Prince Charming. "I wish for him a great sense of humor," one of us said.

"I wish for him passion," said another. Wanting Nicholas to grow into an ideal man, we gifted him with generosity, wit, sensitivity, playfulness, creativity, determination.

Now these gifts are taking hold. Perhaps too soon. Perhaps the qualities of a charming prince don't fit well with a two-year-old boy. They certainly don't fit well with the two-year-old's mother.

Take a sense of humor. When his mother wished for a good sense of humor, she envisioned him telling tasteful jokes, with great punch lines, appropriately delivered. She envisioned a room full of well-dressed people, spellbound by his wit, poise and originality.

Nicholas's sense of humor includes banging a ball against the floor 444 times. He laughs at farts, burps and any bathroom word he comes across.

He laughs when he drops his spoon from his high chair. In fact, this act engenders such hilarity that Nicholas does it again and again.

Nicholas's idea of generosity also differs from his mom's. When Tanya and I held Nicholas within our gentle circle, we imagined him as a man open with feelings, willing to share time, doing his part of the housework and tithing to worthy charities.

At age two, generosity means spitting out peas and offering them to his younger and hopefully less wise cousin. Generosity means leaving his crayons sprawled across the white rug, so the dog can chew on them.

Of course, Tanya wanted her son to be creative. His innate creativity has astounded and confounded her: already he can open childproof lids (something that Tanya herself has yet to master) and take apart the alarm clock. He has figured out a way to create a sound louder than the combined efforts of the dishwasher, washing machine, television and telephone. He has learned to take one cookie and distribute it equally across his anatomy.

Tanya's wish for her son to have determination has haunted her. When smoothed over the frame of a man, determination is an attractive quality, implying stick-to-it-ness, confidence and commitment. Determination means he will not run away when things are difficult.

"What is the difference between being determined and being bull-headed?" Tanya asks. She suspects Nicholas may have inherited her family's stubborn streak. Determination means he will not sleep until he hears *Green*

Eggs And Ham "read with good voices" at least three times.

All of us wished Nicholas would be sensitive to women and treat them as equals. But Nicholas's take on gender equity has an Attila-like quality we didn't envision.

When he wants to ride on the tricycle three-year-old Natalie is pedaling, he accords her the same treatment he would his friend Allen—Nicholas grabs the tricycle and pushes her off. When she hits him, he slugs her back.

And then there's the question of expressing emotions. Many of the women gathered around baby Nicholas had suffered through strong silent men.

We wanted Nicholas to grow up vulnerable and able to express his feelings.

"At this point, I think he could use a little repression," Tanya sighs, as she recounts a scene with Nicholas sobbing incessantly because his older brother did not want to play with him.

I hear the exhaustion in her voice and I wonder if our wishes have gone awry. Did we conjure up a monster or a prince-in-training? How much humor, determination, creativity does a child need to last him through adulthood?

Then I remember how wild my nephew, now a sensitive creative teen, used to be. And my own daughters, once amazingly willful, are now merely determined.

As we continue our phone conversation, I soothe Tanya with tales of wild children who grew up great.

"I feel better," she says. "Nicholas, those candles are not for eating. No, Nicholas, you cannot bang that spoon on the table top. Nicholas honey . . . I have to go," she tells me.

I hang up. In the fairy tales, the prince charming slays dragons and rescues princesses with ease. He is strong, loyal and watches out for children and animals. He is handsome, wise and popular.

Back at the castle, though, his mother is still recovering from raising him.

Deborah Shouse

Hush, Little Baby . . .

Out of the mouths of babes and sucklings hast thou ordained strength.

Psalm 8:2

My husband, Doug, and I had been married for eight years and had tried unsuccessfully for a good part of that time to start a family. So it was with utter delight that we greeted the news that we were expecting. In fact, my doctor's words when he returned with the lab results were, "Pigs flew!"

Doug and I threw ourselves into preparations for the baby, decorating a beautiful nursery overlooking the lake where we lived. Our precious son, Forrest, arrived on a mild spring evening in March. He was absolutely perfect, and I serenely slid into postpartum elation. Forrest was a wonderful baby—calm, contented and happy. He slept through the night early on, and we happily recorded each of his achievements in his baby book, smug in the knowledge that, of course, he was the first baby ever to reach such milestones so well and so swiftly.

We were concerned, however, that despite crawling

very quickly and taking his first steps early on, the "First Words Page" was sparse. Even as an infant, Forrest didn't babble like other babies. People reassured us, relating their own experiences of sons and daughters who suddenly burst into conversation when they were "ready."

Still, it was disconcerting to hear Forrest's little friends and his cousin, born a mere fourteen hours after him, chattering away, while he communicated silently or with the single words of his limited vocabulary.

In every other way, Forrest was a perfectly normal, active little boy who loved building intricate structures with Legos, beachcombing with his dad, and drawing detailed pictures of airplanes, cars and trucks. He loved books, and we read his favorites to him every evening.

Our bedtime ritual also included me singing two songs, "Hush, Little Baby" (the mockingbird song) and "Puff, the Magic Dragon." Singing is not my strong point, but Forrest demanded "Hush" and "Puff" every night before settling down to sleep.

We moved to White Rock, British Columbia, when Forrest was two and a half, and we began consulting physicians and specialists regarding his speech limitation. He continued to struggle with verbal responses and insistence for simple courtesies. For instance, "May I leave the table, please?" was met with tears of frustration. Testing indicated that both his hearing and comprehension were fine, which relieved us both.

When Forrest was four, we enrolled him in a Montessori preschool, hoping that the exposure to other children would help develop his communication skills, since we lived in a secluded area with no children nearby. Forrest enjoyed going to school, made several good friends, participated in all the activities and took pride in all that he learned—but remained silent.

By now, the differences were becoming increasingly obvious. Forrest's little sister, Brontë, born when Forrest was two, was speaking clearly and well.

We enrolled him in kindergarten, again a Montessori program, concerned about his struggle with speech and his viability in an increasingly structured academic situation. We continued to work with him, utilizing the various tools and resources provided by some of the specialists we had met.

One afternoon, when I went to collect Forrest after class, his teacher pulled me aside. With tears in her eyes, she explained to me how, each day, the children had a sharing period, a kind of show-and-tell where they were encouraged to tell their classmates about incidents and events in their lives. While Forrest always listened quietly, he had never volunteered to share. So when Forrest raised his hand that day, both teachers and classmates were surprised. The room fell completely silent as Forrest, in a clear, soft voice, sang "Hush, Little Baby" from beginning to end, perfectly.

Then, months later, on a warm summer evening with sunlight filtering through the trees, Forrest, with a growing confidence, led his fellow classmates in singing "Puff the Magic Dragon," then ended with a solo—"Hush, little baby, don't say a word . . ."

Karin Bjerke-Lisle

What's in a Name?

The smallest children are nearest to God, as the smallest planets are nearest the sun.

Jean Paul Richter

"Are you sure this is the name you want for your baby?" the nurse asked. "Shannon is more of a girl's name." I looked at the newborn boy in my arms. His head was small from the microcephaly, the low muscle tone made his body feel limp, and the doctors said there were probably more disabilities. Tears welled in my eyes, and my heart ached. *What's in a name?* I thought. *Does it really matter that much?*

After some discussion, my husband, Denny, and I thought it best to pick a different name. So we decided to name him Brandon.

While waiting to talk with a doctor, I sat back in a hospital chair and closed my eyes. My thoughts traveled back prior to the birth of our son. Life seemed perfect. We had a beautiful daughter, Rachel, a happy marriage and a bright future ahead of us. When the news came that we were going to have another baby, we were thrilled! My pregnancy progressed normally, and our excitement about the newest addition to our family grew. I noticed this baby didn't move as much as Rachel had, but the doctors didn't seem concerned. The day our son was born, though, we knew our life would never be the same. My heart broke when I realized there were problems, and the doctors worried about our baby's health. Caring for a child with special needs was not going to be easy, and our confidence in our ability to do a good job was more than a little shaky.

Tears streamed down my face. The past few days had been filled with so many tests—so many unanswered questions. I wanted answers from the doctors, but mostly from God. How could he do this to me? Did I do something wrong? Before Brandon's birth, I toyed with the idea of finding a church; now, I wasn't so sure. I was angry with God. First, he gave me a perfect child, and now I had one with so many problems. I didn't know if I had the strength or ability to handle it.

A few days later, Denny and I left the hospital with Brandon in our arms, heading toward a future filled with uncertainties and challenges.

For me, the next couple of months were consumed with doctor visits, caring for a newborn with physical ailments and tending to the needs of a two-year-old. Brandon's life was filled with one test after another. The doctors could name some of his disabilities, and some they could not. Though they admitted it likely would not change his care, they were puzzled and determined to find and name the missing pieces. *What's in a name?* I thought. *Does it really matter that much?* Still, I believed it was my duty to allow the testing, in the hopes it might help other parents. Exhaustion and hopelessness began to take over.

One evening, close to Christmas, Denny was at work, and I decided the kids and I needed to get out. The little church down the street had a live nativity scene, so I bundled up the kids and we headed out. The crisp, clean air felt good. I looked up at the starlit sky and let out a deep sigh. Rachel and I slowly pushed the stroller with Brandon in it down the street. A fabricated star shone in the distance, leading us to the stable in front of the church. As we approached, the star became brighter, bathing my children and me in its light. I looked at Mary, Joseph and baby Jesus. Something opened up inside me—I took a deep breath, and for the first time in a long time, an unexplained feeling of peace filled my whole body. A burden seemed to be lifted.

Not long after, I resolved to attend church every Sunday, along with Denny and the kids. My heart filled with the light of God. I no longer felt it was my duty to put my son through countless tests to name more disabilities they couldn't treat. I then realized my purpose in life was to love Brandon unconditionally, just like God loved me.

I felt enlightened with my new purpose. My world wasn't caving in on me anymore, but opening up. God showed me the light through a special little boy. What's in a name? I learned Brandon means beacon of light.

Joyce Adams as told to Kerrie Flanagan

A Tackle Box of His Own

Remembered joys are never past; at once the fountain, stream and sea, they were, they are, they yet shall be.

James Montgomery

I chose a warm April day to introduce my son Shawn to fishing and thought that a nearby farm would be the perfect place to help him catch his first fish. I should have known that the lesson would last only five minutes; my three-year-old preferred chasing butterflies, picking weeds and running through the tall grass.

We arrived home tired, but happy, until I opened the car door to remove my young butterfly-chaser from his car seat. I spied a tick crawling up his arm and shrieked, quickly dragging him from the car seat and toting him into the bathroom. I stripped off his fuzzy sweatshirt and beheld an army of ticks marching up the seams. Motherly squawks echoed from the bathroom as I picked off critters one by one, flinging them into the toilet. Shawn watched my tantrum and soon retreated to the kitchen. I'm sure the sport declined on his priority list of fun things to do that day!

Before he entered preschool, the two of us visited relatives who lived near a lake, a cherished childhood spot of mine. I remembered catching lunkers the size of semitrucks and hoped this excursion would strengthen my son's love for the outdoors.

We no sooner applied bait to hooks and cast our lines in the water when Shawn announced, in his most entertaining voice, a "call of nature." Stand-up comedy wasn't appropriate, and neither restrooms nor bushes were available. I pondered what my husband, Mike, the hunter, would recommend. I instructed Shawn to sit, hanging his bottom over a log, and explained Daddy's method. The four-year-old shook his head in disbelief, but arranged his clothing and sat across the designated log. Looking sullenly up at me, he loudly proclaimed, "Mom, this is *not* pleasant!"

When my youngster was about seven years old, I once again attempted to instill a love for the outdoors, this time on a vacation on the White River in Arkansas. We rented a boat and watched wildlife while drifting. Shawn couldn't sit still, constantly tangled his line, and hopped up and down from the boat seat like a dime-store pop-up toy. Consequently, he stayed in trouble much of the morning.

Stopping for a break, we stepped out of the boat and rested on a picnic bench. I fretted over yet another failed attempt to ingrain a love of the great outdoors in my first-grader. Sniffling back tears, Shawn leaned his little head on my shoulder and moaned with a sigh of despair well beyond his years, "I don't think fishing is gonna be one of my best hobbies, Mom." His confession brought me to tears.

Eventually, during Shawn's preteen years, he finally gained an appreciation for nature. In our rural neighborhood, a nearby pond contained giant catfish, and I felt secure with Shawn and a buddy fishing there. One evening, they ran home as fast as twelve-year-old legs could carry them. With much hand gesturing and laughter, they described catching a huge catfish whose escape attempts were prevented by their "manly courage." Fishing had at last become his best hobby!

Understanding this special occasion in our son's life, Mike and I decided he might enjoy a tackle box of his own. When we asked, a huge smile gave us the answer. We returned from a trip to Wal-Mart with hooks, sinkers, corks and a small black tackle box. I praised Shawn for perfectly organizing all his gear.

For the remainder of those puppy days of summer, the boys headed to the pond each morning and stayed until the heat changed the atmosphere from a catfish hole to a swimming pool. Each day Shawn returned home with sweaty face, sunburned shoulders and a firm grip on his tackle box, thrilling his mother with fresh sagas of belly flops and tales of Old Whisker's kin who got away.

Life passed quickly from that point. In anticipation of retirement, we sold our house and moved into town. We rented a duplex so small that the majority of our garage items were stored in a friend's shed, including all the fishing tackle. Shawn waited until the last minute to pack. After all, meeting his friends and driving his truck were more important than helping Dad move items to storage.

While Mike left to begin building our dream home in Arkansas on the White River, Shawn and I stayed awaiting my retirement and his high-school graduation. Prom night arrived in April, and this very proud mother watched as her handsome teenager left to collect his date. He never returned. That evening a drunk driver killed our young fisherman.

Mike and I moved that summer and faced our most difficult task—unpacking our son's belongings—including his beloved tackle box, still organized with lures and hooks in separate trays as he had left them.

Months before Shawn's death, the retirement plan was to develop a trout resort called "Angels Retreat." Our idea had been, with our son's help, to teach others about this beautiful place. Stranded in our grief and bitterness, we almost changed the name—angels were the last topic we wanted to confront. Yet, there was a certain peace here, and we kept the title.

Sometimes, when I sit on our back porch swing and look over the river, I smile. I reflect on teaching my little boy to appreciate the offerings of Mother Nature, about picking ticks off little socks, and yarns about old catfish at the bottom of a neighbor's pond. I dream about having my young fisherman here with me on moonlit nights when whippoorwills call and screech owls answer. Explanations never come back to me, but I have my special fishing memories, my picture albums and a small black tackle box to give to some other little boy . . . when the right one comes along.

Rita Billbe

Reconnecting

There is in all this cold and hollow world no fount of deep, strong, deathless love, save that within a mother's heart.

Felicia Hemans

My son Kent and I always had a great bond. Our communications were cemented by his sharing grade-school notes on the refrigerator, long journal entries crammed on the back of postcards during climbs and treks, late-night e-mails that ended with, "Mom, I think I need a woman," and phone calls about interesting females, all of whom were apparently forgotten as soon as he met Janet. The minute he told me, "Mom, she's a park ranger, she paints her toenails and wears a toe ring," I knew that this attractive young woman was a good match for him.

They planned a June wedding in California, unaware that his parents' marriage had unraveled back home in Kansas. I was the one to tell both of the children, living far away, in a letter. My daughter came and worked through communication with both her father and me. Kent did not respond. I finally reached him by phone and was met by a vehement, "I don't want to hear about it, Mom!"

I managed to stay outwardly calm while we finished the conversation as quickly as possible. Asking about their wedding plans was painful and confusing for me, so I ventured, "How's work?" A one-word answer, "Fine," exhausted that subject. Weather was about the only topic that didn't evoke some reference to family or the chasm that loomed between us.

From that day, we exchanged civil calls and e-mails about mundane happenings and family news, but I had no clue what he was really thinking.

Each time I would start to write feelings once easily expressed and received, his denied anger echoed in my head. In fear that I would say something to turn him against his father—or further against me—I would hit *delete*, not *send*.

The grief was almost as heavy as with the divorce itself. I had also lost my son.

Months later, I awakened with the conviction that I must speak from the heart. I wrote an e-mail and hit send:

> *Dear Kent,*
>
> *It came to me this morning that you're possibly having as much of a struggle coming to some kind of clarity over this divorce as I am . . .*

I told him how wounded I felt at first, how I came to realize that the marriage couldn't be "fixed," that I would miss my in-laws until they got comfortable enough with my being outside the clan to reestablish friendship ties, and assured him that neither his dad nor I wished the other ill after thirty-six years.

> *I don't see a single thing you or your sister did or didn't do as affecting our decision to divorce. Dad*

assured me that he loves you both just as much as ever.
I do, too, and always will.

Ramblings from an aging mom or, maybe, insights
from within a cracked cocoon when I'd like to see from
the perspective of a butterfly.

A three-page answer came immediately. Kent's old voice was there, honestly telling me what he thought and felt. He recounted his fiancée's quizzical look when he spoke of his parents' "perfectly balanced marriage," of Mr. Sequential vs. Mrs. Random, taciturn vs. gregarious personalities, nightly TV vs. frequent travel, retiree vs. second-career seeker, stock market vs. spiritual reader. Our breakup had rocked Kent to the core. He was about to commit to a marriage when most of his friends scorned the convention, and his role models had just chopped it all off at their clay ankles. He was anxious about how we'd handle the upcoming wedding.

He wrote that our superficial communication had taken its toll on him, too, but it had given him time to decide what he did and did not want from married life. He would work to keep common interests alive in his marriage and thought he might actually be a better husband from what he had learned from us. Above all, he loved us both.

The sweet relief I felt is difficult to describe. I read his letter over and over, grateful for the healing passage of time that brought insight and courage (or desperation?), that helped me stick my neck out vulnerably, and risk that helped us both to grow. Mostly, I felt thankful for the mother-son bond, mended.

Virginia Fortner

Forwarded Prayer

Remember, whatever warrant you have for praying, you have the same warrant to believe your prayers will be answered.

John Phillips

Like every other Tuesday morning, after driving my middle son to the high school, I returned home at 8:00 to read my e-mails before waking the younger children for school. A woman from our church had sent me a prayer, with the request to pass it on to all those I thought might need it. I sent it to my best friend, a new Christian; to an ill woman in my writer's group; and to my sister, who had just recently acknowledged her belief in the power of prayer. The last person I sent it to was my oldest son, Scott. Just twenty years old, he lived in his own apartment a couple of miles away and was a part-time inexperienced mate on a lobster boat. Scott balked at my fears of him fishing or lobstering. I knew he was at work but would find my e-mail with the prayer when he returned home.

As my day progressed, so did my workload, and I ran errands for most of the morning. When I returned home around noon, I found Scott sitting on our couch with one foot wrapped in plastic and duct tape. He stood up and gave me the biggest hug I'd ever received. I felt him trembling. "What's happened?"

He plopped back on the couch with his arm still around me. "My captain and I went out at three o'clock this morning to pull traps. Around eight, I was in charge of throwing the lines of traps over the side of the boat while he was at the helm. I had no idea my foot was tangled in the line when I threw it." His voice quaked as he recounted the weight of the traps pulling him over the side of the boat, fighting with all his strength to hold on, feeling the icy cold of the black water below, knowing that without immediate help, death was looming.

The captain, oblivious to the situation, had continued steering the boat along its course. After a few minutes, he peeked around the corner to shout to Scott.

"Oh, dear God!" he exclaimed as he hurried toward my son, dangling over the side of the boat. He frantically cut the line holding the traps and pulled Scott to safety.

As I praised God and hugged my son closer, I understood what so many fishermen had told me about respecting the sea, that it was unmerciful to those who failed to learn its power.

After Scott returned to his apartment, I received an e-mail from him. "Mom, the prayer you forwarded came at eight o'clock! That was the same moment I was holding onto life with all my might!"

The moment when God's strength had provided his.

Kimberly Ripley

Ma & Me & Gin

"What's the name of the game?"

That became my mother's tagline. If you heard this phrase you knew you'd had it. Her chin elevated a little, her eyelashes fluttered, and her voice jumped an octave. My mother never exclaimed *"Gin!"* when she won. It just wasn't her way.

For the past twenty years, my mother and I have marked the time with thousands of games of Gin. This simple card game saw my mother and me through all kinds of strife. For years I tried to grow up and accept the world for what it was, mostly unsuccessfully. Mom saw the one thing she lived for disintegrate. Then she spent a few decades putting herself back together. Somewhere along the way, our two lives intersected again, and we developed a loving friendship as mother and son. Through it all, however, we never stopped playing Gin. Through good times and bad, the cards continued to be shuffled and dealt.

I was fifteen when Ma told me I couldn't live at her house anymore. She had every right to get rid of me. I was a rotten kid and completely out of control. She did what most mothers do in her situation: She sent me to live with my father. Pig-headed jerk that I was, I smirked and left my boyhood home. It never occurred to me how much I'd miss it.

Years before that, our family had imploded. Older siblings stayed away at schools. Dad left to start a new life. My mother tried her best to deal with it. She didn't do hospitals very well, though, so it took a good long while for her to fully recover. She uprooted her remaining family and moved 100 miles south. That, she felt, might give her the peace she needed to begin anew.

And that's how our odyssey started. She focused on the sons who moved with her, and I ran wild trying to find anything that might satisfy me for the next moment. I visited her home on occasion, although mostly to see my dog or brothers.

I visited her on Sundays for the express reason of watching *Poldark* on PBS, but we'd always squeeze in a game of Gin between dinner and the show. The games became uproariously competitive. We kept a running score sheet on the refrigerator that never went higher than ten wins. My mother wouldn't allow anything greater than that because of the psychological damage it might inflict should either of us suffer a lengthy losing streak. The champion of each game immediately stalked over to the refrigerator to post another victorious mark on the sheet.

Of course, this was preceded by many emotional outbursts as cards were collected from the discard pile or extensive hands intensified already jittery nerves.

Even the cutting of the deck became a sacred ritual— some perfectly even, others thick or paper-thin, shattering the nerves of either one of us.

My articulation of a hand ending with Gin was, of course, the complete opposite of my mother's. While she composed herself and posed the inevitable question, I would sing out the word "Gin" in a continuous, operatic screech. Throwing my cards face up on the table, I would jump up from my chair and waltz around the room. Using grand strides to mark the magnificence of my feat, I would wring every last ounce of passion from the moment. Sometimes Mom sat there making faces at me; other times she'd just ignore my histrionics altogether until it was time to resume the game.

My mother had her own quirky little game antics, as well. I certainly wasn't the only passionate player. Every time I selected one of her discards, she slammed her hand down on the counter, trying to take it back from me. A look of ghastly dismay swept across her face as she pleaded with the Almighty for a son who wouldn't treat her so horribly. If the ultimate insult befell her and I won, her voice left her and her cards fell to the counter from a hand suddenly gone limp. Conversely, when she was winning, she would cackle like the witch of the west as she shared her surprise with me.

I'm forty-seven now. My mother is almost eighty. We're lucky that we live close enough so visits don't pose too much of a challenge. We still play Gin almost every time I stop over at her house. And every time we play, I see the sparkle in her eyes. She gets to see one of her sons, and she gets a chance to beat the pants off him playing her favorite card game.

My mother took quite a few curves in her life. I took my share of lumps as well. Somewhere along both of those roads, we found each other again. A little card game called Gin helped us on our way back to each other. When she finally passes on, I doubt I'll ever find another opponent who will provide the competitive fire she and I share. For now, though, we'll continue to grow closer with a deck of cards and a loving friendship.

Kevin Kilpatrick

Whoever You Are, I Love You

A child enters your home and for the next twenty years makes so much noise you can hardly stand it. The child departs, leaving the house so silent you think you are going mad.

John Andrew Holmes

I never know who I am going to be when I visit my mother these days.

She has told me, on different days, even from one moment to the next, that I am her husband, her beloved brother-in-law, her grandmother. Then, on her good days, I am just Jim, or Jimmy, her son. Those are my good days, too.

It's confusing and frustrating for both of us. My mother doesn't have much to say to me anymore. She sits in silence, and I try to prod her into saying something. She searches for the right words and knows what she wants to say. I can see it in her blue eyes, still bright, and I know it hurts her when her search is fruitless.

"Why do I call you Mom?" I prodded her one day.

"Because you're my grandmother," she said.

"C'mon," I beseech her, "why do I call you Mom?"

She looks at me, a bit puzzled by my inquisition. It's more than she can handle. Finally, she offers, "Whoever you are, I love you."

I've always known that.

My mother, Mary O'Brien, has resided the past five years in a nursing care center. After some bad falls, she didn't want to walk anymore for fear she'd fall again. She has been in bed or in a wheelchair ever since.

"I like it here," she tells me repeatedly. "They couldn't be nicer to me. I always try to make the best of it. I'm just getting old and rusty. It makes me feel better when you stop."

The feeling is mutual.

The admissions director kisses my mother whenever she sees her in the hallways. "She's one of my favorites." She asked my mother to identify me.

"That's Jim O'Brien, my son," she says, proudly.

"See, she knows," cried the director. "She fools you now and then."

I visited my mother on New Year's Eve, her ninety-fourth birthday. My wife, Kathie, came with me, and we brought birthday and Christmas gifts. I came back the next day to find Mom dressed in one of the new jerseys I had picked out for her. It was embroidered with cardinals on a fence in front of a home in a snow-covered field.

My mother's white hair was combed just right. She was sitting up in her wheelchair, looking lovely in her new outfit. She was smiling and more lucid than usual. She was making sense. I started to cry.

"What's wrong, honey?" she asked. I blamed it on the Christmas season, just getting overwhelmed by it all. She had a concerned look on her face. Once more, for a moment anyhow, she was definitely my mother.

I read her birthday and Christmas cards aloud to her. I recognized the names of relatives and friends and felt grateful for their kindness. Thank God for such people.

"Whatever happened to me and all that stuff I once knew?" my mother asked, feeling bad about her lack of recall. "I'm a complete failure. I forget things I'm supposed to know. I love this place. I just don't love the way I am. Not knowing anything. Jimmy knows I used to be pretty sharp. Don't you, Jim?"

I smiled, delighted for her recognizing me.

Then she added, "I've been so lucky to have the dad I've had." As I prepared to leave, she looked my way. "I love you, Dad."

Jim O'Brien

Pay It Forward

All that I am or hope to be, I owe to my mother.
Abraham Lincoln

I wasn't the first nineteen-year-old girl to have to tell her mother she was pregnant and not likely to be getting married then, or ever, to the baby's father. The confession brought a heavy sigh and probably more than a few private tears. Mom was not one for emotional displays. She was pragmatic. "What is your plan?" was her response to any number of emotional crises.

But in the spring of 1971, when my son made his appearance, she was fully engaged in a plan of her own. I would have to return to work full-time almost immediately, and she was firm: Nobody, nobody but Granny herself was taking care of this little boy. She was small and, at fifty-seven years of age, not terribly strong. Jason challenged her from 6:30 A.M. until 5:00 P.M. every weekday for three years. He was stubborn. She was patient. He jumped and climbed and ran as if he were made of springs rather than muscle and bone. She kept him safe. She taught him to knit and to hand sew. They cooked and baked. She always had supper ready when I arrived after work and would say, "You might as well eat here. I always make too much. What's the point of you going home and cooking, too?"

If she watched the clock or the window wishing for me to get there to rescue her, she never indicated it.

Jason was—and is—charming. He would flash his dimples at us, the sun glinting off golden hair, his crystal blue eyes dancing, and he'd have his way with us. He had two moms: a pretty young one and a pretty tired one. He was adored.

Thanks to my mother, Jason and I were able to spend our evenings and weekends cuddling, playing, getting by with only and exactly just enough, but as secure as two children with one guardian angel in a blanket and couch-cushion tent. He told his Granny one time, "My mom is magic. She can turn hamburger into all kinds of things." We were free of the stress that comes from weak support systems. My little guy and I had a solid one. We did a lot of growing up together.

When he was three, I married a wonderful man, and life took on all that happily-ever-after tone. Mom didn't need to do full-time care anymore, but she missed him and frequently asked to have him for a day. They would again cook, sew and sing together. "Would you like to swing on a star?" was her theme song. I would never deny her a chance to sing it to him.

Years passed, and we all grew up. Now Jason has two young daughters. His rock-and-roll mama is a grandma. My dimpled boy carries those babies into my house, one on each arm, both sheltered and secure. He moves with grace changing diapers and wiping spills as he coos and smiles with sheer delight over their every move.

I am not Granny, but Nanna. My house is now outfitted with a potty chair and a toddler bed. I trip over blocks and

Playskool people again. The babies play with Fisher-Price toys that are over thirty years old and find them joyous. Of course, there are outrageous new toys all over the house and yard.

One recent weekend, my granddaughters came here so Jason could work an extra shift at his second job. When he got here to pick them up, he was exhausted and fell asleep in the chair with a baby on his chest.

I fixed supper and let him snooze. To me, they looked like two babies sleeping together. I woke him to eat and said, "No point in you going home to cook. I always make too much."

As he loaded the girls into his car that evening, bathed, pajama'ed and ready to tuck in, he hugged me. If there is a hug more precious than a son stooped to enfold his mom, I don't know what it would be.

"Mom, you don't know how much your help means to me." Those dimples, those still crystal-blue eyes that always smile.

"Oh, yes, I do. I do."

Beadrin Youngdahl

6

LIFE LESSONS

You give up yourself, and finally you don't even mind. I wouldn't have missed this for anything. It humbled my ego and stretched my soul. It gave me whatever crumbs of wisdom I possess today.

Erica Jong

Happy Father's Day, Mom

Gratitude is the heart of memory.

French Proverb

We know you're not really our dad, Mom, but in so many ways you are. We just wanted to say thanks for all the "dad things" you've done for us, but they don't make Father's Day cards for single moms.

Thanks for teaching us that the screwdriver with that criss-cross point is called a Phillips and for showing us that the handle also doubles well as a hammer.

Thanks for allowing the belching contests we boys needed to display our fledging manhood. Oh, and thanks for letting *us* win sometimes.

Thanks for teaching us to clean up our rooms and telling us that women aren't interested in slobby bachelors, even when we didn't know what a bachelor was at the time.

Thanks for letting us flirt with the girls and test our masculinity without feeling jealous or threatened (you know you were always #1 with us, Mom); and thanks for defending us when their boyfriends came around.

Thanks for taking in stride all our broken bones, cuts, scrapes and emergencies, without fainting or throwing up.

Thanks for teaching us about the birds and the bees when nobody else wanted to and for ignoring the looks we gave you for weeks after.

Thanks for teaching us how to pump gas and check the oil, and thanks for letting us know in your subtle way that cars work best when the man takes care of these things.

Thanks for teaching us how to read a map like a man and how to fold it back up like a woman.

And when the money was tight, thanks for showing us that a little bit of imagination stretches a lot farther than a dollar.

Thanks for showing us that real men had better eat quiche.

And thanks, Mom, for teaching us to trust in God, the one from whom all blessings flow.

Thanks for being a good example of being a provider and for preparing us to be good husbands and fathers from a woman's perspective. We learned how to be men from you, Mom, by your example of what a woman wants a man to be.

And Mom, in spite of what happened to you, thanks for teaching us that marriage is good and that a father is to be honored.

We honor you, Mom.

Happy Father's Day.

Jeri Chrysong

Bundle of Boy

I'm sure there are women who dream of raising boys. I was not one of them.

It always seemed to me that someone who subscribes to *Victoria* magazine, collects perfume bottles and hosts ladies-only garden tea parties was simply incapable of manufacturing a male child.

But an astonishing ultrasound midway through my first pregnancy proved me wrong. First, I saw the unmistakably masculine appendage dangling there on the monitor in black and white—and then I heard a thousand delicate teacups come crashing to the ground.

My bundle of joy was actually a bundle of boy.

The very notion was outrageous. What a shocking violation of my privacy to learn that all this time, the creature sharing my nutrients, occupying my innermost regions and causing me to coo unabashedly at tiny pink sandals in shop windows was a *man*. I could just see him in there, leaving hair in the sink and stinky socks on the floor, decorating my womb with distasteful posters and brick-and-board shelving.

I panicked. What could I possibly have to offer a little boy? I'm dreadful at sports. I detest insects and lizards and other things boys collect in jars. I never could chug a beer, even in college.

Still, I could raise a sensitive boy, I assured myself. His name would be Stone, a simple and earthy sort of moniker. I would encourage his creative and nurturing sides, teach him about flowers and spices, and make sure he's a good dancer.

After all, who's to say boys can't have tea parties with their mothers?

There's no reason my son shouldn't prefer pruning hydrangeas and picking out slipcovers with me to playing Nintendo and shooting hoops with his pals.

Even when Stone was born at an indelicate ten pounds, ten ounces, and it seemed likely he was put on this planet to be a defensive tackle, I held out hopes the boy would be a gourmet chef—albeit a very large one.

But nearly two years later, I know better. Despite buckets of gender-neutral toys like teddy bears, crayons and baby strollers, Stone is an indisputable guy's guy.

He wants nothing to do with dandelions, but hoots with gusto at every passing truck and plane. He leaps into mud puddles. He throws balls in the house. He drinks his own bath water and follows each cloudy gulp with a satisfied "Ahhh."

He wears his baseball cap sideways and has a rather macho attachment to a filthy pair of pint-sized construction boots.

And he dances like his father.

Now, I am not completely sexist. I know there are plenty of girls who do these things, too, but the difference is this: Their mothers can still put them in a gingham sundress with matching bloomers and sigh at the pure sweetness of the sight.

I can't do that to Stone; he and his future therapist would drag my good name through the mud.

So I faced facts. Stone and I will never paint our toenails together and dress up in feather boas. We will never sit at a sidewalk cafe giggling over Caesar salads and flirting innocently with the waiters. We will never share the secret recipes of womanhood.

But we are doing something I never imagined—spelunking the mysteries of manhood. It turns out that guys have their own secret and seductive pleasures, and Stone is giving me private lessons in them all.

For example, there is great pride to be gleaned from knowing a backhoe from a front-end loader crane, and much joy to be had from scooting around the pavement collecting rainbows of sidewalk chalk on the butt of your brand-new blue jeans.

Stone and I dig in the mud and wear our dirty fingernails as badges of courage. We eat French fries and cheeseburgers, then burp and laugh about it. We play rough, sparring on the floor and growling ferociously until we're out of breath. We visit fire stations and marvel at the big red rigs in all their mechanical glory.

And together we beat our breasts in a robust celebration of testosterone, as if to say, "I'll take baseballs over Barbies any day!"

Starshine Roshell
As appeared in The Santa Barbara News-Press

Climbing in the Ring

*S*ports *do not build character; they reveal it.*

Heywood Broun

"Who's better?" I asked my bridegroom of several weeks. "Cassius Clay or Muhammad Ali?"

My new husband looked at me in wide-eyed terror. "You're kidding, aren't you?"

I shook my head meekly, wondering what was so wrong with my question.

"They're the same person!" he said, bursting with laughter as he buried his head back in the sports page.

As a young bride, I was simply trying to acclimate myself to my husband's world of sports. Although my father and two brothers enjoyed sports, their interests were nothing compared to my bridegroom's obsession. He watched all the games, knew all the statistics, analyzed all the coaches and listened to all the sports talk shows on the radio.

He tried his best to draw me into his sporting world. "Watch this replay!" he would shout from the TV room.

Dropping what I was doing, I'd dash through the house to catch sight of yet another spectacular catch, block, putt, run or leap. Although it was great stuff, the action didn't grab my attention like a good book, a long walk, stars on a clear night or a Monet on an art museum wall.

Even when I joined my husband on an occasional sports outing, I found myself paying more attention to the people than the score, the cool breeze than the play, the peanuts than the pop-up.

As our marriage moved through the game plan of life, three sons were born to us. Unwittingly, I had produced the perfect team for a game of pitcher, catcher and batter. While my friends with daughters got all dolled up for outings of lunch and shopping, I threw on jeans for hours of fielding, refereeing and yelling, "Run! You can make it!"

"Aren't you just a little bit disappointed you don't have a girl?" friends often asked.

"Not at all," I answered truthfully.

"Well, there's a special place in heaven for mothers of three boys," they replied, quoting from a popular parenting guide.

Pity is not part of my playbook.

So as each young son grew and took his section of the sports page at the breakfast table, I refused to be benched on the sidelines. So what if I didn't have braids to tie ribbons on, sweet dresses to iron or ballet shoes to polish? I wasn't going to be left in the dugout. It didn't take long to figure out I could be the ball girl, or I could step up to bat.

In short order, I became one of the boys. I pitched; I putted; I fished. And a whole new world opened up to me. Activities I never would have chosen turned into wondrous adventures.

As pitcher for the neighborhood pick-up game, I discovered the joy of a well-hit ball—and the earthy smell of trampled grass on a hot summer's afternoon.

As driver to the putting green, I marveled at the exactness

of nailing a four-foot putt—and the bird song that sere-
naded us from a nearby oak tree.

As threader of the worms, I caught the excitement of a
fish tugging on a line—and the shade-shifting brilliance of
a setting sun.

Just about the time I grew accustomed to these activities, the boys moved into the teenage years, and I found
my middle-aged self thrown into a whole new realm of
challenges. Because I often took the guys where they
wanted to go, I decided there was no point in just sitting
and waiting for them to finish. I joined in the action.

I spent hours on a cool overcast day climbing up a forty-
foot pine tree, swinging from a rope and yelling "Tarzan"
before plunging into the cold waters of a northwoods lake.

I rode the fastest, steepest roller coasters of a theme
park, screaming my head off, amazed that I allowed my
upside-down self to be put in such a precarious situation.

I attended years of baseball conventions, running with
a crush of fans for autographs of players I didn't even
know. (I can beg with the best of 'em.)

I found myself at the top of a snow-covered mountain
peak as a novice skier on a too-steep slope, simply because
my sons knew I'd like the view.

"Go for it, Mom!" they said. "You can do it!"

And I did.

The highlights of my sporting career came, however,
when my sons crossed over into my playing field. I knew
I'd scored when my eighteen-year-old returned from the
city and described the personal tour of the art museum he
gave his friends; when my sixteen-year-old discussed the
contrasting novels of a popular author; when my thirteen-
year-old spotted sparkling Orion in the velvet darkness
of the sky and announced it was his favorite constellation.

Hey, these guys even do lunch.

Not long ago, as we rode home from dropping our

oldest son off for his freshman year at college, my younger sons and husband joined in a game of sports trivia.

"Name three pro basketball teams that don't end in S."

"Who holds the record for most home runs by a catcher?"

I listened vaguely as I watched the silver-beamed headlights of farmers' tractors glide down rows of golden moonlit cornfields. Breathing in the sweet scent of the late summer harvest, I noticed a sudden lull in their questioning. I seized the moment.

"Who was better, " I asked, "Muhammad Ali or Cassius Clay?"

Stunned silence.

"Muhammad Ali?" answered one son.

"Cassius Clay?" guessed the other.

Their father burst out laughing. "They're the same person!"

"Hey, that is a really cool trick question, Mom!" said one son.

"Let's try it on Billy and Greg when we get home," said the other.

Twenty-five years later, I have redeemed myself.

Marnie O. Mamminga

Rewind

The first duty of love is to listen.

Paul Tillich

A few years ago we decided to give my father a surprise birthday party. My son, who was then four, was especially excited about the party for his grandpa. Bryce spent all day making streamers and paper hats and decorating the house. He instructed his brother and sister as to where they should hide and how to yell "Surprise!" with the proper inflection and zeal.

When the moment of Grandpa's long-awaited appearance finally arrived, Bryce led the troops in the noisy revelry. But, as so often happens in life, reality failed to measure up to the great expectations Bryce had created ... the party horns weren't tooting properly; the guests weren't appropriately enthusiastic; the cake wasn't chocolate. Finally, Bryce could take no more disappointment and melted into a sobbing little heap on the floor. Scooping him up in my arms, I took him to a quiet room where he poured out his troubles to me.

"Sweetheart," I asked, as he flopped across on my lap,

"what can we do to help you feel better?"

"Oh, Mommy," he cried between heaving sobs, "can we rewind the party?"

"Honey, I wish sometimes that we could do that, but we can't rewind time," I answered, smoothing his golden hair from his damp forehead. "But we can start from right now and find a way to make the rest of the day better."

"Well," he sniffed, "maybe . . . maybe before we go back we could just 'hit pause' a little while, okay?"

"That's a good idea," I answered.

As I quietly rocked my little boy, smelling his sweet hair and feeling his warm little body relax against mine, I realized what an important lesson I had just learned from my son. Sometimes, when life is overwhelming, the best thing to do is to just "hit pause" for a little while.

Cheryl Kirking

Majestic Moms

*The dignity, the grandeur, the tenderness, the
everlasting and divine significance of motherhood.*
Thomas De Will Talmage

I was nursing my newborn when my middle son
Matthew came in from the thawing front yard. We had had
the Texas version of snow—an ice storm—the night before.

"I got all the ice off your car, Mommy!" he chirped.

"Thank you so much, sweetie! How did you do that?" I
asked.

"With a bat!"

Just another day in a house full of boys.

I should know—my husband and I have been blessed
with three sons, ages three, eight and twelve. I've always
had an inkling that there is something pretty special about
being the only source of estrogen in a household. One
night, during book time, my gut feeling was proven
beyond the shadow of a doubt.

We were reading *The Chronicles of Narnia* when one
line jumped out at me. The Snow Queen was ordering a
minion about, when he replied, "I hear and I obey, my

queen!" Well, I just stopped storytime right there. "What did he say?"

"I hear and I obey, my queen." My chaotic chorus replied.

"What was it again?"

"I hear and I obey, my queen."

"Oh, just one more time because it makes me happy!"

"I HEAR AND I OBEY, MY QUEEN!" they shouted, dissolving into giggles.

That became our battle cry. I heard it when they were being sweet. I heard it said through clenched teeth when they were annoyed because I stopped the fun to remind them about their chores. I heard it when they knew I was having a bad day and needed a smile.

That year on Christmas morning, the boys presented me with my very own tiara. Made of plastic, it had big purple gems, complete with matching earrings. I tried it on; it fit perfectly, and I declared myself queen of the household.

As my reign went on, I felt the need to share my newfound status with other moms of boys. I broadened my queendom, if you will, and re-coronated myself as Her Royal Highness, The Queen of Lakewood, after the lovely neighborhood we live in.

In April 2002, I held a brunch and invited the eighteen women I could name off the top of my head who were also drowning in testosterone. I hired my boys and some of their friends to be my pages for the brunch. As the moms came up the red-carpeted walk, the boys offered them their arms.

"May I escort you to the festivities, your majesty?"

As the queens entered my castle, they were announced. "Presenting Her Royal Majesty Queen Deb!" the boys shouted in the entryway. I then crowned the queens by placing a tiara on their heads and a glass of champagne in their hands and then sent them off to join the fun.

During brunch I listened as the moms traded war stories and got advice from each other. One mom, who was a pediatrician, *our* pediatrician, asked for hints on dealing with her middle son, who was more emotional than the other two. "Wow!" I said to myself. "If she has boy-raising questions and is getting ideas and answers from other moms, I may be onto something here." And the wheels started to turn. "What is our common goal?" I asked my reigning queens. Amassed from that conversation, a quest for queens came to me: Take over the world by raising smart, responsible, spiritual, mom-loving boys and have a lot of fun in the process.

In February 2003, I took my mission to the Internet and launched *www.itsgoodtobethequeen.com*. It started small— just a funny story about my boys posted once a week on the site—then a sign-up to get The Queen of Lakewood's Weekly Address via e-mail. After a profile in a national women's magazine, the queendom grew by leaps and bounds. We have official chapters now, my favorite being in Queensland, Australia.

I added a message board feature and sat back to watch the queens chat. Sometimes it's about favorite TV shows, party ideas or money-saving tips. Sometimes it's about handling temper tantrums and potty training. And sometimes it's about the yearning for a daughter or the overwhelming grief of losing a pregnancy. I am so proud of the fact that a mom can be all alone in the middle of the night with a feverish baby and help is just a mouse-click away. These moms are family, to me and to each other. On this journey through momhood that is the most unexpected blessing.

Recently, a mom, Queen Bethany, e-mailed me:

My husband puts his arm around me and says to our three-year-old, Cole, "This is my wife." Cole's response is always, "No, Dad. She's my life!"

Mission accomplished.

Linda Marie Ford

The Almost Home Run

Baseball is a drama with an endless run and an ever-changing cast.

Joe Garagiola

He stepped up to the plate, a tanned, sturdy six-year-old, for his first time at bat, in his first Peewee baseball game. Jeff shouldered the bat, longer than he was tall, with the composure of a seasoned major-league hitter.

The first pitch went wide. The second, too high. When the third pitch headed straight for him, my heart flip-flopped. He swung the bat, connected with a resounding crack and sent the ball sailing over the second baseman's head.

Flinging the bat to the ground, my son headed for first base, his chunky legs churning. He rounded second, passed third and was almost home when someone yelled, "Jeff, you didn't touch third base!"

With that, he spun around, heading back to third. But before he got there, the third baseman caught the ball. So Jeff dodged him and ran toward second. The ball beat him there, too. Then, not knowing what else to do, the gutsy little guy started running all over the infield, hunting a safe place to land—halfway to the pitcher's mound, a sharp left toward first base, back to third. By now the crowd was laughing so hard, they barely heard, "You're out!"

Talk about no joy in Mudville. I couldn't even enjoy the rest of the game worrying about how I would console my fledgling Peewee. Was he devastated? Would he refuse to talk about it? Quit baseball forever? And what could I, his athletically challenged mother, possibly do to help?

After the game, I gathered up my plucky little player and his older brother and headed for the car. As we pulled out of the parking lot and started down the road, the boys discussed the game, never mentioning the out. Then, on the verge of delivering my pep talk, I glanced in the rearview mirror and saw Jeff grinning broadly, his blue eyes shining.

"I hit that ball, didn't I, Mama?"

"Yes, Jeff, you sure did."

Enough said.

Nancy J. Knight

"Thou shalt not steal . . . except for bases."

©1987 Martha Campbell. Reprinted by permission of Martha Campbell.

It's Not Windy Enough

"Mommy, can we go fly my kite now?" My five-year-old son had asked that every day for a week. I must have had a traumatic kite-flying experience when I was young, because I do not like to fly kites. So when Drew kept asking me if I'd help him fly his, I used every excuse possible to avoid it. My most popular was, "It is not windy enough."

Well, this excuse was not going to work today. Today was one of those "blowing-bubbles days"—you only had to hold the wand out in the air and the wind would do all the work. I had no choice. I told him to go get his kite. Today was the day we would fly it.

We went into the cul-de-sac of our quiet street to begin our adventure. I inhaled a deep breath of wind, hoping to build my confidence. He stood quietly and looked up at me with big blue eyes. I explained, "I'll throw the kite into the air while you hold on to the string and run down the street."

Theoretically, I knew this would work. I asked him if he understood. He nodded.

I handed him the string, threw the kite in the air, and my son started running—toward me! The kite came crashing down. So much for theories.

I had him practice running *down* the street a few times, and then we tried again. I hurled the kite, and he walked backward this time. The kite went up—and right back down.

I stared for a minute. Maybe it would be best if we switched jobs. I'd get it flying, and he could take over string control. I explained my foolproof plan to him and handed him the kite. I walked swiftly in the opposite direction to make the string tight, then called, "Let go!" The kite went into the air. Success! I let more string out. It was still flying! I couldn't believe it! I let out more string. Feeling proud I yelled, "Come and hold the string!"

But it was too late.

The kite string went limp, and the kite started plummeting toward the ground. Panicked, I ran down the street, screaming at the kite, "Stay up! Stay up!" and looking over my shoulder every few steps to see if it was listening.

It wasn't.

Down came the kite and about a half-block of string. Out of breath from my fifty-yard dash, I stood at the end of the block, stared at my son and thought, *This is ridiculous. I'm getting too old for this.* But standing down there was a little boy who looked up to his mom. He had confidence in me—he thought I could really fly this thing—and so for him I would give it one more try.

Hurriedly, I tried again, before I lost my nerve. I didn't see any need to wind the string back up since we would have to let it out again soon enough, so I ran back toward him with a trail of string both in front of and behind me while the kite lay on the pavement. Just then the wind picked up and started to swirl the string around me. *Oh, no,* I thought. I turned around, leaned over, grabbed the string behind me, stood up and raced on. Somehow, though, the string got tangled around my shoes. I bent over to undo it. Then a gust of wind blew string into my hair. When I stood, I had string wrapped around my ankles, waist and head. I frantically grabbed at the strings, trying to get myself out of this snarled mess, all while walking down the block. By the time I reached Drew, I felt and looked like a helpless insect caught in a spider's web.

I peered at him through string-covered eyes and said, "Mommy's not very good with kites." No kidding. "Let's wait until Daddy gets home." Drew stood speechless. From the look on his face, I couldn't tell if he felt sorry for me or thought I was just pathetic. Either way, he didn't argue. He just turned around and went into the house.

As I watched him depart, thoughts raced through my mind: What kind of mother was I? I couldn't even fly a silly kite. I was sure this would have some lasting effect on him. He'd probably never ask me to do anything with him again. I began freeing myself from the web of kite string, but not from the guilt. Then it occurred to me: I was not a bad mother—I gave kite-flying a try—I was being a good example! I knew going into it that I didn't like to fly kites and that I was not very good at it, but I did it anyway. I realized I couldn't be good at everything. I knew my strengths and weaknesses. I knew what I had to work on (kite flying) and what skills I should be using to my full potential. Hopefully next time Drew asked me to do some-thing, I would get to utilize one of my strengths.

With a wad of string in one hand, a kite in the other and a new outlook on life, I went into the house. There stood my son, dressed in full hockey gear and holding two hockey sticks in his hands. Through the black metal hockey mask I heard, "Mommy, will you play hockey with me?"

I took a deep breath. Here we go again.

Kerrie Flanagan

Two Left Feet

It was my very first parents' night at Danny's school. His original kindergarten class had been split in half due to the large enrollment that year, so the teacher I met at kindergarten orientation was not the one he ended up with. A friend who taught at the school sang Mrs. Roberts' praises, and I was pleased to see that Danny was responding to her and to the school environment so well after only a month.

But parents' night—that's a biggie. I hadn't yet met this woman who had charge of my son for eight hours of every weekday. Suppose I said the wrong thing? Suppose she took one look at me and said to herself, *Oh yes, she's the one who didn't volunteer to help with any of the parties or field trips. Well, I already know how little she's concerned with her son's education. I won't waste my time talking with her for very long.*

Would she give me a chance to explain about a single-parent household? . . . and working sixty hours a week? . . . and mortgages? . . . and medical bills? These were all matters that sucked up my time like a big vacuum, leaving me precious little time to volunteer at school. I had explained so much of this to the first teacher. Did she pass on any of the information? Or was this teacher expecting to see some sort of heartless woman eager to pass off her youngster for eight hours every day?

I worked on my cheerfulness for Danny's sake. He was so excited I was going to his school to see his work on the bulletin board and to meet his teacher. His enthusiasm was contagious, and I felt a bit more confident as I dressed to meet his teacher, keeping on my work clothes (a dress suit) but exchanging my high heels for flats since we would be walking around the school.

We arrived right on time. Danny grabbed my hand as soon as I was out of the car; he wanted to introduce me to Mrs. Roberts right away. We were about twenty yards from his classroom when I realized my right foot felt funny. I sighed to myself, figuring I had grabbed the older pair of flats, not the new identical ones. I looked down to confirm my suspicions and stopped dead in my tracks. I did not have on the older pair of flats. Well, to be correct, I didn't have on a *pair* at all! I had on the left shoe from the newer pair and the left shoe from the older pair!

Danny was tugging on my hand to get me going again, so I swallowed my mortification and hoped against hope that his teacher didn't ask us to dance the Hokey-Pokey!

The humor of the situation finally hit me about the time I shook hands with Mrs. Roberts, so all she saw at first was a woman with a giggle in her voice and eyes that were dancing (even though those two left shoes couldn't have possibly done that!).

Needless to say, all my fears about her impressions of me as a parent were unfounded, indeed. Danny's first teacher had explained about our family of two and my working hours. Mrs. Roberts said, "Danny is such a joy because I know you are raising him in a joyful household."

Even though I had on two left shoes, we got off on the right foot!

Ginny Dubose

My Mother's Piano

The future of society is in the hands of the mothers. If the world was lost through woman, she alone can save it.

Louis de Beaufort

Music was my mother's life, and she always loved the piano. However, playing one was a dream she could never realize because, as a child of three, she'd lost her left arm below the elbow and her left leg below the knee in a tragic trolley car accident that nearly cost her life.

When she was five, she began taking tap-dancing lessons with her two sisters, and they became so proficient that seven years later the three were appearing at the Curran Theater in San Francisco. Yet, even with this early success, she wanted to *make* music, and through the kindness of a member of the orchestra, she was shown that it took only one hand to play the trumpet. For her twelfth birthday, her father presented her with a shiny cornet. It didn't come easy, but through perseverance she became an accomplished musician, and at sixteen became the youngest member of the San Francisco All Girl Symphony Orchestra.

In 1936, she married my dad, and two years later I was born. During WWII my father worked in the shipyards, and Mom formed an all-girl band that entertained amputee servicemen in hospitals and USOs. Through her inspiration, many of them realized their injuries weren't the end of their lives, but rather a challenge they could overcome.

Two years after the war, my parents divorced, and to supplement our income, Mom once again took up the trumpet, this time as a teacher.

When I was ten she bought a piano. I came home from school one day and just stared at this huge upright monster filling an entire corner of the living room.

"What's the piano for, Mom?" I asked.

"Oh, nothing. I just thought a piano would look good in this corner of the room. What do you think, Gary?"

"Uh huh," I shrugged. "Yeah, I guess."

Numerous cigarette burns had scarred and pitted its rough surface. Mom noticed my frown. "Oh, it will look much better with a couple of coats of polish."

Nothing more was said, but the piano was still on my mind, and later that evening I sat down on the bench, opened the battered lid and frowned. The ivory keys were yellowed and nicked from years of use. I hit a note. Then I hit several more. Hey, this was fun! Soon all ten fingers were pounding on the keyboard in a cacophony of discordant sound.

Mom came into the room. "So you like it, huh?"

"It's neat, Mom. Can I play it some more?"

She smiled. "Under one condition. You have to take lessons."

Lessons? I hated school, and now she was offering the tedium of *more* lessons? Still it would be so neat if I could really play it. Without much hesitation I agreed, but she made me understand that it would be difficult, and once I committed myself I couldn't quit.

"How long do I have to take lessons, Mom?"

"Oh, a few years," she replied as she sat down on the bench with me. With her right hand she began playing "Alexander's Rag Time Band," a tune that was still popular in the late forties. I didn't know she could play, and she explained that she'd always wanted to learn to play it properly, but because of her accident it was impossible. Yet I marveled at how fast her fingers flew over the keys.

"Someday you'll play this, but you'll play it with both hands."

I was hooked. For several weeks Mom and I would sit at the piano after dinner while she taught me scales, the rudiments of rhythm and a few simple songs. The following month I began taking lessons.

It was fun, but after a year the lessons became a chore. Yet Mom kept telling me I'd made a commitment and would have to stay with it. And I couldn't fake it either. She was an accomplished musician and corrected all the mistakes I made.

Teaching trumpet wasn't as lucrative as playing professionally so, when I was thirteen, Mom took a job with a band working three nights per week at a popular Dixieland club nearby in addition to her teaching during the week. And, as predicted, I learned "Alexander's Rag Time Band," though somewhat grudgingly.

After a particularly heated argument about continuing with my lessons, she agreed I could quit if I'd give it another month without complaining. Then, if I still wanted to stop, it was okay with her. No arguments. I quickly agreed.

One evening the phone rang, and she asked me to hop on my bike and bring her the jacket she'd forgotten. I arrived at the club a few minutes later and told the doorman that I had to give the jacket to my mom.

"Okay, but you can't stay here long. They frown on kids being inside without supervision."

Wending my way through the tables and over the dance floor, I waited until the band finished the number they were playing and then handed the jacket to my mom. Instead of her taking it, the piano player grabbed my hand, pulled me on to the stage and led me to the piano.

"Your turn," he said, and unceremoniously sat me down. "Let's see what you can do with 'Alexander's Rag Time Band.'"

"I can't play that!" I panicked as I looked over the crowded club.

"That's not what your mom told me."

I looked at my mother, who simply grinned and winked at me. I was trapped!

Reluctantly I started the first few bars of the song, when suddenly the rest of the band began playing. Then Mom performed a trumpet solo on the next chorus, and the place rocked. It was the first time I'd seen her playing professionally, and I was actually a part of it. I was overwhelmed and thrilled, and suddenly taking piano lessons didn't seem so bad.

Years later, Mom told me she wanted me to learn to play not for her, but just in case work was hard to find. "This way, you'll always have the piano to fall back on."

And, you know, she was right.

Gary Luerding

What Will I Be?

Being a full-time mother is one of the highest salaried jobs in my field, since the payment is pure love.

Mildred B. Vermont

After twenty years of working full-time, I found myself with an opportunity to quit my job and be a stay-at-home mom. As I faced this decision, I felt the stirrings of longing to be more of a mother than a career woman. My seven-year-old daughter and four-year-old son had grown up in the daycare system since they were both six weeks old. At the time, I never felt any regret in handing my children over to them each morning. I had a great job that I loved and had worked my way up to being the Assistant to the Vice-President of Sales at an Internet company.

I decided to resign and begin my new job as a full-time mom, but it felt strange to lose this part of my identity. The first time I needed to fill out an application for online banking, I came to the line that asked my occupation. I stared at it, not wanting to write "N/A." Ultimately, I threw the application away rather than label myself as a "nonworker." I continued to struggle with this feeling.

However, after a few months of waiting at the bus stop, volunteering in the classroom and making good dinners, I began to get into the whole idea. My daughter was in school, but my son Cobi was with me all day. For the first time in his life, I was all his. We Rollerbladed, took walks, played soccer and made crafts. He thrived on this alone time with me, and I began to see what I had missed.

One day as we kicked the ball in the park, Cobi looked up at me and said, "Mommy, do you know what I want to be when I grow up?"

"A professional soccer player?" I asked.

"No," he smiled at me. "I want to be a stay-at-home mom."

My heart melted. I've never looked back since.

Cheryl Kremer

Not Jeffrey's Mom

Taking joy in life is woman's best cosmetic.

Rosalind Russell

"Jeffrey Wilson's mom makes pancakes, scrambled eggs and bacon every morning," my eight-year-old son informs me, through a mouthful of Captain Crunch.

"Umm," I grunt, wiping sleep from the corners of my eyes and reaching for my coffee cup.

"Jeffrey Wilson's mom puts *six* things in his lunch every day, *plus* snack money," my son continues. He looks suspiciously at his lunchbox and then lifts it up and down.

"This doesn't feel like it has six things in it. And you never give *me* snack money!"

"Do you have a lunch?" I growl.

"But Jeff's mom . . ."

"Do . . . you . . . have . . . a . . . lunch?"

Sighing, he slumps out of the kitchen. I stuff my nightgown into my jeans, slip on my battered Keds and grab my husband's coat.

Jeffrey Wilson's best friend looks at me and rolls his

eyes. "Jeffrey's mom puts makeup on her face every day—even nail polish," he announces.

"Get in the car!"

He scoots out the door. When I join him in the van, I'm informed that when Jeffrey Wilson's mom drives for a field trip, kids don't have to worry about getting out of her Mercedes with a half-chewed sucker stuck on the back of their shirt.

I pull the sucker off his shirt as he gets out of the van and hand it to the baby while I gaze through sleep-blurred eyes at the parade of shiny SUVs and minivans streaming into the parking lot. I see many well-coiffed mothers wearing the suburban mom uniform of pressed jeans, blouses and leather loafers. Mrs. Wilson glides past in her lemon-yellow dream car and waves a carefully manicured hand at me. I slump lower in my seat and pretend I don't see her. I know there are other moms in this parking lot just like me, but when Mrs. Hicks drives by in her floral-print bathrobe, I don't even smile. Today the burden of not being Jeffrey Wilson's mom weighs heavily on my shoulders.

I wish Mrs. Wilson was a tight-lipped old hag, but she's not. She's very sweet. She has two well-behaved, spotless little darlings. I have four wild, noisy male offspring who, despite my pleas, often escape from the house with their cowlicks waving in the morning breeze.

Her children wear designer labels. My children wear whatever I can buy in bulk and on sale. Her three-year-old has been potty-trained for almost a year. At least my three-year-old dresses himself. Unfortunately, he prefers to wear red corduroys and purple sweatshirts.

Jeffrey Wilson's mom bounces out of bed and gets her children off to school so she can go to Junior League meetings and coordinate blood drives for the Red Cross.

I can't bounce out of bed. I'm afraid of hurting myself.

The only time I have for writing are the hours between 10:00 P.M. and 1:00 A.M. When the alarm rings at seven o'clock, it's truly a painful sound to me. Six hours of sleep don't cut it anymore. I tried donating plasma, but they told me my blood was tired. I knew that.

I rarely wear makeup around the house. When you spend most of your days with a three-year-old in red pants and a purple shirt, it seems pointless.

I'm usually very happy to be me. I watch the Mrs. Wilsons of the world in awe, much like I watch the *Crocodile Hunter* on TV. Exotic and interesting, but not a lifestyle I'd choose to emulate. This morning, however, the knowledge that I'm not Jeffrey Wilson's mom follows me through my day, like Pooh's little black rain cloud.

I sweep our cracking linoleum and think about Mrs. Wilson's glossy Pergo hardwood floors. The toilet overflows, and as I plunge, I picture the Wilsons' four spacious bathrooms. I doubt they even own a plunger.

At naptime I lie down with my mismatched three-year-old. He twists my hair around his finger as he drifts off, and soon I'm asleep as well. I dream I'm Jeffrey Wilson's mom, driving just two angels home in my Mercedes sedan. As I unlock the front door, I savor the scent of lemon-oil the cleaning service left in its wake. The phone rings. It's Nils at the spa, calling to confirm my weekly massage . . .

I wake to find Sam's drool has left a sticky mark on my cheek. The thought occurs to me that if I were Jeffrey Wilson's mom, there would be no Sam. I sit up and slip off the bed. I go to the door of each child's room and wonder—if I could only have two children, like Mrs. Wilson, which two would I choose not to have?

I imagine not needing a minivan. I think about how much it costs to raise four sons, knowing we could afford a much larger home if we had two fewer children. But then, we wouldn't need a larger home, would we? My thoughts become unbearable, and I'm glad when Sam wakes up.

We munch graham crackers and milk. I watch the crumbs trickle down to the just-swept floor. Before we leave to pick up the older boys, I carefully curl my hair and put on some makeup.

At school, my boys cram into the van, each one stopping to give me a kiss. I'm glad I left off the lipstick. Little boys don't want any visible evidence of their mother's kisses.

"Are you still going over to Jeff's house after school tomorrow?" I ask Zack.

"No," he sniffs. "His mom is having the carpets cleaned and the lawn landscaped, so no more boys can come over to play."

"Why don't you invite him over here instead?" I suggest. "One more boy is no problem."

"Thanks!" He musses my curls with his grimy hand. "I'm glad you're our mom!"

Me, too.

Cindy Hval

Popcorn and Dirty, Bare Feet

Many children, many cares; no children, no felicity.

Christian Nestell Bovee

"Don't slam that door!" I yelled at the boys for the fourth time. The screen door slammed again.

My sons were five and six that hot, sticky August afternoon. School was out, and they were home for the summer. I was constantly wiping fingerprints off the refrigerator door, scrubbing the kitchen floor, picking up dirty dishes and doing loads of laundry. I strived to make a perfect house, a perfect yard, perfect dinners on the table at night and perfect kids. It was so hard to keep up, though, and I was exhausted.

When my husband came home, he announced at the supper table, "Let's go to the drive-in movies tonight!" The last thing I wanted was more work to do.

"Yippee! We're going to the drive-in," both boys hollered in unison as they threw up their arms in glee.

"Oh, Stan, does it have to be tonight? I'm so tired."

"Come on, it'll be fun," he coaxed.

Yeah, it was fun for him, but who had to get the boys in their pajamas, pack the car with pillows and blankets, and pop the giant bowl of popcorn to bring along? "Okay, boys, you go upstairs and get your PJs on, and I'll make the popcorn," I said grudgingly.

Bringing out the old popcorn kettle, I added oil, then just enough kernels to cover the bottom. Slowly I moved it back and forth across the flame on the stove, and the kernels slowly popped. My mind raced. *Why do I have to do more work tonight? All I want is a bubble bath away from everyone and everything.* The kernels began popping all at once, pushing the lid of the kettle up and spilling popcorn out the sides. My emotions were bubbling over, too, but I shoved the feelings of anger aside. The wonderful smell filled the house, and the boys came running.

"Can we have some now?" they pleaded.

"Wait until we get to the drive-in," I answered, as I finished pouring melted butter over the popcorn that now filled a huge green bowl. After shaking salt over the top, I put on the lid and stowed the bowl in the back of the station wagon.

"It's almost dark. Let's go," Stan yelled to the boys, and they ran to the car and climbed in.

It was only a ten-minute ride to the drive-in theater. We found a spot toward the front, pulling close to a metal pole that held a speaker. Right after the car stopped, the kids ran to the swings to play. "Be careful and don't get dirty," I called out to them.

As the first cartoon melody began playing on the big screen, they crawled into the back of the old wagon, huffing and puffing. They propped themselves against the bed pillows and munched popcorn and giggled with delight as first one cartoon character and then another danced across the screen. It was a pleasure to see them having so much fun; I bit my tongue from saying anything to spoil the messy moment.

After a while it grew quiet; both boys were sound asleep. I cast a glance at the back of the car and saw the huge green bowl now spilling the last of its contents. Amid the popcorn lay our two children with the dirtiest bare feet I'd ever seen. Oh, how I wanted to scrub them right then and there, but then I looked at the smiles on my sons' faces as they lay in a peaceful slumber.

Why am I so worried about perfection? Does it really matter if the house isn't perfectly clean or the dirty laundry is piling up? Would it hurt to relax and enjoy them while they are here with me instead of trying to bend them to fit into the mold of what I think perfect children should be?

It was at that moment I realized those two little boys were already perfect. Those dirty bare feet could be washed in the morning, along with the empty popcorn bowl.

"This was a good idea, honey," I told Stan as I snuggled up close while we watched the final movie in the triple feature. "It was just what the boys—and I—needed."

B. J. Taylor

"Cleanliness may be next to Godliness,
but with Jimmy it's next to impossible."

©2000 Patrick Hardin. Reprinted by permission of Patrick Hardin.

Sliver of Silence

Let us be silent that we may hear the whisper of the gods.

Ralph Waldo Emerson

I crave quiet.

I feel starved for silence; like an Atkins dieter in a bakery, it's the one thing I long for but am constantly denied. My husband and I are raising four sons. They don't even *sleep* quietly. I've got two who snore and two who wake up talking, fall asleep talking and continue to chatter while they slumber.

Silence is so rare in my house that it gets my mommy radar buzzing. It usually means someone's tied up, something is being disassembled, or something's broken and no one wants to take the blame.

I wake up to boy noises—the din of TV, GameCube and computer mixed with the general hubbub of male rowdiness. They chew cereal loudly, and despite my best etiquette instructions, I can hear them slurping milk, though my bedroom door is shut and I've pulled the sheets over my head.

I'd love to wake to civilized conversations or giggling whispers instead of belching competitions, but my boys are rarely voluntarily muted. Whispering is right up there with silence on my mommy radar.

And then a miracle occurred. My oldest son signed up to be a camp counselor at the same camp that two of his younger brothers were attending. Okay, I *made* him volunteer, but he was pretty happy about it once he saw the cute girl counselors. For five whole days I would have an only child. That's when I had an idea of staggering genius. It was like a blazing chandelier glowing over my head instead of a fifty-watt bulb. Why couldn't I farm Sam out to his two doting grandmas for a few days and enjoy an empty house?

I placed two calls and made two grandmothers very happy. Sam had been feeling sad as he heard his siblings talk about all the fun they'd be having at camp. Then I told him he was having a *Two Grandma Sleepover Extravaganza* while his brothers were gone. He was delighted to be leaving home and packed his backpack immediately.

On Monday morning bright and early, I deposited three of my offspring at the church to catch their bus to camp. I took Sam to his first sleepover destination and hurried home to my blissfully quiet house.

I shut the door behind me and leaned against it, savoring the silence. All that day the house was still. The boys told their friends that they'd be gone for the week, so my doorbell was mercifully mute. No neighbor boys came to see if Alex or Zack could play. The phone didn't ring for my teenager.

Most wonderful of all, I had no chauffeuring duties. No soccer, play-dates, malls or movies. Even my car was quiet. It was a wonderful day.

Tuesday felt a bit like the day after Christmas. A little of the glow had worn off. I let the answering machine take my calls and sat down to get some writing done. The silence was starting to make me nervous. I tossed the rap CDs and loaded the stereo with *my* music. I played it really loud. The empty computer screen glared accusingly at me. I called my husband at work and let him listen to the silence of our home.

"Isn't it great, honey?" he said.

"Yeah, I love it . . . it's just . . . really . . . you know . . . quiet."

"Well, you enjoy every minute of it. You deserve it," he said as he hung up.

I wandered through the boys' rooms, marveling at their cleanness. Their beds were neatly made, all their toys and books on the shelves, and no dirty socks on the floor. The silence felt unnatural, so I spent the rest of the day at the mall.

That night I found myself drawn to those empty bedrooms. I really did enjoy the quiet and the tidiness, but it felt like indulging in too much rich food after a long fast. Tomorrow Sam would be home, making enough noise for at least three children. In a couple more days, these rooms would be overflowing with stinky laundry and dirty boys. And *noise . . .*

Someday these rooms will empty for good, and quiet will come, not as a temporary visitor, but as a permanent resident. I'll have my fill of silence then.

Lying on Sam's bed, I clutched his forgotten teddy bear and promised myself that I wouldn't complain about the shrieking, shouting rambunctious behavior that floods my home when the boys are here.

I'd had my sliver of silence. It was refreshing, but a taste of stillness left me sated, and I wasn't hungry for more.

Cindy Hval

"Those Kids"

*Few things are more satisfying than seeing your
children have teenagers of their own.*

Doug Larsen

The switch from a small, private Christian school to a
public eighth grade had been difficult for my son. Now he
faced the challenge of a new high school, with his new
friends zoned to attend another school.

"Can I please repeat junior high?" Jim begged.
"Everyone thinks I'm in seventh grade anyway. I won't
know anyone at my new high school."

"Best to push him through," his junior-high principal
advised.

My heart ached, but my husband and I agreed to force
our son to face his deepest fears—another new school and
making new friends.

The first day I picked him up, he waved good-bye to
a kid with short dark hair, baggy pants, an earring and
tattoo.

"Who's your new friend?" I asked, trying not to sound
alarmed.

"Just some kid named Jerry." I could tell his first day in a school with over two thousand kids hadn't been easy.

"Still planning to go out for football?" I asked. It had always been his dream.

"Yeah."

Then you'll find better friends, I thought, *and not hang around with these kids who probably get into trouble.*

When football sign-ups came, I dropped him off at the school, and week after week I picked him up after freshman practice. One day while doing laundry, I noticed his football clothes looked brand-new. As did his football cleats.

A quick phone call to the coach confirmed what I had suspected: Jim was staying after school, but he wasn't on the football team. He was hanging out with his new group of friends until practice was over, then timed it just right to meet me at the curb.

"I called your coach today," I said after picking him up.

"Yeah?"

"I understand you're not playing football."

Silence.

"What's going on?"

"I tried to go out," he said. "I just couldn't. The other kids were better than me. And I didn't know anyone. I just couldn't do it."

"So you hang out with your new friends during practice?"

"Yeah."

"Doing what?" I could only imagine. Smoking? Shoplifting? Skipping classes? How could my son be hanging out with "those" kinds of kids?

"I'm sorry, Mom," he said. "I'm sorry I lied."

The decision not to hold him back in junior high ate at my heart. *We should have listened to him. Another year and he would have had more confidence. Then he would have gone out for the football team. Then he wouldn't be with "those" kids.*

The following years were no different. I'd drop him off for spring football tryouts, but he'd come home defeated. "I'm not good enough," he'd say. "I should have played my freshman year. It's too late now."

My heart ached.

By his senior year, his dream to play football seemed over. To our surprise, Jerry, one of "those" kids, knew his desire and understood the fears and insecurities that had held Jim back.

"You're going to do it this time," Jerry insisted on the day of tryouts, as he walked Jim to the locker room. "This time you're going to stay!"

Daily Jim worked out with the varsity team, coming home with his cleats and uniforms covered with grass stains and mud.

"I'll never get to play in a game," he said. But game after game, he suited up, ran onto the field with the other varsity players and cheered them in victory or defeat.

Near the end of the season, his school played the cross-town rival in their homecoming game. As floats were driven off the field and the band settled, my husband and I wedged in among the packed parents sitting in the visitors' section. Blinding lights filled the night sky.

By the fourth quarter, our team held a twenty-point lead. Suddenly, a low chant rose from among the varsity players on the sidelines. Some picked up towels, turned to the stands, started waving to the crowd and shouting, "Jim, Jim, Jim, Jim . . ."

The crowd joined the chant, and other mothers turned to me, smiling with tears in their eyes.

With four minutes remaining on the clock, the coach signaled out the starting quarterback and motioned Number Sixteen, my son, into his first varsity game. The crowd went wild. I looked around and saw Jim's friends, the kinds of kids who don't normally attend football games, on their feet and crazy with excitement.

It was because of "those" friends that Jim was on the team.

The crowd jumped to its feet clapping and cheering as Jim threw his first pass. No, it didn't end in a touchdown, but his determination and courage prevailed.

A few months later, the varsity players, coaches and parents met for the Annual Awards Banquet. After three hours of speeches and acknowledgments, the head coach stood.

"Finally, we come to the most important award of the evening, The Most Inspirational Player. This award is selected by the team, not the coaches, and goes to the player who has most influenced his teammates."

The coach opened a piece of paper and read, "This year The Most Inspirational Player Award goes to Jim Pallos."

Jim stumbled to the podium in a stupor, grinning from ear to ear.

After the ceremony, one of his coaches approached me. "When Jim first came out for the team," he said, "I wanted to laugh. A senior who has never played football wanting to be a quarterback? He was so bad at catching the ball that we had to hand it to him during practice. But he taught me one thing: I'll never again laugh or make fun of any kid who wants to play football."

And I knew I'd never again judge a teenage boy by the clothes he wears, the rings in his ears or the tattoos on his arms. I smiled at my son, who was surrounded by his teammates.

Now I wished "those kids" were here.

Jeanne Pallos

A Mother of a Job

Son, Mother's Day is a week away, and I imagine you're weaving, sculpting or painting some brilliant little treasure for me at school and plotting a clandestine trip to the card store with your dad.

And while I look forward to choking up over these sentimental trinkets and tucking them gently into my box of beloved keepsakes, I'm not entirely convinced I deserve them.

Let's face it, you are only four, and even you know that I'm not always an exemplary mother.

I drive aggressively. I cuss occasionally. I refuse to play Monopoly. I let you go to sleep with sand in your bed. When you splashed in a rain puddle, I barked at you for getting mud on my work clothes. Once I trusted your friend's word over yours, only to find out he lied. I accidentally gouged a chunk of flesh from your cheek with my fingernail. I broke my own "no spanking" rule in a moment of pure, wit's-end outrage. (You remind me of it every time I tell you, "There's no hitting in this house.")

That's not the worst of it, either. Here are some things you don't even know:

I have hidden a few of your favorite books, the ones I can't bear to read again. I have thrown away some of the less-inspired drawings from your endless racecar series. I have dipped into your Halloween candy when you weren't looking. Well, not dipped so much as dove in, touched the bottom and did the backstroke.

I buy nonorganic fruit because it's easier and cheaper. I've got you hooked on *American Idol*. I've convinced you the "real" way to bake cookies is to scoop frozen dough from a tub.

And sometimes, I'm so sorry, sweetheart, I literally count the minutes until your bedtime in delirious anticipation of having an hour or two all to myself.

But I've tried to impart you with a strong sense of justice, so in the interest of that, let's talk about the things I do right.

I leave "sweet dreams" notes on your pillow every time I'm out too late to tuck you in. I play hide-and-seek till my bones ache from scrunching into too-tight spaces. I help you make lemonade from scratch, turning our entire kitchen into a sticky mess just so you can take a sip and say, "Ew. No, thank you."

I suppress my own intense squeamishness long enough to squash a spider hanging out in your bathtub, waiting to freak you out.

I come into your room every night just to listen to you breathe, smell your neck, memorize your profile and run my fingers over the dimples on the back of your hands, where proper knuckles will someday form.

I live for the warmth that spreads through my chest when I catch a glimpse of your perfect little naked body rifling through your overstuffed pajama drawer. I physically ache when my covert attempts to let you win at Go Fish fail.

For every time I've asked you not to climb on me or

cling to my legs while I'm making dinner, there are twice as many times I've secretly fought back foolish tears simply because you let go of my hand first or pulled away from a hug before I was ready.

I know it bothers you that I can't spend as much time in your classroom as the other moms do. I know I'm really rigid when it comes to cleaning up your own spills. I know you wish I would drop the eat-your-vegetables rant and let you subsist on cheeseburgers and brownies.

The truth is, I'm hoping my annoying habits will teach you the value of hard work, self-reliance and discipline.

I'm seeking the balance between giving you a fun childhood and molding you into a charming and responsible adult. I'm watching you learn things I don't know how to teach, like how to walk, read, hit a baseball, express frustration and demonstrate kindness. With each of your breathtaking, independent successes, I'm slowly forgiving my own occasional (and apparently innocuous) failings.

This week, while dropping you off at school, a teacher came to the car door to help you out. She seemed to know you, and I wondered if she had ever scolded you for throwing sand on the playground or comforted you when you scraped your elbows on the pavement and I (your preferred Owie Empathizer) was behind a desk on the other side of town.

The teacher took your hand, and you scampered off to class. Before she closed the door, the woman looked me in the eye and smiled.

"Nice boy you have," she said.

"Yes, he is," I replied.

Yes, he is.

Starshine Roshell
As appeared in The Santa Barbara News-Press

Our Mom:
A Book by David and Paul

Don't worry that children never listen to you; worry that they are always watching you.

Robert Fulghum

My brother and I don't listen to the same music. We don't always listen to the same teams, but we have always listened to the same mother. I've had seven more years of listening, but for over twenty-five years, we have listened together.

As most parents do, from time to time, she repeated herself in her everyday admonitions to us both. We always said she could write a book about the things she has said to us over and over. Somewhere on the journey, we decided that WE needed to write that book . . . if for no other reason than to offer proof that we had heard every word.

Our parents' twenty-fifth wedding anniversary afforded us that opportunity. Our gift to her was to start on our book. What we produced was only the table of contents, but it tells the whole story.

Our Mom
A book by David and Paul

Chapter I	How Many Times Have I Told You?
Chapter II	How Many Times Do I Have to Tell You?
Chapter III	I Shouldn't Have to Tell You!
Chapter IV	I'm Not Telling You Again!
Chapter V	Listen to Me When I'm Telling You Something
Chapter VI	I Don't Remember Telling You That
Chapter VII	I Don't Remember You Telling Me That
Chapter VIII	Well, Somebody Tell Me Something!
Chapter IX	I Don't Want to Hear It . . .
	but our favorite is
Chapter X	We Could Always Tell You Anything!

Happy Twenty-Fifth Anniversary, Mom!

This now hangs framed on a wall of our home where the echoes of each reminder can still be heard, even though my ears have moved on to listen to new women in my life—my bride and three little girls, who have lots to say.

Now when my brother and I listen to Mom, it is often through the words of an e-mail or over the phone lines . . . but always, in our hearts, we can hear those things that weren't always said, but daily lived . . . lessons that would fill more pages than any one book could hold.

I would share some of them with you, but I need to check on my girls who are making too much noise in the other room. How many times have I told them . . .

David Skidmore

$\overline{7}$

LETTING GO

The thought of our past years in me doth breed a perpetual benediction.

William Wadsworth

Don't Blink

*To my embarrassment, I was born in bed with
a lady.*

Wilson Mizner

To prepare for motherhood, I read all the current books
by Dr. Spock, Penelope Leach and T. Berry Brazelton. I
spoke to new and "seasoned" mothers and received a
wealth of information and parenting tips. But one piece of
advice I wish I had received was, *"Don't blink."*

One morning I was delighting in listening to my toddler
son's chatter as we talked on his Fisher-Price telephone—
I blinked—and one afternoon I called home to realize the
deep voice saying "Hello" was my son.

I helped him when my preschooler begged me to turn on
Sesame Street—*I blinked*—and my teenage son was the only
one who could operate the multiplying number of remote
controls for the TV/DVD/Cable/PlayStation/Stereo system.

I gave my son colorful Playskool keys to play with on
our way to the grocery store, the park and the zoo—*I
blinked*—and our Toyota car keys were taking him places
to explore on his own.

I spent wonderful hours helping him learn the alphabet—
I blinked—and in high school he learned new and frightening combinations of those letters—SAT, GPA and AP.

Many a day I commiserated as my little boy complained that there was no one to play with since only the girls in our neighborhood were home—*I blinked*—and he was asking for my advice on finding the best dozen roses to send his sweetheart for Valentine's Day.

On the first day of kindergarten, I dropped him off and worried for three *hours* until I could rush back to pick him up—*I blinked*—and I was dropping him off at college, knowing I wouldn't see him for three *months*.

When he was in first grade, I packed a bag for him to take to a sleepover two houses down—*I blinked*—and he was packing his own luggage to spend six months studying halfway across the world.

On a spring day I took the training wheels off the shiny new bike for my determined four-year-old—*I blinked*—and an even more determined young man had saved enough money to buy his own shiny new car.

Surely it was only last night that I was tucking him in and heading for bed myself at 10:00 P.M.—*I blinked*—and my bedtime now coincides with the hour he's heading out the door for a night out with his friends.

I photographed his adorable end-of-preschool pageant when he donned his paper-plate mortarboard and proudly accepted his graduation certificate—*I blinked*—and he was striding confidently to shake hands with the university president and accept his college diploma.

I always bent down to give my son a bear hug and smother him with kisses—*I blinked*—and now I reach up to show this young man my love.

I relented when, as a sophomore in high school, my son made an impressive case for why he absolutely had to have a cell phone—*I blinked*—and as a sophomore in college he was the first family member whose cell phone finally reached me on 9/11 to be sure I had made it out of the World Trade Center. "Mom! Are you okay?"

So to all the new mothers, take it from this seasoned one. *Don't blink.*

Pamela Hackett Hobson

"They grow so fast. Today he's in diapers
and the next thing you know, he'll be shaving
the hair on his chiny chin chin."

©2002 *Martin Bucella. Reprinted by permission of Martin Bucella.*

The Last First Day

The mother's heart is in the child's schoolroom.

H. W. Beecher

This was my last first day of school. My baby Rob, the youngest of my three sons, was starting kindergarten. I had already gone through this twice before with his older brothers, but this time it was different. I knew this was my last time. Being the third boy in our family, he was more than ready for his first day of school. I, on the other hand, was not. I was a wreck.

What if he was scared? What if he missed me? What if he needed me? I decided to try and do the grown-up thing and not tell him how I felt. I assured him that he was a big boy now and that everything would be just fine. He, on the other hand, knew that everything would be fine—but he wasn't absolutely sure I would be.

The night before school started, Rob and I went into his bedroom, just the two of us. I wanted to have a few minutes alone with him. I sat down with him, hugged him and asked if he had any questions about what he could expect tomorrow when he went to his big new school. We had visited the school, been to his classroom and met his teacher.

"I'm really excited, Mommy, but I'm a little worried about what I should do if I miss you," he confided sheepishly.

I had just the answer for him.

I opened my hand and showed him a brand-new, shiny penny. "This is a lucky magic penny you can take to school with you. If you're scared or lonely or if you miss me, just put your hand in your pocket and hold on to this lucky penny. Every time you hold it and think of me, I will know and be thinking about you, too."

It was absolutely true. I'd be thinking about him every minute.

School started bright and early the next day. Tucked in the pocket of Rob's new jeans was that lucky penny. As he entered his schoolroom, he looked back at me, put his hand in his pocket and smiled. My baby looked so sure of himself. I smiled back at him and hoped that he didn't see the tears in my eyes.

The hours moved slowly, but finally it was time to pick him up. Out of the room he bound, still smiling.

"I had a great day!" he cheered. "There were a few times I was worried, but I held on to my lucky penny, and I knew you were thinking about me and that made me feel all better."

Rob carried that lucky penny to school with him for about a week. Then, one day after I had dropped him off and returned home, I found it on his dresser. I guessed he was secure enough in his new situation that he didn't need it anymore.

I, on the other hand, tucked it in my pocket for a few more days.

Barbara LoMonaco

School Days

Remembrances last longer than present realities.

Jean Paul Richter

When my twin sons started kindergarten, I followed in my mother's footsteps. I sang the song "School Days" while we were getting ready to go. I don't know if I sang it to make the boys laugh or if I was simply singing if for myself. There was one thing that I knew for sure, however: The more I sang, the less likely I would cry. I guess you could say it was a way to cope with the fact that my sons were growing up.

That year sped by, and the first day of first grade was quickly upon us. Again, the morning was filled with my "off-key" version of "School Days."

"Oh, Mama," the boys moaned, fighting back the smiles. Luckily, that simple song turned that bittersweet day into a joyous occasion for me.

Every year on the first day of school, the scene was the same. Second grade, third, fourth, fifth . . . all the way up through high school. The boys groaned and rolled their eyes, but I didn't care whether they liked it or not. The more they opposed, the louder I sang. Each year the song was a little easier to sing as I was learning to accept the fact that they were getting older.

Tears filled my eyes as I sang for their twelfth grade, knowing that the next year they would be off to college, and I would probably not see them on the first day of school.

The night before the first day of their college classes, Chad called home. He was so excited and wanted to share with us all about his new books and the professors that he had met. Before we hung up, Chad said, "Classes start at 8:00 tomorrow, Mama. Are you going to call me? We have to leave at 7:30."

"Do you want me to call, son?" I asked.

"Yes, Mama, I do," Chad said. "You have to sing 'School Days.'"

Nancy Gibbs

Back-to-School Blues

The future destiny of the child is always the work of the mother.

Napoleon Bonaparte

The house is too quiet. The phone has stopped ringing. The TV sits silent. No mind-maddening video-game music comes from the porch. Outside, the basketball hoop stands like a lonely sentry on an empty driveway court. The laughter and shouting that rebounded there this summer are just echoes.

Three basketballs, a dented whiffle ball and bat, a pile of muddy golf balls, one rusty golf club and two worn footballs are scattered like confetti across the yard, where they were all abandoned for the next game of choice. In a brief second of time, the action has all stopped. Today is the first day of school.

Although many parents look forward to this day after a long summer of kids underfoot, I find it somewhat unsettling. Perhaps it's because my three boys are teenagers, only a few ball bounces away from their own independent lives. I know that this quiet I hear today will be a permanent sound in the not-too-distant future.

To be honest, there's a lot about the summer teen scene I won't miss—like the aforementioned messes. Frequent and repetitive, they appear with amazing regularity no matter how many orders to the otherwise. Remnants of orange Kool-Aid sprinkled on the counter, pop cans deserted exactly where the last sip occurred, a minefield of shoes scattered at every entrance, newspapers left lazily throughout the house, chip bags tucked in a variety of obscure places, like under the bed or in the bathroom.

Add to this mess the scramble of their summer activities. Band camps, golf team practice, summer jobs, sport camps, vacations with family and friends, and our calendar looked like a spider's web gone haywire.

Throw in the evening summer social schedule of three teens, and our house resembled a summer camp, with their dad and I as designated counselors for the midnight shift.

So what will I miss about the boys' summer time at home? A lot. I'll miss the energetic sound of a basketball thumping on the driveway. The chance encounter of a good one-on-one visit in the kitchen. The kids' lively banter as they play pool on the porch.

I'll miss glimpsing the sweet innocence of young love as my oldest and his girlfriend cuddle on the couch for a night of video viewing. I'll miss my younger sons' sleepovers with their buddies, the late-night smell of pizza and popcorn, the low rhythm of their rock music, the voices of happy boys drifting upward through the house.

But most of all I'll miss the daily opportunities to witness my sons' gentle metamorphoses into young men. Under the fertile freedom of soft summer skies, I observed firsthand their joy at trying something new, their courageous comebacks in facing failure and adolescent disappointments, their delight in accomplishing a goal.

Sometimes, in a quiet moment, they spoke to me of an individual summer experience and cultivated it into deeper expressions of thoughts and feelings. As a gardener tending the most precious of blooms, I gathered the essence of their youthful spirits and held these bouquets close to my heart.

But every growing season must come to an end. One bright, sunny morning the school bell beckoned, and out the door, one by one, they left.

With the back end of his used pick-up truck piled high with boxes, a worn stuffed chair and his computer, my oldest son pulled confidently out of the driveway and headed off to his second year of college. As he turned the corner, the early morning light caught the gleam of his brass trombone perched on a laundry basket, and in a sparkle, he was gone.

A few minutes later, my second son eagerly backed the car out of the garage to begin his junior year in high school. My youngest son, a freshman, jubilant at long last not having to ride the bus, climbed in next to him. Their faces beamed with delight in a bond of mutual anticipation and camaraderie at this new sense of independence. With a happy honk and blasting radio, out the driveway they went.

As I re-enter the house, the quiet grips me. All is still. Even the dog senses in the silence that something has changed. He posts himself by the front window and begins his school-year vigil of watching and waiting for the boys' return.

At a momentary loss as to what to do, I grab a sponge and slowly scrub the last of the orange Kool-Aid stains from the kitchen counter. This simple chore gives me a moment to regroup and reflect. With my youngest off to high school, I know that in four short years, this phase of my life will be over.

Much like their first day of kindergarten, there's an exciting sense of new beginnings for both parent and child, but also a longing look back at a time together that will not pass this way again.

So on this first day of school, although a myriad of responsibilities await me, I think I'll bounce this stillness away and go shoot a few baskets. Besides improving my shot, the sound will soothe my soul.

Marnie O. Mamminga

My Sunshine

A mother's arms are made of tenderness, and children sleep soundly in them.

Victor Hugo

I am a proud mother of two loving children. Ray, my five-year-old, is vibrant and imaginative. Savannah, my one-year-old, is inquisitive and always in good spirits. Together they are the perfect pair, but still I try to spend quality time alone with each of them. Sometimes I put off the housework, and we escape to the movie theater or down the street to the park. Ray tells me I'm his best friend, and my heart melts . . . no award or fame can compare to that status. He is my best friend, too.

No one else kisses me with a milk mustache, rubs their sticky hands on my face and tells me, "You're the bestiest mommy in the whole world."

One day he said, "I would rather cuddle with you than watch TV or play with my toys."

I smiled and quickly climbed into bed with him. As we lay there, I relished the true meaning of motherhood. I live for these moments when I can hug and kiss my children any time I want. My heart suddenly grew sad, and I said without thinking, "I'm going to miss these hugs when you get older because sometimes grown-ups don't like to hug and kiss their mommies that much."

We both lay there silent for a few seconds when I felt his little body tremble.

Quickly, I turned him over to discover tears streaming down his face. He could barely speak in between his sobs. "Mommy, I don't want to be a grown-up like that, who doesn't hug and kiss his mommy all the time."

I squeezed him tight and shed a silent tear for the enormity of love my son possessed and for the sad reality that I thought was destined to be.

That day I put my fears to rest because I know that Ray is my sunshine, and no matter where I am, he can warm my heart, with or without hugs.

Our hugging and kissing years are not numbered.

They're only beginning.

April Garcia

Manual Training

Throughout our parenting years, my husband and I read everything we could get our hands on—popular baby magazines, church literature, pediatrician pamphlets, Dr. Spock—determined to parent "by the book."

And we took the expert advice that we read. We sterilized; we purchased safety-tested, doctor-recommended car seats; we locked away dangerous cleaning solvents. We studied each new stage as our child grew: the terrible twos, puberty and adolescence. Until we reached a new stage: teenagehood.

And our teen discovered cars.

"Don't worry," my husband comforted. "I read an article, 'Parenting Teenagers,' and it said to let your child earn the money for his first vehicle. It will be years and years before Kyle can afford anything."

Meanwhile, Kyle was doing his own reading: *Blue Book* and the classifieds. And my husband was wrong. It didn't take years and years to afford something because Kyle found a "bargain." A used Jeep. His dream car.

The vehicle was a bargain because it was previously owned by another teenage boy who had obviously never read anything. He drove the Jeep without oil. Check in

hand, Kyle raced out to make his purchase and promptly
. . . towed it home.

Have you ever really looked at a twenty-eight-year-old
Jeep?

Up close?

It was put together with zippers and snaps. I've seen
Matchbox cars that looked sturdier. Had I known exactly
what Kyle wanted, I would have offered to sew him a
vehicle. How could I ever trust the safety of my once
securely-seat-belted child to such a flimsy vehicle? It was
a decade older than he was, and it didn't even run!

And Kyle, who had never even changed a spark plug,
was going to install an entire engine?

"Don't worry," my husband reassured. "The owner's
manual came with the Jeep. We'll let him study it out and
tinker with this awhile. He'll never be able to take it to college. It will be ages and ages before his Jeep is road
worthy."

With bad weather settling in, the Jeep was shoved into
the garage—my stall, of course—where it took up resi-
dency. For the entire winter.

Meanwhile, Kyle rolled up his shirtsleeves and began
dismantling. If it was loose, he wiggled it off. If it had
pieces, he separated them. If it could be removed, he disassembled it. We were reminded of his Lego years. Only
now the pieces were bigger. Costlier. Greasier.

Soon, the Jeep bled onto the other side of the garage (his
dad's stall this time). My husband was right. It had been
ages and ages, and still the Jeep wasn't running.

"Don't worry," Kyle soothed. "I'll just hoist in this rebuilt
engine, and you'll have your garage back in no time."

Then he consulted experts of his own. Strange boys in
dirty sneakers and sweaty T-shirts huddled over the Jeep.
Parts catalogs, engine diagrams and wiring manuals lit-
tered the kitchen counter. Margarine tubs housed Jeep

entrails, and peculiar odors, loud noises and greasy finger-prints were everywhere.

Meanwhile, I consulted a how-to book of my own, *Keeping a Clean Nest,* and memorized the chapter on stain removal. Did you know that teenage boys leave grease on everything? Refrigerator doors, milk jugs, showers and sinks, light-switch plates, ceilings, and . . . toilet seats.

This job was bigger than Baby Wipes. I unlocked every cleaning solvent we owned. I tried everything. Some things worked better than others.

It was a long winter.

But, wonder of wonders, one fine spring day the slumbering Jeep stretched and yawned, grumbled a little, then rolled from its winter bed. We held our breaths when, after several false starts, Kyle coaxed it from hibernation.

We heaved a joyous sigh of relief. At last, the end of a stage. The Jeep was out and going, the house grease-free, the garage once again our own.

Now Kyle would leave the safety of our home for college. Driving a . . . twenty-eight-year-old vehicle . . . with a carburetor that hiccupped . . . and an engine that stuttered . . . when it was running!

And run we did—to the nearest bookstore . . . to buy a new how-to manual for a new stage, *Surviving an Empty Nest.*

Carol McAdoo Rehme

OFF THE MARK, *Mark Parisi,* ©1995. *Reprinted by permission of Mark Parisi.*

Changing Course

Grown don't mean nothing to a mother. A child is a child. They get bigger, older, but grown? What's that supposed to mean? In my heart it don't mean a thing.

Toni Morrison

It's hard to see down the road. The pouring rain and hot summer mist create a veil across the fields of corn as I drive my youngest child to his two-day college orientation.

It's been a week since his high-school graduation, and we've hit a lull. The excitement and anticipation of the ceremony are over. The future hovers with uncertainty. In the fall he will leave all that he has loved and known for a new life, and I will return to an empty nest.

With jangled nerves, we pull into campus and check into his overnight dorm. As he heads upstairs to his room, I pace nervously around and somehow enter the men's bathroom. I don't know who looked more surprised: the two young men or me. Meanwhile, my son has mistakenly walked into the wrong room and met the wrong roommate. We are off to a shaky start.

The day improves, however, when my son makes small talk with the kid behind him in line and coincidentally discovers it's his roommate for the fall. Big sigh of relief. He has a friend.

Next I check into my dorm across campus. I'm not happy anticipating sharing a room with a stranger after our kids dump us off at 9:00 P.M. for their evening of activities. I'll just want to read my book and go to sleep, not make small talk.

As I unlock my dorm door, my roommate just happens to arrive at the same time. Her friendly smile and easy conversation put me at ease. We both head out to our separate activities, a little less anxious.

The first orientation session with my son is on planning the students' fall schedule. Until this point, he has wanted to major in history education. As we listen to the information, my kid casually turns to me and whispers he wants to switch his major to acting.

Acting?

I remain calm.

Although he has nonchalantly mentioned this once or twice in the past few weeks, he is now seriously testing the waters. We both know the odds for success are about one percent, which means the $18,000-a-year tuition bill might lead to a career as head waiter.

Yet who am I to say, "No, you have to be a history teacher."

"Acting?" he asks with hopeful eyes as he gets up to leave with his academic advising group.

"Go for it, kid," I say as he heads out the door.

Waiting for the parents' session to begin, I think back to the start of my own college days. I can clearly remember what I wore my first day on campus: a navy-blue shirtwaist dress with a red apple pin anchored to my Peter Pan collar and red flats to match. However, since the year was

1967, I soon traded the dresses and pins for bell-bottoms and beads. The anti-establishment attitude, feminist movement and Vietnam protests were just heating up.

Being at a university during this poignant period of history led me through all sorts of twists and turns, disappointments and failures. Yet looking back, I am grateful for the opportunity to grow, the exposure to vastly different viewpoints and the challenge to really think on my own. I cannot say, as many do, that it was the happiest time of my life, but I can say that I learned a lot about myself and the world. In that sense, my college experience was a huge success. I can only hope the same for my son, no matter what choices he makes or opportunities he chooses.

Later that night, when my roommate, Darlene, and I are back in our room, we discover we are both 1967 high-school grads. We compare notes and laugh about the similarities of our own college days. Soon we are discussing the dreams for our children about to embark on theirs.

When I mention my son wants to major in acting, Darlene is encouraging. When she discusses her daughter's desire to balance soccer, a business honors program and poems, I respond in kind.

We talk late into the night, finally drifting off to sleep, no longer strangers but friends and mothers with similar hopes for our children. Both our books lie unread by the side of our beds. We would have made good college roommates.

The road is sunny and clear as my son and I leave campus late the next day. The kid drives. He is now an official acting major. We enthusiastically fill each other in on information we gathered about this adventure at our different sessions.

Winding our way back home through the cornfield highways, we listen to each other's music. He plays for me two versions of Bob Dylan's "Knockin' on Heaven's Door" by Eric Clapton and Guns N' Roses. I play for him Carole

King and James Taylor. He sings to his tunes. I sing to mine. Sometimes we sing together.

Yet the song I hope he listens to the most, this dear child of mine, is the melody of his heart. As he flies away and empties my nest, it matters not if he becomes an actor on the big screen, a history teacher in a small town or head waiter in a fancy restaurant. I'll be there, applauding.

Marnie O. Mamminga

Saturday Mornings

I hate it when that happens . . . you know, it's Saturday morning, and the only plans you have made are to sleep in; but you are suddenly brought into the day by the sound of a too-early phone call. There's no recapturing that wonderful feeling of being suspended between the past worries of yesterday and the eagerness of tomorrow. You're awake, and you might as well put your feet on the floor and begin the journey for today.

When we were first married, our Saturdays were spent mowing lawns or heading for the river to fish and picnic. Our family grew. Our treasured weekend time began with early morning feedings, giving baths in the bathroom or kitchen sinks and some great one-on-one time in coos, song or patty-cake.

As the boys grew, Saturdays were days you were awakened by cold, little noses pressing to your cheek. With their warm breath and in a faint whisper, they would cup your ear in their hands and say loving things like, "Mom, I can't reach the Count Chocula." Lesson well taken, you would rearrange the shelves so that the cereal was within their limited reach.

Assuming more responsible roles, the boys would get up, fix their cereal to hold them over until something warm, like pancakes, could be prepared. They would find solace in the only babysitter available at 7:00 on Saturday mornings and watch their favorite cartoons. They would keep the volume down, but their giggles and laughs would float down the hall to remind you that sleeping late was a definite thing of the past.

Saturdays were often filled with scouting events or school-related commitments. I remember the time we hiked four miles on a park trail and finally sat down at its end on the base of a monument bearing the inscription, "May they rest in peace." Or the Saturday soapbox race where one of the boys ran off the ramp at the start, dropping about three or four feet to the pavement. I prayed that wouldn't be an indication of his driving abilities later in life. There were river-raft races, ballgames, camping trips and our very favorite—high-school band competitions. October was band month. Every weekend was a trip to some competition, and it always began early, early on Saturday morning.

When schedules did allow us to be at home on Saturday morning, it often turned into washing the dog, changing oil in the cars or their very favorite—cleaning their rooms. As any parent knows, cleaning the room of a teenager usually takes more than the morning hours. No matter how early they start, it seems they manage to draw it out through the entire day. This frequently results in a bit of banter about why this is necessary, as it will all have to be done over again next Saturday.

The boys are grown now. One's room has been completely redecorated to accommodate guests as he has moved with his sweet wife to another town. The other boy's room, while he's away at college, still bears evidence of his "youth" by posters, movie memorabilia and a massive Star Wars collection. The lights may go for days without even being turned on in their rooms. The carpet is visible, no clothes scattered here and there. The things on the shelves remain on the shelves in their respective places. The beds stay made for weeks.

So I guess I've come full circle. Saturday mornings are mine again. Sleep late, get up and sit on the screened-in porch with a cup of coffee and listening to music (my choice) on the local radio station. In all the quietness of the morning, I can read or write without interruption. If I choose to watch television, I can flip over the cartoons and go straight to the Discovery Channel. I don't have to watch for toys on the stairs or shoes in the hallway. The towels in the bathroom hang where I last put them, and the tub has no ring. The refrigerator is always full. Our kitchen cabinets aren't cluttered with cereals that are pink or multicolored. When I get in the car, the gas tank is full. The house is free of brotherly squabbles, no frantic schedules to meet, no emptying my wallet for gas money or spending money to take on trips. But you know what—I hate it when that happens.

Andy Skidmore

"I feel so empty since my son left home."

©2004 Bob Zahn. Reprinted by permission of Bob Zahn.

Who Gives This Son?

My son, on your wedding day, the minister will ask, "Who gives this woman to be married to this man?" and your bride's father will answer, "Her mother and I." Shouldn't the next question be, "Who gives this man . . . this son?" For sons do not just spring from the ground. They, too, are nurtured under the protection of a mother's rib and enter this life through the veil of water and blood.

My body shook violently as I lay on the delivery table in the minutes just after you were born. While I was wrapped in warmed blankets, the nurses assured me the shaking was a natural reaction to the trauma of childbirth. It was my first "giving" of you, when your body was pulled from mine and you forever lodged in my heart.

As the years went by, the "givings" continued to be required of me. I could not stop them. And the trembling has not ceased.

As you grew, like any other little boy, you had your share of bumps and bruises, scrapes and cuts. But when you were ten, I was asked to give you to an open-heart surgeon's knife. After you were taken to surgery, all who loved you waited prayerfully. The doctor appeared, finally, to report the success of the operation. Thankfully, your recovery was uneventful, and a long scar is the only outward evidence of that day. What cannot be seen is the patch permanently sewn on your heart. Nor the pain in mine when it is grazed by the memory of that day.

There have also been many happy times of giving. The whole family applauded the appearance of the first hairs on your chest when you proclaimed they made you a man, or so you told your still hairless younger brother. He, no longer smooth-chested but a man now himself, will stand up with you this summer.

I vividly remember giving you the keys the first time you took the car out, alone, at night. You were so excited, it made my heart shudder. I was greatly relieved to see the car and you pull back in the driveway, both still in one piece.

I tried to leave you to your own unique style, without excessive commentary. My plan was to save the speeches for the important issues like morals and character (although, as you know, speech-making is my forte!). I didn't say too much about the baggy "skater" shorts you loved. I only insisted they be worn around your waist, not six inches below. And I attempted not to appear shocked, but only pleasantly surprised, when you got a permanent in your hair. I still chuckle when I come across the only picture we have of you in all your curled glory.

I gave in to your taste in music. Rap was your love, and the louder the bass, the better. My heart literally shook, along with the windows. But I was very proud when you and a friend won first place in a state-fair rap contest, performing original lyrics and music. You two shared a trophy, two hundred and fifty dollars, and my respect.

But not all the times of giving have been delightful. Against my wishes, our family changed from four to three—just you, your brother and me. My heart trembled with sorrow as I witnessed your suffering. I had to give you to the pain and entrust you to the One who gave you to me, since I was powerless to shield you.

Then, the summer you turned sixteen, I had to give you to the will of the One who made you, again. You had just returned from a week of church youth camp. When I tried to release you from a welcoming embrace, you held on, struggling to speak. Finally, in a choked voice, you told me that God had called you into the ministry. It was an awesome, humbling giving, and so it remains.

The training for your calling led you to a college six hundred and fifty miles away. The day you left was hectic. Friends called with good-byes. Family dropped in for one last hug. You and your rap-contest buddy were traveling together in a tightly packed car. All day long, the rhythm of my heart repeated, "My son . . . is leaving home . . . today." I refused to acknowledge its message. I wanted your departure to be a joyful occasion.

A prayer, a fierce hug, a watery-eyed wave, and you were gone. The overwhelming aching I felt reminded me of the day you were born. Neither time did my willingness to release you protect me from the pain of the giving.

All throughout history, mothers have been asked to give their sons for noble causes. With quiet joy, as a seasoned giver now, I am following in that tradition. Though the question will not be asked on your wedding day, I have already replied. Softly my trembling heart will whisper, as it has many times before, "I do . . . I give this son."

Leslie T. Britt

The Day My Son Became a Marine

A better world shall emerge based on faith and understanding.

Douglas MacArthur

"'Bye, Mom," he said as he quickly planted a kiss on my cheek and gave me one last firm hug.

"'Bye, Son," I managed, then watched him fold his broad-shouldered, six-foot frame into his friend's tiny green sports car. *I will not cry*, I told myself. *Not until he's out of sight.*

I had dreaded this day ever since he was born—this day when our last child would leave home. His enlistment into military service caused even more gnawing fear.

He wouldn't let me see him off at the airport. "No emotional scenes, please."

I'll stay busy, I told myself. *Try not to think.* No matter. My eyes kept glancing at the clock. Was it time yet for Flight 304?

At the appointed hour, I could stand it no longer. Running by the closet, I grabbed my heavy coat and hurried out to the backyard. *We're only fifty miles from Atlanta*

International. Maybe I can see his plane from here. I realized I probably couldn't. But I just had to try. I yearned for one more glimpse, even if at 20,000 feet.

I raced down the hill behind the house to a large clearing with a view of the sky in all directions. I barely noticed the near-perfect weather of an autumn afternoon. Instead I saw the old oak tree farther down in the backyard, looking forlorn, stripped now of its leaves. I knew how the tree felt. A part of my life had just ended as I said good-bye to twenty-two years of happiness. My chest hurt so from the burden, I wondered if perhaps the heart *does* break.

While my ears strained for the sound of an airplane, thoughts of past, present and future played leapfrog in my brain. *Where have the years gone?* I wondered. *Wasn't it just yesterday that we brought the blue bundle home from the hospital? Now he's going off to become a Marine Corps officer, with all that implies.* I kept seeing him as a curly-haired toddler with huge brown eyes shining in a cherubic face, all love and innocence. *By training him to fight, will they destroy all the tenderness that I've nurtured?*

I wanted him to grow up to be independent, and I was proud of his willingness to serve his country. But I didn't want him to go so far from home. *Do a good job as a parent, and you put yourself right out of business.*

Tortured with these conflicting sentiments, I'd shrunk from this day. Now it had arrived, and I stood searching the sky. Only a few clouds floated in the huge expanse. I clutched my coat tighter around my neck as the chilly air signaled the coming of winter, both to nature and to me.

Dear Jesus, help me, I sobbed, grasping for the comfort I had learned to expect from my faith. *Take away this awful pain.*

The distant drone of a jet engine broke my reverie. *There it is! That must be it! Rick's plane. It's climbing and heading north.*

Then, just as suddenly as it appeared, it slid into the heavens, out of sight. He was out there alone somewhere . . .

I stared at the vacated space in the sky. *Good-bye, son. Good-bye.*

Reluctantly I trudged back into the house, pleading, *Dear God, you tell us in your Word to cast all our cares on you because you care for us. So, Lord, here, I give you my burden. I can't carry it alone.*

But after I gave God my burden, I took it right back. The next day I was back in the grips of deep sorrow and self-pity. I refused to clean Rick's room until his dad could be in there with me. I avoided his radio workbench and the weights stacked neatly in the basement.

I was unable to do anything constructive. Rather, I walked from room to room, tears coursing down my cheeks. It was more than pain of separation. I sensed that Rick could never be the same; and my grief for that loss was wrenching, tearing.

Late that afternoon, I found myself standing at the kitchen window, gazing out at another afternoon sky. I don't know how long I stood there, lost in memories. But finally my eyes focused again on the old oak tree in the backyard. With its bare branches it looked as sad as I felt.

But this time I saw something I hadn't seen before. Those bare branches reached expectantly upward, confident of new life next spring. They presented a picture of faith, of trust. I felt a surge of hope, for it was as if God himself had shown me that picture when I needed it most. Surely I had known that I could trust my son to God. And that I could trust God to heal my hurt. Had I failed to reach up to him, in trust?

Forgive me, Lord, I prayed as I bowed my head and my heart before him. *Teach me, once more, to trust you in all things.*

A calmness filled my consciousness as I gradually yielded to our Lord's tender care. Finally, I could add the close to my prayer. *Now, God, I turn Rick over to you. I guess you had him all the time, though, didn't you? Thank you, Father, for those beautiful twenty-two years.*

Once again I studied the old oak tree down the hill. Now we had even more in common, that old tree and I. For I, too, reached expectantly upward. My burden felt strangely lightened. And though the tears were still in my eyes, I knew that this, too, would pass. That tomorrow— or the next tomorrow—I would smile again.

At last, across the miles, I whispered my benediction. "Good-bye, my son. Good-bye. May God, who loves you, hold you in the palm of his hand."

And I knew now that he would. Yes, God would take care of Rick. And me.

Gloria Cassity Stargel

Momma's Memorial

Stars of earth, these golden flowers; emblems of our own great resurrection; emblems of the bright and better land.

Henry Wadsworth Longfellow

February has been terrible here in the foothills of the Great Smoky Mountains. The sun hasn't shone more than two days this month. Wet weather is miserable stuff, and I am suffering from sun deprivation.

Yet, all hope is not lost. Mother Nature is beginning to pop plants out of the ground, waterlogged though it may be. One thing that has come unscathed through the wet weather is a group of bushes in my front yard. They are full of blooms already. I don't know the botanical or standard name for these bushes. I just call them "Momma's bushes."

They came from one piece that I dug from my mother's yard several years ago when I was still young and limber enough to crawl, yank and otherwise force things out of the ground. I brought home that one digging, set it out, and waited for it to grow. From that one start, seven more have grown. Each one is healthy and hearty, just like the one at Momma's house.

The fragrance of their blossoms is beyond words, permeating the yard and even the yards across the street. My brother Jim was visiting today, and he stopped suddenly, sniffed the air, and said, "Your yard smells fantastic! Momma's bushes are blooming! I need to get home and see if mine have started."

That bush's perfume—sweet-smelling stuff that makes the air thick and palatable—serves my family with wonderful memories. We think back to being kids and hunting Easter eggs. That bush always yielded several Easter treasures, since its branches bowed to the earth and offered a fine, although not surprising, hiding place.

It also reminds us of throwing ball in the front yard. Neither my brother nor I was much of an athlete, and our throws were often off target. We spent as much time crawling under that bush and playing tug of war with it as we did actually throwing to each other.

More than anything, the lingering scent of Momma's bushes always brings back the memories of my mother. She has been gone ten years, but the blooming of her bush brings her back to us. Mother loved warm weather, and as I do now, she hibernated during the cold months and leaped to action at the first signs of spring. I can see her working in her flowerbeds in the yard as she put out new plants, moved and divided old ones, or pulled weeds. She could take her crooked index finger, dig out the soil, and place a small plant or cutting into the ground. I can guarantee this much: If she put a plant in a hole dug with her crooked finger, that plant would flourish. She had God's touch in her green thumb . . . or, I should say, finger.

Momma's bush is special to so many of us. I have given "starters" to folks who have asked for them. I figure that my family shouldn't be the only ones who are blessed with such a wonderful, make-you-feel-glad-that-it's-spring shrub. Besides, we shouldn't try to keep mother or her spirit to ourselves; she was wonderful enough to bless the whole world.

Joe Rector

8

BECOMING A MAN

It is not what he has, or even what he does, which expresses the worth of a man, but what he is.

Henri Frederic Amiel

My Son

As a lad you held my hand
You walked with me
You sat upon my knee
I sang to you
You came to me
I wiped your tears
You needed me, I needed you.

Then my son, you grew
You dropped my hand
You chose friends to walk beside you
My knee became too small
You had not the time
For a rock or a song
Your tears subsided
You needed them, they needed you.

Then my son, you grew
There were other hands to hold
You took long walks
But not with me
You held others upon your knee

Rocked and sang love songs
You wiped away their tears
You needed them, they needed you.

Then my son, you grew
You took her hand in yours
You walked the aisle with her
Built with your hands
Your own rocking chair
She sang love songs to you
You wiped each other's tears
You pledged your love
You needed her, she needed you.

Then my son, you grew
A little one held your hand
You walked with her
She sat upon your knee
You sang lullabies
You wiped her tears
She called you, "Dad"
She needed you, you needed her.

Then my son, you grew
You became wise
You held my hand
You walked with me
We sat together
We talked of days gone by
You wiped my tears
I needed you, you needed me.

Betty King

Being a Man

If a man has been his mother's undisputed darling he retains throughout life the triumphant feeling, the confidence in success, which not seldom brings actual success along with it.

Sigmund Freud

I am absolutely convinced that male behavior and thought processes begin the instant the X meets the Y chromosome. How else to explain giving birth to a fully formed, bona fide *guy*?

Our daughter, Annie, emerged into the world feather-soft, sweet-smelling and light as a kitten. Her brother, Sam, on the other hand, came out raging and struggling. When I lifted his muscular little body for the first time, it felt like I was picking up a bulldog. Even his newborn aroma had a husky quality. And what an enthusiastic appetite! No doubt about it, we had a son.

As Sam grew, so did his instinctive maleness—using Barbies as weapons of aggression, finding delight in all things gross and disgusting, hiding his tears when a beloved pet died. Skinned knees and elbows were barely acknowledged with momentary winces, and my maternal fussing was dismissed with a mildly annoyed, "I'm *fine*, Mom!" Then he was off again at the speed of tennis shoes. Eventually, I figured out how he wanted to be treated—like a boy.

But I soon discovered more aspects to his emerging masculinity than just toughness and machismo. He was protective of animals, solicitously attentive toward little girls, and quietly perceptive of pain or sadness in people who mattered to him. The first time he grabbed my arm at a crosswalk with an urgent warning about fast-moving cars, I was impressed by his manly assumption of responsibility for a lady's safety. He was in kindergarten at the time.

One hectic fall day when my husband was out of town, I decided to take the kids to our favorite family restaurant. Just as we were about to pull out of the driveway, seven-year-old Sam suddenly unfastened his seat belt and said, "Wait a minute, Mom! I have to get something." Annie and I grew impatient with hunger while he searched for his GameBoy, Legos, Pokémon cards or whatever it was he couldn't last the evening without. He finally returned, pocket bulging, and we were on our way.

"So what did you decide to bring?" I asked at a stoplight.

"Well . . ." he replied with measured words, "I went back to get my wallet because I want to take you girls out to dinner." His voice had a hopeful inflection, the kind of laying-his-heart-on-the-line sincerity I hadn't heard from a young man since high school.

I was stunned. What prompted this? His offer was sweetly touching, but I knew that such an act of chivalry would wipe out his entire summer's worth of saved allowance. My first instinct was to kindly decline, insisting that he keep his hard-earned money for something he wanted for himself.

But a strong force of guidance stopped me short, and a

voice much wiser than my own urged me not to reject his loving offer. *He wants to be a man . . . let him.*

I looked back at my son's earnest face and saw that what he truly desired more than toys or candy was to be the provider, just like his dad, and to take care of his women. The sudden rush of love I felt for him was so powerful I thought I would burst.

"Oh, Sam . . ." I stammered. "Thank you! I'd love for you to take us to dinner." He beamed with pleasure, and I found myself floating on a cloud when the light turned green.

From that moment on, the evening was infused with enchantment. I couldn't have wished for a more charming escort than this little man with a missing front tooth. When he leafed through the bills in his wallet (mostly ones) and magnanimously announced, "I want to leave a nice, big tip for the waitress," I could barely contain my pride. The magic remained even when he spilled his water, got in a loud argument with his big sister—and picked up the check, looking horrified. (I discreetly slipped a ten-dollar bill to him under the table, much to his relief.)

No dinner could ever have been appreciated more . . . but I was concerned by his silence and somber expression on the drive home. Did he regret the generous impulse that bankrupted him? I was strongly tempted to reimburse him for the tab, but thought better of it. Maybe I could find some pay chores at home to get him out of the red, while leaving his dignity intact.

"Mom . . ." he said solemnly as he slid out of the car, "I'm going to need a really good job when I grow up."

I couldn't help smiling. In spite of his worries about the daunting responsibilities in his future, he was willing to accept the challenge.

"You know," I replied, "there's more to being a man than

just earning money. It takes a lot of love, and you already have plenty of that to give!"

I squeezed him with a long, enveloping hug, and this time he returned it instead of squirming away.

Jean Harper

Going to the Dance

An adolescent is both an impulsive child and a self-starting adult.

Mason Cooley

The spring night is cool and rainy. The kid is hot and sweaty. It's the eighth-grade graduation dinner dance, and adolescent anxiety is in high form. As I walk down the upstairs hallway to see if my just-turned-fourteen-year-old son is ready to go, I am enveloped in the strong scent of cologne rafting from his room.

"Do you think this tie goes with these pants?" he asks nervously.

He is dressed in his sixteen-year-old brother's clothes. Rather than wear his own for this special occasion, he banks on big brother's tried and tested "coolness." I glance at his pant cuffs sweeping the floor, his shirt hanging loose and baggy, and his brother's suede loafers ready to slide off his feet.

"The tie looks good," I say. "It's a perfect match."

With only a few minutes until blast-off, there's no point in starting over. If he's satisfied, then so am I. Time to go.

Heading off to his "date's" house for group pictures, I use this car-captured moment to remind him about good manners. He nods absently. His nervousness at this first formal social has taken his mind elsewhere.

As we park the car in his date's driveway, he whispers his own parting advice. "Mom, don't take too many pictures."

I get the message. Don't talk too much. Don't laugh too loud. Basically, don't do anything to embarrass him in front of his friends.

My son's "date" is a longtime friend he has known since first grade. Fresh from the beauty parlor, she is near tears because she thinks her hair is a disaster. Her short pretty dress, my son says, looks just fine. (He's obviously paid close attention to his father's finesse with his mother over the years.) I'm proud of him.

Chatting and laughing amicably, the gathered parents direct the photography session like a Hollywood shoot snapping off rolls of film. I am a muted mom, muffling my chuckles and taking only four pictures. My son slides me a secret smile. He's proud of me.

Like a gaggle of giggling geese, the adolescents finally head out to the waiting van. Awkwardly, they debate where to sit. The end result is girls in front, boys in back. With a quick and casual wave that belies the bittersweet beat of our hearts, we send our babies off to their first dance.

Three hours later, I'm back on the scene as pick-up chauffeur. By this time, the "dates" have split up, the girls heading off to a sleepover. I watch as dozens of adolescents stream euphorically from the banquet hall. Teachers grin broadly as they wave good-bye to their charges. I overhear one remark to another, "Three hours is way too long!"

"How was it?" I ask as four hot, sweaty neighborhood buddies pile into the van.

"Too short!" they answer in unison.

"I wish it had lasted at least another hour!"

"It was so awesome!"

"Even the food was good!"

The cacophony of conversation and body heat immediately steams up the car. Though the night is cool, I crack all the car windows halfway down. The boys think it is so they can wave and holler good-bye to their friends, which they do with great gusto.

"Whom did you and your dates sit with for dinner?" I ask.

"Oh, we just ate with the guys," answers my son.

"You didn't eat with the girls?" I ask in amazement.

"Naw, we all split up as soon as we got there," he says. "Our dates wanted to talk to the other girls, so we guys just sat down."

So much for the seriousness of an eighth-grade first date. Nevertheless, the mention of the girls brings on a sudden moment of quiet reflection.

"The girls were, well, they were something else!" muses one.

"They were awesome!" says another.

"They looked, like, so different!" ponders the third.

"Yeah, they were . . . really pretty!" gushes the fourth.

Having seen these same girls at 8:00 A.M. on school mornings when I drop off my son, I can understand the boys' surprise. Dressed in blue jeans and baggy flannel shirts, the girls, like the boys, come dressed for school in casual comfort.

For their first dance, however, the girls pulled out all the stops: pretty necklines, feminine dresses, heels, makeup, jewelry, beauty-parlor hair, the works. They have sampled the well of feminine mystique. The eighth-grade boys are delightfully dazed.

"Did you dance?" I ask.

"Yeah, but was I ever nervous!" says one.

"I didn't have a clue what I was doing!" admits another.

"I've never even danced before!" confides a third.

"I just went out on the floor and started dancing," says the fourth. "I think by the end I was actually pretty good!"

With good food, beautiful girls and no embarrassing moments on the dance floor, how could the evening be more perfect?

"You know," says one thoughtfully, "after all that dancing, I don't even think I smell too bad!"

"I just checked," says another. "My deodorant is still working!"

"I sprayed cologne all over my clothes before I left just in case!" admits a third.

"I even put some in my shoes!" says the fourth.

Laughter rocks the car.

I lower the windows all the way.

Exhilarating, crisp spring air blows across my face. Happy, octave-changing voices float like music out onto the night wind. As I drive my nest of fledglings home, I savor their joyful spirit toward life's transitions.

Partnered with humor and honesty, they have gingerly taken their first awkward steps across the dance floor from boys to young men.

Marnie O. Mamminga

Snips and Snails
and Puppy-Dog Tails

Every child born into the world is a new thought of God, and ever-fresh and radiant possibility.

Kate Douglas Wiggin

Some women seem to have a sixth sense predicting the sex of the child they are carrying. During my second pregnancy, I thought I was one of those women. I just knew the baby inside me was a girl. Everyone else agreed.

"Oh my, you're carrying that baby high," one neighbor commented. "It's bound to be a girl."

"The heart rate is high—165. I bet it's a girl."

I was already convinced. My sixth sense told me we'd have a second daughter.

Then came my surprise. After five short hours of labor and two pushes (I know, I know, you don't want to hear about it), a robust nine-pound, eleven-ounce baby presented itself to the world.

"Lynn, you have a healthy boy," my doctor proclaimed, as she placed him on my chest.

"A boy? Oh, a boy!" I gushed, surprise turning to delight.

I was prepared for a girl. How much different could raising a boy be?

Well, God had another surprise waiting for me. I first really noticed the differences when my son was about a year old.

"*Vrroomm, vrroomm,*" he would say while pushing his cars around the room.

I had never heard my three-year-old daughter punctuate her play with such noises. "Did you teach him that?" I asked my husband.

"No, I thought you did."

"Oh, sure," I mocked. "I always say *vrroomm, vrroomm.*"

As my son grew older, I noticed other differences. He adored me. While my daughter had gone through that "I want my daddy" phase, he wanted "his mommy." My daughter would hug me gently, cuddle sweetly next to me or stroke my face softly, and he would literally jump into my lap, try to climb my body and hang ten from my hair.

"I assume it's normal for a four-year-old boy to run from across the room, tackle his mother and nearly knock her to the ground?" I questioned the doctor at my son's check-up.

"Yep, I'm afraid so," he said. "It's all that testosterone. You know, snips and snails and puppy-dog tails."

That same year, I became a mother for the third time—a second girl.

As they all grew, the differences became more noticeable. I watched my son as he gently played Barbies—or, as he called them, action figures—with his sisters. But put him with another boy and look out!

"Could you watch Sammy after kindergarten two days a week?" a neighbor asked.

"Yes, I guess so." How hard could it be? I had watched little girls before, and frankly, two five-year-old girls were easier than one. The girls quietly played house for hours.

Sometimes my "mommy radar" would be alerted, and I'd go upstairs to make sure they were still alive and not getting into mischief.

With the boys, my radar was alerted for another reason. BOOM, BANG, SCRAPE, KERPLUNK.

"Hey, you two, what's going on up there?"

"Nothing," two little voices replied.

"Well, nothing sure is loud. You think you can keep it down?"

They couldn't. I'd find them locked in friendly combat, rolling around on the floor.

Gray hairs sprang forth from my scalp.

The difference that was the most difficult to deal with, though, was my preteen son's attitude toward me in public. When I volunteered in the girls' classrooms, they came rushing toward me, locked their arms tightly around my waist and planted soft kisses on my cheek. But not my son. He'd acknowledge my presence only with a nod or crook of the head. If I moved toward him, he'd give me the "kiss me and you die" look.

In their teen years I noticed several other differences. While the girls often plopped down and told me every little detail of their day, including how their latest boyfriend dumped them, my son was tight-lipped. I wouldn't even find out about his latest girlfriend until after they had broken up. He was evasive about everything.

"How was your day?" I would ask.

"Fine."

"What did you do?"

"Stuff."

"What kind of stuff?"

"You know, stuff stuff," he'd say and walk away, impatiently.

Another big difference between the girls and my son was food consumption. I had heard that boys eat a lot, but I never imagined that meant gobbling an entire package of hot dogs in one sitting. He grew a full foot taller in one year.

In just the blink of an eye, my name went from "Mama" to "Mommy" to "Mom" and now to "Muuther." There are no more chubby little hands reaching up asking for an "uppie." Those chubby hands and stubby fingers have been replaced by a manly version replete with bulging veins, and now I'm the "little one" reaching up.

"I tower over you, Muuther," my still-growing six-foot-two son brags proudly, as if he had something to do with the genetic code at work inside of him. As if he were the one buying the two tons of food he eats each week.

Today, if I want to kiss him, I have to catch him first—not an easy task, as he's so quick and agile. Sometimes I try to sneak up on him and kiss his not-yet-fuzzy cheek, but all too often his keen hearing alerts him to my approach, and he deliberately jerks around, scaring me out of my wits.

But every now and then, I get a glimpse of the gentle, loving man he will soon be—his arm placed firmly around my waist while guiding me away from temptation at the clothing store, raspberry lips blowing on a giggling toddler's tummy or his curly head darting behind a baby blanket for a game of peek-a-boo.

Recently I learned yet another difference between him and his sisters. When the girls began driving, they preferred the simplicity of an automatic. With the enthusiasm of Mario Andretti, my son could hardly wait to get behind the wheel of a stick shift. When I asked him why, he said, "I feel one with the car."

Then, with me in the front passenger seat, he slid behind the wheel.

"Hang on, Muuther. *Vrooom vrooom!*"

Lynn Dean

Driving Lessons

*Never lend your car to anyone to whom you
have given birth.*

Erma Bombeck

"Slow down! Slow down!" my father yells, a distinct
edge of panic in his voice. As a novice fifteen-year-old
driver, I am trying to downshift around a curve on a gravel
country road. "Slow down!" I immediately respond by hitting the brake, which sends the car sliding, kills the engine
and jerks us to an abrupt halt. We sit in surprised silence
as a cloud of dust sifts slowly down upon the car. I wait for
an angry reprimand, but instead my father takes a deep
breath and calmly suggests I restart the engine. The driving lesson resumes.

That was thirty years ago. My father is gone, and I am
now the parent of three teenagers. I wish he were here to
share his secret to remaining calm time and time again
with his own brood of five kids.

Today, I am the parent scheduled for the road test. I
click on my seat belt and watch as my own fifteen-year-
old son climbs joyfully behind the driver's wheel.

"This is so cool!" he says.

"Have you got your permit?"

"Of course," he says, waving it before my eyes.

"Do you realize, Mom," he continues, "that I am the only one in my class who has never driven before?"

"Well, that makes you the only one who didn't break the law," I say.

"No," he says, "that makes me the only dork who doesn't know how to drive. Are you ready?"

I watch as he starts the engine with a roar, adjusts the rearview mirror to check his hair, flips on the radio to his favorite rock station, flips it off, checks the mirror/hair again, and finally, after what seems like an eternity, puts the car in reverse.

Slowly and with much caution, he backs down our long, narrow driveway, which is no easy feat. I am impressed and begin to relax.

Entering the street, he snaps the car into forward and steps on the gas.

"Watch the mailbox! Watch the mailbox! WATCH THE MAILBOX!" I scream as my foot slams an imaginary brake.

Misses it by a centimeter.

"See," he says, "no problem."

I rub the cramp in my braking foot as my inexperienced driver pulls out onto a main road with giddy delight.

"Wow, this is fun!" he says, a smile beaming across his face.

Enjoying the new power of his moveable beast, he starts to pick up speed. I tense. Suddenly, all the mailboxes, lightposts and assorted garbage cans seem really close to the road. Really close!

"Watch your speed," I say calmly. "Slow down on this curve. Slow down ON THIS CURVE!"

My right foot floors the fake brake.

"I'm not going that fast," he argues.

I let out a deep breath. "Just turn right at the next road."

Flipping on his signal, he makes a wide turn directly into the opposite lane. Luckily for our insurance rates, there is no oncoming car.

"You've got to stay in your own lane," I snap.

Silence fills the air.

He grips the wheel. I grasp for patience.

Heading down a long stretch of country road in a tension-filled car, I struggle to keep quiet and just let him experience the driving.

Looking around at the countryside for the first time, I notice the fields are awash in a golden light. The late afternoon sun hangs low in the rich blueness. The warm breeze blowing through the open windows brings a calm caress against our faces and a soothing grace to our mutual tension.

After a period of quiet, my son turns to me with an eager face, happiness shining in his eyes. "How am I doing?" he asks proudly.

"Very well," I reply.

"See, Mama," he says, "you just need to give me more time."

"I know," I say. "You're going to make a great driver."

Smiling brightly, he steps on the gas.

I keep silent. He slows at the curve.

Looking over, I watch the innocent profile of my man-child whose soft cheeks sport the beginnings of light peach fuzz. Radiating an awakening confidence, his face glows with the joyful realization that vast horizons and new beginnings are stretching out before him just like the wide-open road we are on.

For a fleeting instant, I feel the magic.

I am no longer the weary forty-six-year-old mother of three with a sometimes overwhelming assortment of eclectic responsibilities, but once again the young girl in the driver's seat. And through this blurry mist of time, a beam of knowledge shines dimly out to me. Thirty years ago, as gravel dust floated down upon us in a stalled car, did my father's own memory of a youth-gone-by come sparkling back to him?

Gingerly tucking my brake foot under the seat, I notice the sky has turned a rosy hue. I turn and look out the back window.

"Is there a car behind us?" my son asks nervously.

"No, but there's a spectacular sunset," I say. "The sky is filled with beautiful colors. Keep your eyes on the road, and I'll describe it to you."

"Hey, I can actually see it my rearview mirror," he says. "Cool."

Through the open windows, the dropping coolness of the evening breeze blows in the sweet pungent scent of country dusk. It refreshes and invigorates us. I take a deep breath. My son checks his hair. Cruising on down the road, we both admire the fields glowing in the twilight.

Marnie O. Mamminga

Grown Up

And a little child shall lead them.

Isaiah 11:6

It had been a long summer day on the farm, filled with hard work as we continued to harvest the crops for our animals. I was waiting for the haying crew to come for the evening meal when our middle son, Andrew, just eighteen years old, was the first one in. He paced anxiously.

"Do you have something to tell me?" I asked.

He blurted, "I'm going to be a father!"

Mother and son stood motionless, suspended in time, staring into each other's eyes. An overwhelming panic crept up inside of me. In an instant, I saw my blond, tanned three-year-old wearing Spiderman shorts, my five-year-old making pretend roads with his toy tractors outside, my six-year-old returning home from his first day of school so proud beside his big brother. This couldn't be possible. How could my baby become a father? How would he ever cope? In the next instant I saw the confusion in my son's eyes, and I knew without a doubt his announcement was no mistake; it was a reality. Summer holidays were drawing to a close, and in a few weeks he would be starting his senior year—a year that was supposed to be full of fun and freedom. My heart broke into a thousand pieces.

In the confusion, the first words out of my mouth surprised even me. "We will move forward one day at a time. Your dad and I, your brother and sister will be there for you."

Days led into weeks. His father and I felt exhausted from walking beside him and holding him up while he marched to the beat of his own drum. We struggled to get him to school every day. His behavior seemed to defy all we'd taught him in the past.

Weeks led into months. Finally, on a cold February day, we gathered in a hospital room. All the struggles over the past seven months were forgotten as we hovered over the teenage mother-to-be. Minutes slipped into hours as we anxiously waited. Although various family members and friends filled the halls, Andrew never left the room. He was gentle. He was calm. I faded into the background in awe as I marveled at the wild, young boy now showing so much tenderness.

By early evening the doctor arrived, and we heard the first cries of the child we had been waiting for. Love surrounded the room. A baby girl was wrapped in a blanket and placed in my son's arms. Amid the tears, I heard the nurse say to him, "Come carry her down the hall with me to weigh and measure her."

For the second time in so many months, my son and I seemed to be suspended in time as we stared into each other's eyes. *Can he walk with her? Do I dare trust this little boy to carry something so precious?*

And then I saw Andrew hold his daughter close in his strong arms. I watched as he turned away from me to follow the nurse down the hall. He walked tall and straight,

the stride of a protective father. Once again my heart
broke into a thousand pieces, only this time it was with
joy and pride because in the eyes of my son, I saw the
wonder of a miracle.

Darlene Lawson

And Now a Man

*M*en are what their mothers made them.

Ralph Waldo Emerson

It is early on a Friday morning. Careful not to make a sound, I ease open the door and peek into the room. Sunlight creeps around the edges of the drawn shade, making bright streaks dance along the wall. I tiptoe in and look down at my sleeping son with his arm tucked under the pillow and his legs tangled in the covers. His toes touch the end of the bed.

It's been a long time since I watched my youngest sleep. He probably wouldn't like it if he knew I crept in to study him. After all, he is not a little boy who needs his mother to shake him awake in the morning or tuck him in at night.

In fact, it is rare for him to sleep in this house, in the room that was his when he was growing up. Wasn't it just yesterday when I came in to wake him for school or a tennis match or just because it was time to get up? But now I'm quiet, hoping to steal one more moment watching . . . and remembering.

I listen to the rhythm of his breathing. I know this is the

last time he will sleep in this house as a single man. This is my third child to marry, so I should be prepared for the feelings sneaking up on me this bright morning. I've felt them before, but somehow forgot how the grown person right in front of me can instantly become a three-year-old child again in my mind—how the memories rush in.

He moves, tightens his grip on the pillow, and I resist the urge to touch his cheek as I did when he was a baby sleeping in my arms.

In his face, I see that baby who grew into the boy, then the teenager, and finally the man. A fine man and, next, a loving husband. He is so in love with the woman who will be his wife.

I've seen the two of them, my son and my future daughter-in-law, grow up. I remember the middle-school crushes and the breakups. Now I see the look in his eyes when she walks into the room, and the private smiles that pass between them.

It's time to start my day, but I stand glued to my spot at the foot of his bed.

Soon a new picture will be among those filling my head. Family and friends toasting Meredith and Tim and their life together—another memory snapshot to add to those I treasure in my heart.

But, for now, my son sleeps, and I watch.

His eyes sweep open. He sees me and gives a half-smiling yawn. I take a step backward.

"Good morning," I say, turning toward the door. "Time to get up. It's going to be a beautiful day."

Nancy Blackmon

The Charming Con

*In praising or loving a child, we love and praise
not that which is, but that which we hope for.*

Goethe

We should have known we were in trouble when he
had to be forced into the world almost three weeks late,
and we missed our tax deduction. Joshua pretended to
sleep the entire hospital stay. This was his first great con.
Once home, the only way he slept was while in motion, so
we took many a midnight ride, rocked until the sun came
up, and cranked his mechanical swing until it wore out.
We even put his infant carrier on top of the dryer, and he
slept as long as the dryer ran. His father snored loudly, his
head bouncing on top of the humming dryer with the
infant carrier clutched in his arms.

If you tried to put Joshua in his crib, one eye would open
and glare as if to say in Dirty Harry fashion, "Do you feel
lucky today, punk? Well, do you?" By three years old he
had a charming, innocent smile down pat. His entire con
routine was a thing of beauty. While shopping at the store
known for "blue-light specials," he explained to a running,

screaming salesclerk how gerbils, hamsters and other assorted critters escaped from their cages, and she *believed* him. Thank God the fish tanks were too heavy to overturn.

At five, he convinced his gullible father that he would not ask for candy if he could go to the neighborhood store with him. Joshua knew Miss May, the store's owner, had always been a sucker for his smile, hug and twinkling blue eyes, and always gave him a handful of candy. Josh, of course, had counted on this, and his father was furious. His defense was, "Dad, you know you can't trust me." His father, who still had smoke coming out of his ears, was not amused.

At seven, his second-grade teacher called to tell us that Josh did not qualify for their free-lunch program. It seems that the lunch money we had given him every morning had been used for some other "worthy cause." Joshua explained that we had always emphasized saving his own money for the video arcade and that he was just doing what he had been told. His father did more than fume this time!

Joshua honed his skills from seven to nineteen. Enthralled with reggae music, he tried to achieve the Bob Marley look. He grew shoulder-length dreadlocks and explained to us that women thought his dreads and his raggedy jeans were extremely sexy. His clueless grandmother still went shopping with him while his dad and I walked a few steps behind and told our friends that he was exploring world cultures for one of his college classes.

For the next several years, Josh conned his way in and out of several colleges where he majored in "party-hardy." He explained that "nobody graduated in four years anymore." Our friends thought he was going straight through for his Ph.D. or possibly he was in medical school. We did little to discourage this assumption. When he finally graduated, his father and I danced in the streets.

Joshua's most amazing con occurred a couple of years later when he convinced a lovely girl named Amanda that she was in love with him and they should marry. His dad and I not only danced in the streets but anywhere we could without being carted off to jail. A couple of years later we all excitedly awaited the arrival of a baby boy.

There were problems with the delivery, and Kaleb Maxwell Jordan entered the world a very sick baby. With piercing, luminous blue eyes and the longest lashes the nursing staff had ever seen, he looked like a healthy eight-pound baby. But Josh and Amanda were told he wouldn't live past four months. They were to take their baby home to die.

Today, three years later, Josh and Amanda still take shifts with Kaleb. He requires twenty-four-hour care. Cerebral palsy makes it impossible for him to swallow, and he has to be suctioned often to avoid choking. Our charming con grew up overnight to become the most caring, loving father I have ever known. Josh's shift is early morning. Kaleb and he watch that famous squarepants sponge at 6 A.M. Josh has mastered all the songs from the show, and Kaleb seems to recognize them when his daddy sings. Both faces radiate love when Joshua comes home from work and says, "Hi, Buddy," and kisses him.

Kaleb has had numerous surgeries and late-night visits to the hospital. Through all of this, Joshua and Amanda have refused to give up hope that Kaleb will be with us for a long time.

The little boy in footed pajamas, who once watched Spiderman cuddled up on the couch with his dad, will soon be thirty-two. We have watched with pride as he has discarded his charming con façade for the billowed cape of a real super hero. Our hearts soar as we dance in the streets.

Brenda Jordan

Answering the Call

There are only two lasting bequests we can hope to give our children. One of them is roots; the other, wings.

Hodding Carter

I'm a writer. Putting words on paper is what I do. Ads. Newsletters. A monthly humor column for a family magazine. An occasional opinion piece for the op-ed page of the local daily.

But the words I'm looking at right now on the paper are unlike any I've ever written. The handwriting is mine. The paper's familiar. But the words are different.

They're not mine. They belong to my son, Roman, a private in the infantry of the U.S. Army.

Originally, Roman's after-high-school plan had been to make it on his own as a Web designer.

But a lot of things changed after 9/11, including the dot.com world. And times turned hard for independent nineteen-year-old Web masters. So in the summer of 2002, Roman decided to join the Army, "see the world," put college on hold even longer and figure things out for himself in the meantime.

I couldn't help but wonder how military life would change the funny, cheeky kid who had once decorated his bedroom door with a sticker that said, "Wake for food." The kid I used to remind to eat his vegetables and pick up his socks, the same kid who balked at wearing a bike helmet, the teenager who played his hard-rock CDs way too loud.

Roman chose the Army partly because it offered him a say in where he'd be based. When he picked Germany, I was relieved, thinking for sure that his unit, the 1st Armored Division, wouldn't be involved in conflict in the Middle East.

But when bombs begin falling, I've learned, all bets are off.

He was in the Middle East the morning he called, the morning I wrote those words on that pale yellow paper. His unit had arrived in the desert staging area of Kuwait a week earlier, just after Baghdad fell. The region was far from stabilized.

"We'll be leaving here soon. We're already packed. So this will be my last call for a while," he said. "There are no phones where we're going. No Internet either."

"And where's that?"

"Can't say. It's a secret," he answered.

With some coaxing, I did learn that he and the rest of the men of Bravo Company would reach their ultimate destination fifteen hours or so after their convoy headed north.

"Does the place start with a 'B'?" I pressed.

"Mo-om," he answered with feigned exasperation. During his years as a teenager, I'd often heard the real thing. Back then it had been my job to ask the questions. "Homework finished? What time does the movie end? Who's driving?" And it was his job, or so it seemed, to answer with as few syllables as possible.

"Is Dad there?" he asked.

"No. He's at a biotech conference today."

My husband had been laid off from his job as Director of Engineering at the big computer company where he'd worked for twenty-seven years. He'd been looking for work while dreaming of starting his own company. This in-between-time year had been as challenging for him as it was for our son.

"Dad's not there? Shoot," Roman said, adding in a voice that trailed off, "There's something I really need to talk to him about."

"Can I help?" I asked.

No answer.

"Roman?"

"Well, okay. I guess so," he sighed from half a world away.

I waited for the rest and wondered what it could be.

"Got a pen, Mom?"

"Yes."

"And a piece of paper?"

With each question, his voice gained authority.

"Yup. Right here," I said.

"I've taken out a life insurance policy for $275,000, the maximum the Army offers. If anything happens to me, here's what I want done with that money."

I jumped in to stop that kind of talk. What mother wouldn't? "Don't be silly," I sputtered. "Nothing's going to happen to you. You'll stay safe. And when you come home, you'll have lots of stories to tell. Some day your grandchildren will ask about the time . . ."

"Mom, please. Just write this down."

And so, cradling the phone between cheek and shoulder, I took my son's dictation, writing first a few words about his big sister: "Pay for Anne's college." Then a line about taking care of me. And, finally, a phrase for his father: "Help Dad start his company. Did you get all that?" he asked.

"Yes," I whispered.

"Good."

We chatted a few minutes more. Maybe it was about the weather or the food or the fellas he now hangs out with. I don't remember. My mind was still reeling with a changed reality; my heart twitching with a strange, new sadness and a growing pride.

When I'd answered the phone that day, I heard the voice of a boy.

But it was a man I said good-bye to.

Sue Diaz

That's My Son!

When you teach your son, you teach your son's son.

The Talmud

There's just something different about a bond between a mother and son. There is a feeling you get that tingles in your heart when you see your little boy coming toward you, flowers in hand (picked no doubt from the neighbor's yard). He holds them up to you, his face glowing with delight as you take them from his hand. You kneel and give him a gentle kiss on the cheek. Then you stand by and watch as he runs off to play with his friends.

You see his first touchdown, and as the crowd roars, you say to the person next to you, "That's my son."

You see him at school talking to his first true love, and in your mind you say to her, "That's my son. Don't hurt him."

He walks across the stage and reaches for his diploma, and sobbing you say, "That's my son."

Standing at the head of the aisle, tall and handsome in his tuxedo, looking toward his new bride, in your mind you say to her, "That's my son. Take good care of him."

Pacing outside the waiting room, hoping for good news, you see your son and the mother-to-be with worried looks on their faces, and you put your hand on her shoulder and tell her, "It'll be okay. Your son, he'll be okay."

Now you are in their home helping the new mom and, as much as you'd like to take over, you hand this small and familiar little one to her and say, "Here is your son. I know you'll take good care of him."

As you walk out the door, you smile to yourself, and then you're startled when you hear the words, "Mom, I love you!" You turn to look at the handsome man standing in the doorway, and before your eyes he is transformed back into the little boy who just handed you the flowers. You wipe the tears from your eyes and say, "I love you, too." You feel that warm tingle in your heart, and then you say to yourself, "That's my son!"

Dianna Foxcroft

More Chicken Soup?

Many of the stories and poems you have read in this book were submitted by readers like you who had read earlier *Chicken Soup for the Soul* books. We publish at least five or six *Chicken Soup for the Soul* books every year. We invite you to contribute a story to one of these future volumes.

Stories may be up to twelve-hundred words and must uplift or inspire. You may submit an original piece, something you have read or your favorite quotation on your refrigerator door.

To obtain a copy of our submission guidelines and a listing of upcoming *Chicken Soup* books, please write, fax or check our Web site.

Please send your submissions to:

Chicken Soup for the Soul
P.O. Box 30880
Santa Barbara, CA 93130
fax: 805-563-2945
Web site: *www.chickensoup.com*

We will be sure that both you and the author are credited for your submission.

For information about speaking engagements, other books, audiotapes, workshops and training programs, please contact any of our authors directly.

Supporting Others

The *Just for Mom Foundation* is a nonprofit corporation dedicated to enriching the lives of families, today and tomorrow. They fuse the accessibility of tools (such as the Internet) with their network of corporate, nonprofit and personal partners to create opportunities for moms to fulfill their own dreams and properly nurture their families. The exhilarating and exhausting role of mother proves to women that they are needed and valuable and that they have the power to shape and nurture the lives of those around them. *Just for Mom Foundation* helps moms refill their reserves—not only for their families but also for themselves.

The *Just for Mom Foundation* is dedicated to:

• Offering support and encouragement to mothers.
• Sharing the tools and creating opportunities for personal and professional success.
• Enriching a mom's life with the power of accomplishment.
• Providing the resources that allow moms to earn a living while nurturing their family.
• Helping mothers cultivate their personal passion and inspire the lives of their children.
• Supporting efforts that are important to family dynamics and the growth and rearing of their children.

The *Just for Mom Foundation* exists to help moms embrace what is universal and begin a journey of self-discovery, accomplishment and joy. They are the resource to a path that allows moms to fulfill themselves and their dreams as women, mothers, wives, sisters, friends and individuals. They have begun that journey by developing programs that support literacy for their children through their efforts to help Save Reading Rainbow (*www.SaveReading Rainbow.org*) and by selecting quality products and books moms can trust for their families through the Mom's Choice Awards™ (*www.MomsChoiceAwards.org*).

Just for Mom Foundation
P.O. Box 241
Round Hill, VA 20142
contactus@thejustformomfoundation.org
Phone: 571-242-1288

Who Is Jack Canfield?

Jack Canfield is one of America's leading experts in the development of human potential and personal effectiveness. He is both a dynamic, entertaining speaker and a highly sought-after trainer. Jack has a wonderful ability to inform and inspire audiences toward increased levels of self-esteem and peak performance.

He is the author and narrator of several bestselling audio- and videocassette programs, including *Self-Esteem and Peak Performance, How to Build High Self-Esteem, Self-Esteem in the Classroom* and *Chicken Soup for the Soul—Live.* He is regularly seen on television shows such as *Good Morning America, 20/20* and *NBC Nightly News.* Jack has co-authored numerous books, including the *Chicken Soup for the Soul* series, *Dare to Win* and *The Aladdin Factor* (all with Mark Victor Hansen), *100 Ways to Build Self-Concept in the Classroom* (with Harold C. Wells), *Heart at Work* (with Jacqueline Miller) and *The Power of Focus* (with Les Hewitt and Mark Victor Hansen).

Jack is a regularly featured speaker for professional associations, school districts, government agencies, churches, hospitals, sales organizations and corporations. His clients have included the American Dental Association, the American Management Association, AT&T, Campbell's Soup, Clairol, Domino's Pizza, GE, ITT, Hartford Insurance, Johnson & Johnson, the Million Dollar Roundtable, NCR, New England Telephone, Re/Max, Scott Paper, TRW and Virgin Records. Jack has taught on the faculty of Income Builders International, a school for entrepreneurs.

Jack conducts an annual seven-day Training of Trainers program in the areas of self-esteem and peak performance. It attracts entrepreneurs, educators, counselors, parenting trainers, corporate trainers, professional speakers, ministers and others interested in developing their speaking and seminar-leading skills.

For further information about Jack's books, tapes and training programs, or to schedule him for a presentation, please contact:

Self-Esteem Seminars
P.O. Box 30880
Santa Barbara, CA 93130
phone: 805-563-2935 • fax: 805-563-2945
Web site: *www.jackcanfield.com*

Who Is Mark Victor Hansen?

In the area of human potential, no one is more respected than Mark Victor Hansen. For more than thirty years, Mark has focused solely on helping people from all walks of life reshape their personal vision of what's possible. His powerful messages of possibility, opportunity and action have created powerful change in thousands of organizations and millions of individuals worldwide.

He is a sought-after keynote speaker, bestselling author and marketing maven. Mark's credentials include a lifetime of entrepreneurial success and an extensive academic background. He is a prolific writer with many bestselling books, such as *The One Minute Millionaire, The Power of Focus, The Aladdin Factor* and *Dare to Win*, in addition to the *Chicken Soup for the Soul* series. Mark has made a profound influence through his library of audios, videos and articles in the areas of big thinking, sales achievement, wealth building, publishing success, and personal and professional development.

Mark is the founder of the MEGA Seminar Series. MEGA Book Marketing University and Building Your MEGA Speaking Empire are annual conferences where Mark coaches and teaches new and aspiring authors, speakers and experts on building lucrative publishing and speaking careers. Other MEGA events include MEGA Marketing Magic and My MEGA Life.

He has appeared on television (*Oprah*, CNN and *The Today Show*), in print (*Time, U.S. News & World Report, USA Today, New York Times* and *Entrepreneur*) and on countless radio interviews, assuring our planet's people that "You can easily create the life you deserve."

As a philanthropist and humanitarian, Mark works tirelessly for organizations such as Habitat for Humanity, American Red Cross, March of Dimes, Childhelp USA and many others. He is the recipient of numerous awards that honor his entrepreneurial spirit, philanthropic heart and business acumen. He is a lifetime member of the Horatio Alger Association of Distinguished Americans, an organization that honored Mark with the prestigious Horatio Alger Award for his extraordinary life achievements.

Mark Victor Hansen is an enthusiastic crusader of what's possible and is driven to make the world a better place.

Mark Victor Hansen & Associates, Inc.
P.O. Box 7665
Newport Beach, CA 92658
phone: 949-764-2640
fax: 949-722-6912
Web site: *www.markvictorhansen.com*

Who Is LeAnn Thieman?

LeAnn Thieman is a nationally acclaimed professional speaker, author and nurse who was "accidentally" caught up in the Vietnam Orphan Airlift in 1975. Her book, *This Must Be My Brother*, details her daring adventure of helping to rescue 300 babies as Saigon was falling to the communists. An ordinary person, she struggled through extraordinary circumstances and found the courage to succeed. LeAnn and her incredible story have been featured in *Newsweek Magazine*'s "Voices of the Century" issue, FOX News, CNN, PBS, BBC, PAX-TV's *It's A Miracle,* and countless radio and TV programs.

Today, as a renowned motivational speaker, she shares life-changing lessons learned from her airlift experience. Believing we all have individual "war zones," LeAnn inspires audiences to balance their lives, truly live their priorities and make a difference in the world.

After her story was featured in *Chicken Soup for the Mother's Soul*, LeAnn became one of Chicken Soup's most prolific writers, with stories in eleven more Chicken Soup books. That, and her devotion to thirty years of nursing, made her the ideal co-author of *Chicken Soup for the Nurse's Soul.* She went on to co-author *Chicken Soup for the Caregiver's Soul, Chicken Soup for the Father and Daughter Soul* and *Chicken Soup for the Grandma's Soul.* Her lifelong practice of her Christian faith led her to co-author *Chicken Soup for the Christian Woman's Soul* and now *Chicken Soup for the Christian Soul II.*

LeAnn is one of about ten percent of speakers worldwide to have earned the Certified Speaking Professional Designation awarded by the National Speakers Association and the International Federation for Professional Speakers.

She and Mark, her husband of thirty-five years, reside in Colorado, where they enjoy their "empty nest." Their two daughters, Angela and Christie, and son, Mitch, have "flown the coop" but are still drawn under their mother's wing when she needs them!

For more information about LeAnn's books and tapes or to schedule her for a presentation, please contact her at:

LeAnn Thieman, CSP
6600 Thompson Drive
Fort Collins, CO 80526
1-970-223-1574
www.LeAnnThieman.com
e-mail *LeAnn@LeAnnThieman.com*

Who Is Barbara LoMonaco?

Barbara LoMonaco has worked for Chicken Soup for the Soul Enterprises, Inc., since February 1998 and is their Story Acquisitions Manager and their Customer Service Representative. She grew up in Los Angeles and received her bachelor of science degree in education from the University of Southern California. After graduation she taught at the elementary-school level.

Barbara "retired" from teaching when she became pregnant with the first of her three sons and was lucky enough to be able to be a stay-at-home mom while her boys were growing up. During that time, she spent many hours doing volunteer work at the schools her sons attended. When the last one left home, Barbara started her job at Chicken Soup for the Soul Enterprises. Over the years she has worked there, she has seen, firsthand, how one story or the actions of one person really can make a big difference in someone's life. She feels very blessed to be involved with the *Chicken Soup for the Soul* group.

Chicken Soup for the Mother and Son Soul has been a labor of love for Barbara. Her sons, John, Michael and Robert, are her proudest accomplishments, and they are the true inspirations for this book. Her husband, Frank, has been her soulmate since they started dating when Barbara was in high school. He has always stood behind her and has been her biggest supporter in whatever she has wanted to do. Her mother, Frances Berres, has been her mentor and role model, showing her that it is possible to be both a fabulous mother and have a successful career. Barbara and Frank live in Santa Barbara, California. Two of her sons also live in Santa Barbara. Her third son lives close by in Los Angeles. If you wish to contact Barbara, please e-mail her at *blomonaco@chickensoupforthesoul.com*.

Contributors

Several of the stories in this book were taken from previously published sources, such as books, magazines and newspapers. These sources are acknowledged in the permissions section. If you would like to contact any of the contributors for information about their writing or would like to invite them to speak in your community, look for their contact information included in their biographies.

The remainder of the stories were submitted by readers of our previous *Chicken Soup for the Soul* books who responded to our requests for stories. We have also included information about them.

Barbara Adams was an English major at Bates College. She has written extensively for newspapers and magazines and wrote jokes for Phyllis Diller. She has six grown adopted children. Barbara enjoys writing, contests, sweepstakes, antiques and the Internet. She plans to continue writing. Please e-mail her at *mainegal@megalink.net*.

Linda Apple lives in northwest Arkansas with her husband, Neal, and their children. She is a speaker for Stonecroft Ministries and a contributor to several *Chicken Soup* books. She's currently working on her first novel, a historical novel set during the gold rush in 1850. Contact her at *www.lindacapple.com* or *psalm10218@cox-internet.com*.

Anita Biase is a freelance writer and a former elementary teacher. Her specialties include topics pertaining to children, education, family, pets and technology. She can be reached at *emilyrose2342000@yahoo.com*.

Rita Elaine Billbe loves White River fly fishing near her resort, Angels Retreat. Singing alto in her church choir is her passion. Her personal mission statement is to serve and encourage others through the love of Jesus Christ. Her memberships include the Christian Writer's Guild and Write Partners of North Arkansas. Visit her Web site at *www.whiteriver.net/angels-retreat/*.

Karin Bjerke-Lisle and her husband, Doug, live on British Columbia's west coast. Despite a busy career, she most enjoys being with their four children: Forrest, Brontë, Paige and Hunter. They love the beach and the mountains, traveling and *Gemütlichkeit* with their family and friends. Please e-mail Karin at *lisle_crew@shaw.ca*.

Jean Blackmer is a co-author of *Where Women Walked: Powerful True Stories of Women's Perseverance and God's Provision*. She has also written numerous freelance articles for publications, including *Guideposts, Today's Christian Woman* and *Christian Parenting Today*. She lives in Boulder, Colorado, with her husband, Zane, and their three boys.

Nancy Blackmon is a former newspaper reporter and editor. She still writes a weekly newspaper column. Nancy lives in south Alabama and is an avid gardener.

She is also interested in issues relating to autism and advocating for autistic children. Please e-mail her at *blackmon@alaweb.com.*

Cynthia Briggs celebrates her love of cooking and writing through her nostalgic cookbook, *Pork Chops & Applesauce: A Collection of Recipes and Reflections.* She enjoys writing book reviews and food columns. Her newest endeavors include publishing a series of cook-booklets and writing children's books. Contact Cynthia through her Web site, *www.porkchopsandapplesauce.net.*

Leslie T. Britt is an accountant with the state of Alabama. She enjoys working with youth, especially in the area of Christian drama. She loves being a grandmother to Chloe and Ethan, the children of her son, Jason (in the story), and his beautiful wife, Crystal.

Karen Brown is a New Jersey native who's lived most of her adult life in the midwest. Among her mixed bag of professions: radio host, newspaper columnist and copywriter. Karen credits her three boys (husband, Ron, and sons, Casey and Jesse) with her joys and exasperations. Contact her at *rumsonmom@yahoo.com.*

Martin Bucella is a full-time cartoonist/humorous illustrator whose work has been published over 100,000 times in magazines, newspapers, greeting cards, books, Web sites and so on. To see more of Marty's work, visit his website at *memebers.aol/mjbtoons/index.html.*

Debi Callies is the author of *Stay Strong, Stay Safe My Son,* a book describing her challenges in sending her son, Robert, to war. Debi is also the proud mother of three other children, Demi, Kaila and Drew. Debi received her Master's in Educational Technology and is currently a professor at Ottawa University.

Martha Campbell is a graduate of Washington University St. Louis School of Fine Arts and a former writer/designer for Hallmark cards. She has been a freelance cartoonist and book illustrator since 1973. She can be reached at PO Box 2538, Harrison, AR or at *marthaf@alltel.net.*

Jeri Chrysong, a legal assistant, resides in Huntington Beach, California, with her two pugs, Puddy and Mabel. She has a newfound love for traveling and photography and hopes to combine them with her writing. Jeri enjoys watching football games and spending time with her family. E-mail Jeri at *jcpugs2@aol.com.*

Margaret P. Cunningham lives on Alabama's beautiful gulf coast with her husband, Tom. Her short stories have placed in several national contests and have appeared in *Beginnings* magazine, the anthologies, *Hello, Goodbye* and *Gardening at a Deeper Level,* and *Chicken Soup for the Dog Lover's Soul.* Please e-mail her at *peggymob@aol.com.*

G. E. Dabbs is a schoolteacher in Bibb County, Alabama. He's married to Patty, and they share six children: Joseph Aaron, T. J., Amanda, Joshua, Carmen and Edward. He's published one novel, *Lucy's Treasure,* and is a contributing author in *God Answers Prayers, Military Edition.* Please e-mail him at *dabbsge@juno.com.*

Lynn Dean is a Colorado writer and mother of three. Lynn specializes in the areas of parenting, education, lifestyle and women's issues. As a published writer for more than twenty-five years, she has written more than 500 articles that have appeared in over 100 different publications in thirty-five states. When Lynn is not writing or chasing teenagers, she spends her time grant writing and fundraising for local non-profits. You can e-mail Lynn at *LynnDean@frii.com.*

Robin Geller Diamond is a pediatric nurse practitioner who loves being at home with her three teenaged children and husband, Ted, in Amherst, Massachusetts. She enjoys travel, yoga and gardening and is an avid Red Sox fan. She is also an active volunteer in her local community. This is her first published story! Contact her at *gemmom3@aol.com*.

Sue Diaz is an author, writing teacher and essayist whose work has appeared in numerous regional and national publications, including *Newsweek, Family Circle, Christian Science Monitor, Woman's Day* and *Reader's Digest*. She is also a frequent on-air essayist on National Public Radio's "On Point," produced by WBUR in Boston. Feel free to e-mail her at *sue@suediaz.com*.

Angela Thieman Dino is a cultural anthropologist living in Colorado with her loving husband, son and daughter. Her human rights work, locally and internationally, is made especially rewarding by survivors of war and human rights abuse. She encourages others to learn more from organizations like the Rocky Mountain Survivors Center (*www.rmscdenver.org*).

Ginny Dubose graduated from Florida Southern College in 1980. She is an administrator for a booming company in central Florida. Her hobbies include writing, reading and watercolors. She looks forward to retiring to write full-time. Ginny and her son, Danny, spent the first fourteen years of his life as a family of two.

Kerrie Flanagan is a freelance writer from Colorado. She has two sons and one daughter. Kerrie enjoys being the commisioner of a fantasy football league, hanging out with friends and family, and traveling. You can contact her at *kerrief@frii.com* or *www.kerrieflanagan.com*.

This is **Deisy M. Flood**'s second contribution to *Chicken Soup for the Soul*. She is a Sales Coordinator for VKM International, Inc., in Lakeland, Florida, where she lives with her two spoiled dogs that run her life. She enjoys golf between hurricanes and reading. Please e-mail her at *deisy_f@hotmail.com*.

Linda Marie Ford is the queen of three royal subjects and one hubby. She is the creator of *www.itsgoodtobethequeen.com*, an Internet group for moms of boys. She is also a co-founder of Echo Theatre, a Dallas-based feminist theater company, and a voiceover talent. E-mail her at *thequeenoflakewood@itsgoodtobethequeen.com*.

Texas born and raised! **Dianna Foxcroft** writes about her own experiences, things that touch her heart and any underdogs that need defending. Her two beautiful children are the very air that she breathes. It is because of them that Dianna continues to push forward and not give up!

April Garcia has dreamed of being a mother since childhood. She is blessed with two wonderful children, Ray and Savannah. Her greatest accomplishments in life are being a mother and a wife to her husband, Michael. She enjoys spending time with her children and making them smile.

Nancy B. Gibbs is a pastor's wife, a mother and grandmother. She is an author, a weekly religion columnist and freelance writer. Nancy has been published in numerous *Chicken Soup* books, along with hundreds of other publications. She may be contacted at *Daiseydood@aol.com* or *www.nancybgibbs.com*.

Sylvia Gist, a teacher of many years, lists freelance writing among her pursuits, which also include gardening, beekeeping, sewing, cooking, canning and preserving.

Her life includes a husband of thirty-seven years, a son, two stepsons and four grandchildren.

Gloria Givens is a freelance journalist published in magazines, newspapers and two *Chicken Soup for the Soul* books. Her writing reflects life experiences and her faith in a better tomorrow. She enjoys camping with her children, grandchildren, friends and various family animals.

Theresa Goggin-Roberts is an RN, author and proud mother of Frank and Sarah. She is the creator of the "Strong & Wise" workshop and upcoming book. Teri lives with her husband, James, whom she adores! You can contact Teri at *IndigoMuse63@aol.com.*

After having a story published in *Chicken Soup for the Fisherman's Soul* in 2004, **Rosalie P. Griffin** sharpened her pencil to write another. In retirement she's doing what she always wanted to do right after having a family—writing! And writing about family brings back the most nostalgic memories.

Scott Halford is an Emmy Award–winning writer, speaker, author and internationally recognized expert on emotional intelligence at work. Known for his quick wit and depth of knowledge, every encounter provides lessons that stick and lessons that you will use for a lifetime. Please e-mail him at *scott@completeintelligence.com.*

Carolyn Hall is a freelance writer from Shawnee, Kansas. She received her Bachelor of Science from Kansas State University and her MOM degree from raising her children.

Patrick Hardin is a freelance cartoonist whose work appears in a variety of publications around the world. He may be reached at 810-234-7452.

Jean Harper is a wife, mother, public speaker and pilot for United Airlines. She is currently a captain on the Boeing 757. She considers storytelling to be her finest talent and enjoys quilting and cake decorating. Jean and her family live in Centennial, Colorado.

Laurie Hartman is the mother of sixteen-year-old Connor Hartman and the co-author of *Chicken Soup for the Single Parent's Soul.* She loves to write and cook and is a charter member of the Laguna Niguel Soroptimist Club.

Jonny Hawkins loves creating cartoons. Over the last twenty years, his work has appeared in over 300 publications and in over one hundred books. He has several books out including *Laughter From the Pearly Gates* and *The Awesome Book of Heavenly Humor.* He can be reached at *jonnyhawkins2nz.@yahoo.com.*

Pamela Hackett Hobson is the proud mother of two terrific sons. Pam's first novel, *The Bronxville Book Club,* was featured in the *New York Times* article, "Buzzzz, Murmurs Follow Novel." The sequel is entitled *The Silent Auction.* To find out more about Pam, visit *www.pamelahobson.com* or e-mail her at *author@pamelahobson.com.*

Cindy Hval is a freelance writer and the mother of four sons, ages 5–15. Her sons are her inspiration and exasperation, usually both on any given day. Her work has appeared in the *Spokesman Review, Northwest Woman* magazine and *ByLine* magazine. Contact her at *dchval@juno.com.*

Daniel James lives with his wife in Colorado. He is an observer of nature and human nature and is cursed or blessed with a dictate to wrestle with the wily wood, which one day he hopes to do well.

Pamela Jenkins lives in rural Oklahoma with her husband and four children. She is the office manager of her husband's veterinary practice. Pamela is a supporter of 4-H and FFA Youth activities and enjoys writing inspirational stories.

Louise Tucker Jones is an award-winning author and popular speaker. Author and co-author of three books, her work has been featured in numerous magazines and compilation books, including *Guideposts* and other *Chicken Soup* titles. Married for forty years, mother of four and grandmother of two, Louise resides in Edmond, Oklahoma. E-mail her at *LouiseTJ@aol.com*.

Brenda Jordan is a retired public schoolteacher who now teaches at a children's museum. She is married to a teacher and a coach. Brenda enjoys spending time with her grandson, Kaleb, and her beagle, Trey.

Shirley Kawa-Jump writes romantic comedies for Kensington and Harlequin. A Bookseller's Best Award winner, she often uses the embarrassing and hilarious things her children do to add humor to her work. Visit her Web site at *www.shirleyjump.com*.

Kevin Kilpatrick teaches sociology and statistics for California State University. He lives in San Diego with his wife and has nearly completed a five-book series for the young-adult fiction fantasy market. He is actively seeking publishers for what he believes is the American answer to Harry Potter.

Betty King is an author, speaker and newspaper columnist who has lived with MS for thirty-eight years. She and her husband, Bill, have four children and ten grandchildren. Visit her Web site at *www.bettyking.net* or e-mail her at *baking2@charter.net*.

Cheryl Kirking is an author, songwriter and conference speaker who tickles the funny bones and tugs at the heartstrings of audiences nationwide. Her many books include *Crayons in the Dryer: Misadventures and Unexpected Blessings of Motherhood* and *Ripples of Joy*. She is also the mother of triplets! For booking information, visit *www.cherylkirking.com*.

Nancy J. Knight, a singer, speaker and freelance writer, lives in Fayetteville, Arkansas. In her book, *From New Jersey to Joy*, she shares her unusual life story with humor and hope. Nancy has two sons and three grandsons and enjoys music, reading, shopping and Arkansas Razorback basketball games. Please contact her at *www.nancyjknight.com*.

Cheryl Kremer, of Lancaster, Pennsylvania, lives with husband, Jack, and her two children, Nikki and Cobi. She has been published in several *Chicken Soup* books and enjoys recognizing "Chicken Soup Moments" in her daily life with her family. She is the #1 fan of her kids' sports teams, including soccer, field hockey and gymnastics. She can be reached at *j_kremer@msn.com*.

Darlene Gloria Lawson writes from her farm in rural New Brunswick. She especially enjoys the lessons she learns from spending time with her family and her one princess granddaughter. Her writing experiences continue to move her into new areas. She plans to publish a series of inspirational essays. She can be reached at *antenna@nb.sympatico.ca*.

Judy Leger works in higher education in southwest Louisiana. Judy loves writing, reading and eating bowls of popcorn with her sons while watching movies. Please email her at: *jleger314@yahoo.com*.

James W. Lewis lives in southern California. He has several publication credits, including a first-place win in a short-story writing contest. James enjoys DJing, sports, reading and hanging with friends. Please e-mail him at *biglew@ jameswlewis.com* or visit his Web page at *www.jameswlewis.com*.

Gary Luerding resides in southern Oregon with Lynne, his wife of forty-three years. He is a frequent *Chicken Soup* contributor with "Beyond the Breakers" (*Fisherman's Soul*), "The Honeymoon Is Over" (*Military Wife's Soul*) and "The Sunny Side" (*Cup of Comfort for Mothers and Sons*), and author of *Inshore Ocean Fishing for Dummies*. Contact him at *garyluer@frontiernet.net*.

Marnie O. Mamminga is the mother of three joyous sons and has been married to her high-school sweetheart for thirty-five years. In addition, she is a professional writer whose works have appeared in a variety of publications, including *Reader's Digest*, *The Christian Science Monitor*, *Chicago Tribune*, *Chicago Tribune Magazine*, *Detroit Free Press Sunday Magazine* and *Lake Superior Magazine*. Currently, Marnie is a columnist for *The Daily Herald* newspaper and also a presenter of memoir-writing workshops and programs. She can be reached at *marnie@mamminga.com*.

After brief sojourns in Germany and southern California, **Maryjo Faith Morgan** is writing full time in gorgeous Colorado. She enjoys reading, hiking, and tandem biking with her husband. Extended family and friends enrich her life, including her now grown son and his family. For contact information visit *www.maryjofaithmorgan.com*.

Risa Nye is a San Francisco Bay Area writer and college counselor. She is the author of a journal for college-bound students called *Road Scholar*. Her articles and essays have been seen in several Bay Area publications, which pleases her no end.

Jim O'Brien has authored twenty-one books and has written for *The Philadelphia Evening Bulletin*, *The Miami News*, *The New York Post*, *The Pittsburgh Press* and *The Sporting News*. He writes a weekly column for two suburban weeklies, *The Almanac* and *The Valley Mirror*. You can e-mail him at *jpobrien1@earthlink.net*.

Motivational humorist **Jennifer I. Oliver** resides in Copperas Cove, Texas, with her househubby and four kids. Author of *Four Ears: Works of Heart*, her stories have appeared in various *Chicken Soup for the Soul* books, *Don't Sweat the Small Stuff*, *Heartwarmers*, *Stories for a Woman's Heart* and *Half Full*.

Linda L. Osmundson lives in Fort Collins, Colorado, with her husband of forty years. She writes for parenting, grandparenting, teaching, travel, religious, children, *Family Circle* and *Chicken Soup* publications. She enjoys golf, crafts, travel, books, art and Dixieland jazz. You can e-mail her at *LLO1413@msn.com*.

Cheryl A. Paden is a wife and mother of three sons, Isaac, Jordan and Aaron. She works part-time as a local pastor and part-time as a freelance writer. Cheryl and her husband own and manage their own business in Fremont, Nebraska.

Jeanne Pallos is the author of several published articles for adults and children. Her workbook, *Circle of Love*, has been used by churches that deal with recovery issues for women. Jeanne lives in Laguna Niguel, California, with her husband, Andrew, and is the proud mother of two adult children.

Mark Parisi's "off the mark" comic panel has been syndicated since 1987 and is distributed by United Media. Mark's humor also graces greeting cards, T-shirts, calendars, magazines, newsletters and books. Please visit his website at: *www.offthe mark.com*. Lynn, is his wife/business partner and their daughter, Jenny, contributes with inspiration (as do three cats).

Kathleen Partak has been writing a weekly e-mail column for the past six years called the *Monday Motivator*. She writes for her family and mostly for herself. Kathleen has done several short-term columns on telephony and today's technology. She also has several children's books in the works.

Susan Jane Pasztor is a fifty-three-year-old nurse who loves to read and occasionally write short stories. This is her first work to be published, but she hopes to write some stories for children in the future. Susan loves spending time with her family and fishing.

Perry P. Perkins was born and raised in the Pacific Northwest. His debut novel, *Just Past Oysterville: Shoalwater Book One*, was released in February 2004. Visit *www.perryperkinsbooks.com* to read chapter one. Perry and his wife, Victoria, live in the Pacific Northwest.

Gloria Helen Plaisted is an author, freelance writer, Bible study teacher and popular speaker at churches and in the corporate arena. She and her husband, Rick, have been co-entrepreneurs for over thirty years. The title she cherishes most is "Silliest Grandma on the Planet," given affectionately by her two grandsons. Gloria can be reached by e-mail at *glorybee@starband.net*.

Joe Rector is a veteran high-school English teacher of twenty-nine years. He also writes a weekly column for a small suburban newspaper. Joe and his wife, Amy, have been married for thirty-one years and have two children, Lacey and Dallas. Please e-mail him at *joerector@comcast.net*.

Carol McAdoo Rehme, one of *Chicken Soup's* most prolific contributors, believes it is easier to build a boy than to mend a man. Carol directs a nonprofit, Vintage Voices, Inc., which brings interactive programming to the vulnerable elderly. Contact her at *carol@rehme.com; www.rehme.com*.

Kimberly Ripley has written for many editions of *Chicken Soup for the Soul*, several anthologies and is the author of six books. She lives in New Hampshire with her husband and children and is a homeschooling mom. Visit her Web site at *www.kimberlyripley.writergazette.com*.

Dan Rosandich operates the popular online cartoon catalog *www.dans cartoons.com*. Images are available for use in presentations, newsletters, books, magazines and Web sites. Rosandich also specializes in creating "custom" cartoons for any professional projects. Michigan-based, Rosandich can be reached anytime at *dan@danscartoons.com*. Webmasters can also include Dan's daily web comic on their Web sites. For more info, contact Dan at the address mentioned.

Starshine Roshell is an award-winning columnist and entertainment editor at *The Santa Barbara News-Press* in California. She is the mother of two boys, Stone and Dash. E-mail her at: *sroshell@newspress.com*.

Sue-Ellen Sanders is a family newspaper columnist and radio talk-show host living in Fort Pierce, Florida. A 1981 graduate of the University of Florida College of Journalism and Communications, she is devoted to running, reading and raising her family. E-mail her at *tothemoon@bellsouth.net*.

Linda Saslow is a contributing reporter for *The New York Times* on Long Island. She is also the author of three published nonfiction books and a yet unpublished novel based on a true story. When she is not writing, she enjoys yoga, exercise, theater and hanging out with her beautiful baby granddaughter.

Harriet May Savitz is the award-winning author of twenty-four books, including *Is a Worry Worrying You?* (Tanglewood Press), co-authored with Ferida Wolff. Reissued books by AuthorsGuild/iUniverse about the disabled can be found at *iUniverse.com*. Visit *www.harrietmaysavitz.com* or contact Harriet at *hmaysavitz@aol.com*.

Duane Shaw has been previously published in *Chicken Soup for the Nurse's Soul* and the *Christian Woman's Soul* books. He is currently writing an autobiography of short stories about his combat experiences in Vietnam. His grandchildren, Shantel, Ethan, Colton and Shae, are the loves of his life. Contact him at *dbshaw1947@sbcglobal.net* or 707-793-8420.

Deborah Shouse lives and writes in Prairie Village, Kansas. She is a speaker, writer and creativity catalyst. Her writing has appeared in *Reader's Digest, Newsweek, Woman's Day, Family Circle* and *Ms*. Visit her Web site at *www.thecreativityconnection.com*.

Andy Skidmore is a freelance writer who has appeared in several *Chicken Soup* books, as well as having her work published in newspapers and magazines. She enjoys writing, photography and public speaking. Her greatest accomplishments are being a wife, mother and grandmother. Contact her at *AndySkid@aol.com*.

David Skidmore lives in Tennessee with his bride, Melissa, and their three beautiful daughters, Daisy Sue, Anna Belle and Lila Mae. David serves as a youth minister at the North Boulevard Church of Christ. He can be contacted at *jdskidmore@aol.com*.

Gloria Cassity Stargel writes for *Guideposts, Decision, Today's Christian Woman* and other publications. Her book about her cancer-survivor husband, *The Healing*, like a fine antique, gains value with age. Read portions at *www.brightmorning.com*. Order online or phone 1-800-888-9529 or write Applied Images, 312 Bradford St., N.W., Gainesville, GA 30501.

Polly W. Swafford's career began as a business journalist and next as a social studies and language arts teacher. Most recently she served for fifteen years as Senior Editor/Publisher of *Potpourri, A Magazine of the Literary Arts*. Now retired, she enjoys traveling and writing creative nonfiction and haiku poetry.

B. J. Taylor has two grandsons, and, just as she learned long ago, they are also perfect just the way they are. B. J. is a *Guideposts* writer and has been published in numerous collections, newspapers and magazines. You can reach her at *bjtaylor3@earthlink.net*.

Suzanne Vaughan has a B.S. in education, and is the author of the book *Potholes and Parachutes*. She is a motivational speaker who has delivered personal growth programs to corporations and associations for over twenty-five years. She is Past President of the Colorado Speakers Association. To contact her, call toll-free 866-303-7222 or visit her Web site at *www.suzannevaughan.com*.

Joseph Walker is the author of *ValueSpeak*, a nationally syndicated newspaper column that has been looking at contemporary issues from the perspective of traditional values since 1990. He and his wife, Anita, are parents of five children and grandparents of three granddaughters. He can be reached via e-mail at *ValueSpeak@msn.com*.

Linda Watskin teaches creative writing workshops and recently, along with another writer, ventured into the publishing field with A Measure of Words Press. She's a coffee shop aficionado and enjoys hiking in Maine, the Southwest and her community. Some of her poetry and short stories have appeared in small press journals.

Lois Wencil, mother of two, has published many nonfiction and three romantic fiction books. She loves travel, concerts, the theater and movies. You can e-mail her at *lois.wencil@earthlink.net*.

Arthur B. Wiknik, Jr., served in Vietnam with the 101st Airborne Division and fought in the battle for Hamburger Hill. His wartime memoir, *Nam Sense,* was published by Casemate in 2005. Arthur has written a wide variety of articles for publication, including *Chicken Soup for the Veteran's Soul* and *Chicken Soup for the Father and Daughter's Soul.* An active community volunteer, Arthur frequently shares his wartime experiences at schools and civic organizations. Visit his Web site at *www.namsense.com*.

Beadrin Youngdahl is a lifelong resident of Minnesota, grandmother to four perfect kids, and works as a registered nurse to support her passions for reading, writing and knitting. She has published poetry, short fiction and essays and has completed her first novel. Contact her at *Beadrin@aol.com*.

Thousands of **Bob Zahn**'s cartoons have been published in all the leading publications. He has over a thousand greeting cards to his credit. Several of his humor books have been published. His e-mail address is *zahntoons@aol.com*.

Permissions *(continued from page iv)*

Happy Feet. Reprinted by permission of Risa Nye. ©2005 Risa Nye.

Listen to What I Hear. Reprinted by permission of Margaret Oatman Mamminga. ©2004 Margaret Oatman Mamminga.

Getting Even! Reprinted by permission of Suzanne Lowe Vaughan. ©2001 Suzanne Lowe Vaughan.

The Mother's Day Note. Reprinted by permission of Jeri Chrysong. ©2000 Jeri Chrysong.

Chalk It Up. Reprinted by permission of Barbara Ann Adams. ©2002 Barbara Ann Adams.

It Is What It Is. Reprinted by permission of Karen Brown. ©2004 Karen Brown.

Making the Grade. Reprinted by permission of Susan Jane Pasztor. ©2005 Susan Jane Pasztor.

A Place in the Sun. Reprinted by permission of Rosalie P. Griffin. ©2004 Rosalie P. Griffin.

The Gotcha Game. Reprinted by permission of Pamela Sue Jenkins. ©2004 Pamela Sue Jenkins.

The Cowboy Suit. Reprinted by permission of Glenn Edward Dabbs, Sr. ©2005 Glenn Edward Dabbs, Sr.

My Hero. Reprinted by permission of Anita Biase. ©2005 Anita Biase.

A Heart of Compassion. Reprinted by permission of Judy L. Leger. ©2002 Judy L. Leger.

Wassup? Reprinted by permission of Linda Carol Apple. ©2003 Linda Carol Apple.

Raising Eyebrows. Reprinted by permission of Scott Garfield Halford. ©2005 Scott Garfield Halford.

Sounding Bored. Reprinted by permission of Carol D. Rehme. ©2005 Carol D. Rehme.

Ready or Not. Reprinted by permission of Shirley Jump. ©1999 Shirley Jump.

A Girl. Reprinted by permission of Laurie Jo Hartman. ©2005 Laurie Jo Hartman.

The Threads That Bind. Reprinted by permission of Kerrie L. Flanagan. ©1999 Kerrie L. Flanagan.

The Bedtime Story. Reprinted by permission of Sylvia Kay Gist. ©2000 Sylvia Kay Gist.

Coach for a Day. Reprinted by permission of Linda Saslow. ©2005 Linda Saslow.

Spencer's Mom. Reprinted by permission of Robin Geller Diamond. ©2004 Robin Geller Diamond.

The Rustic Rink. Reprinted by permission of Joseph Brent Walker. ©1991 Joseph Brent Walker.

The Yellow Boat. Reprinted by permission of Harriet May Savitz. ©2002 Harriet May Savitz.

Homecoming. Reprinted by permission of Arthur B. Wiknik, Jr. and Casemate Publishing. ©2003 Arthur B. Wiknik, Jr.

Welcome Home. Reprinted by permission of Debra Callies. ©2004 Debra Callies.

A Mother's Bond. Reprinted by permission of Berniece Duello. ©2005 Berniece Duello.

Voicing My Wish. Reprinted by permission of Theresa Goggin-Roberts. ©2000 Theresa Goggin-Roberts.

The Necklace. Reprinted by permission of Gloria I. Givens. ©2004 Gloria I. Givens.

Reel Love. Reprinted by permission of Jean Blackmer. ©2005 Jean Blackmer.

Sharing Flowers. Reprinted by permission of Carolyn Hall. ©2003 Carolyn Hall.

Tea Party. Reprinted by permission of Gloria Helen Plaisted. ©2005 Gloria Helen Plaisted.

Paul's Bike. Reprinted by permission of Linda L. Osmundson. ©2005 Linda L. Osmundson.

The Love of His Life. Reprinted by permission of Sue-Ellen Apte Sanders. ©1999 Sue-Ellen Apte Sanders.

A Swing of Fate. Reprinted by permission of Carol D. Rehme. ©1999 Carol D. Rehme.

Song-and-Dance Man. Reprinted by permission of Maryjo Faith Morgan. ©2004 and ©2002 Melanie Howard Music, Inc. (ASCAP) Murrah Music Corporation (BM). Used by permission. International copyright secured. All rights reserved.

Captain Kirk. Reprinted by permission of Perry Phillip Perkins. ©2000 Perry Phillip Perkins.

Goodnight, Mom. Reprinted by permission of Daniel J. Reust. ©2001 Daniel J. Reust.

His Mother. Reprinted by permission of Angela Lea Theiman Dino. ©2005 Angela Lea Theiman Dino.

A Constant Presence. Reprinted by permission of Kathleen D. Partak. ©2005 Kathleen D. Partak.

No Limits. Reprinted by permission of Deisy Maria Flood. ©2005 Deisy Maria Flood.

Hearts in Our Eyes. Reprinted by permission of Jennifer Ilene Oliver. ©2003 Jennifer Ilene Oliver.

Cerebral Chaos. Reprinted by permission of James William Lewis. ©2003 James William Lewis.

The Optimist. Reprinted by permission of Margaret Pearson Cunningham. ©2004 Margaret Pearson Cunningham.

Wishing Upon a Son. Reprinted by permission of Deborah H. Shouse. ©1995 Deborah H. Shouse.

Hush, Little Baby . . . Reprinted by permission of Karin Bjerke-Lisle. ©2004 Karin Bjerke-Lisle.

What's in a Name? Reprinted by permission of Kerrie L. Flanagan. ©2002 Kerrie L. Flanagan.

A Tackle Box of His Own. Reprinted by permission of Rita Elaine Billbe. ©2002 Rita Elaine Billbe.

Reconnecting. Reprinted by permission of Virginia Fortner. ©2004 Virginia Fortner.

Forwarded Prayer. Reprinted by permission of Kimberly A. Ripley. ©2001 Kimberly A. Ripley.

Ma & Me & Gin. Reprinted by permission of Kevin Gerard Kilpatrick. ©2004 Kevin Gerard Kilpatrick.

Whoever You Are, I Love You. Reprinted by permission of James Patrick O'Brien. ©2000 James Patrick O'Brien.

Pay It Forward. Reprinted by permission of Beadrin Youngdahl Urista. ©2004 Beadrin Youngdahl Urista.

Happy Father's Day, Mom. Reprinted by permission of Jeri Chrysong. ©1994 Jeri Chrysong.

Bundle of Boy. Reprinted by permission of *The Santa Barbara News-Press* and Starshine Roshell. ©2002 Starshine Roshell.

Climbing in the Ring. Reprinted by permission of Margaret Oatman Mamminga. ©1996 Margaret Oatman Mamminga.

Rewind. Reprinted by permission of Cheryl Kirking Kilker. ©2000 Cheryl Kirking Kilker.

Majestic Moms. Reprinted by permission of Linda Marie Ford England. ©2005 Linda Marie Ford England.

The Almost Home Run. Reprinted by permission of Nancy Jane Knight. ©2003 Nancy Jane Knight.

It's Not Windy Enough. Reprinted by permission of Kerrie L. Flanagan. ©2002 Kerrie L. Flanagan.

Two Left Feet. Reprinted by permission of Gina Marie Dubose. ©1999 Gina Marie Dubose.

My Mother's Piano. Reprinted by permission of Gary B. Luerding. ©2004 Gary B. Luerding.

What Will I Be? Reprinted by permission of Cheryl Marie Kremer. ©2004 Cheryl Marie Kremer.

Not Jeffrey's Mom. Reprinted by permission of Cindy Sue Hval. ©2003 Cindy Sue Hval.

Popcorn and Dirty, Bare Feet. Reprinted by permission of B. J. Taylor. ©1997 B. J. Taylor.

Sliver of Silence. Reprinted by permission of Cindy Sue Hval. ©2004 Cindy Sue Hval.

"Those Kids." Reprinted by permission of Jeanne Pallos. ©2005 Jeanne Pallos.

A Mother of a Job. Reprinted by permission of *The Santa Barbara News-Press* and Starshine Roshell. ©2002 Starshine Roshell.

Our Mom: A Book by David and Paul. Reprinted by permission of James David Skidmore. ©1993 James David Skidmore.

Don't Blink. Reprinted by permission of Pamela H. Hobson. ©2004 Pamela H. Hobson.

School Days. Reprinted by permission of Nancy B. Gibbs. ©2000 Nancy B. Gibbs.

Back-to-School Blues. Reprinted by permission of Margaret Oatman Mamminga. ©1996 Margaret Oatman Mamminga.

My Sunshine. Reprinted by permission of April Dawn Garcia. ©2004 April Dawn Garcia.

Manual Training. Reprinted by permission of Carol D. Rehme. ©1995 Carol D. Rehme.

Changing Course. Reprinted by permission of Margaret Oatman Mamminga. ©2000 Margaret Oatman Mamminga.

News from College. Reprinted by permission of Linda Sultan. ©1997 Linda Sultan.

Saturday Mornings. Reprinted by permission of Andrea Sue Skidmore. ©1997 Andrea Sue Skidmore.

Who Gives This Son? Reprinted by permission of Leslie T. Britt. ©1996 Leslie T. Britt.

The Day My Son Became a Marine. Reprinted by permission of Gloria C. Stargel. ©2001 Gloria C. Stargel.

Momma's Memorial. Reprinted by permission of Joseph Theodore Rector. ©2003 Joseph Theodore Rector.

My Son. Reprinted by permission of Betty Ann King. ©1986 Betty Ann King.

Being a Man. Reprinted by permission of Jean Harper. ©2004 Jean Harper.

Going to the Dance. Reprinted by permission of Margaret Oatman Mamminga. ©1997 Margaret Oatman Mamminga.

Snips and Snails and Puppy-Dog Tails. Reprinted by permission of Lynn M. Dean. ©1998 Lynn M. Dean.

Driving Lessons. Reprinted by permission of Margaret Oatman Mamminga. ©1996 Margaret Oatman Mamminga.

Grown Up. Reprinted by permission of Darlene Gloria Lawson. ©2004 Darlene Gloria Lawson.

And Now a Man. Reprinted by permission of Nancy Blackmon. ©2001 Nancy Blackmon.

The Charming Con. Reprinted by permission of Brenda Jordan. ©2003 Brenda Jordan.

Answering the Call. Reprinted by permission of Susan Bindas Diaz. ©2003 Susan Bindas Diaz.

That's My Son! Reprinted by permission of Dianna Foxcroft. ©2004 Dianna Foxcroft.